'Oh, what happened to you?
Whatever happened to me?
And what became of the people we used to be?
Tomorrow's almost over,
Today went by so fast,
Is the only thing to look forward to – the past?'

WHATEVER HAPPENED TO THE LIKELY LADS?

'Oh, what happened to you?
Whatever happened to me?
What became of the people we used to be?
Oh, what happened to you?
Whatever happened to me?
What became of the people we used to be?
Oh, what happened to you?
Whatever happened to me?
And what became of the people…'(fade)

THE MOPPET GIRLS
ARE COMING YOUR WAY

Richard Webber

WHATEVER HAPPENED TO THE LIKELY LADS?

ORION

This book is dedicated to all my nieces and nephews, with love. R.W.

First published in 1999 by Orion Media
An imprint of Orion Books Ltd
Orion House, 5 Upper St Martin's Lane,
London WC2H 9EA

A CIP catalogue record for this book
is available from the British Library.

ISBN 0 75281 815 5

Printed in Italy
by Printer Trento srl

CONTENTS

ACKNOWLEDGEMENTS

There are many people who have helped make this book possible. Without the consent of Dick Clement and Ian La Frenais the project wouldn't have got off the ground, so I'd like to thank them for allowing me the chance to write about their classic programme, agreeing to be interviewed and writing various pieces for the book.

I am grateful to all the actors, including Rodney Bewes, Brigit Forsyth and Sheila Fearn, for sharing their memories with me, and to numerous members of the production team, especially Jimmy Gilbert, the late Bernard Thompson, Evan King and Michael Tuchner.

Several of Ian and Dick's friends – including Terry Taylor, Brian Flint, Maurice Hardaker, Vin Welch, Mike Thompson, Horace Jeffcock, Patrick Tilley and David Hallwood gave up time to talk, and were generous in supplying photos. I'd also like to thank Don Smith for not only helping supply pictures of the show, but for taking many of the shots used.

Many other people helped in various ways, including Neil Somerville at BBC's Written Archive Centre, David Porter, Simon Hall at the BBC, David Hamilton for helping compile the episode listing, Stephen Wagg for contributing to the book, Dr. Les Gofton, Jenny Clement, Briony Hood, Mike Hugg, Brenda Punshon, Laurie Asprey, John Rich, Philip Jones, Graham Whalan and Charles Garland – thanks to you all.

Finally, special thanks to Trevor Dolby and Pandora White at Orion, who I've enjoyed working with again, Simon Nye for talking to me and writing the foreword, my agent, Jeffrey Simmons, and Hilary Johnson, for her advice. Most of all, I'd like to thank my wife, Paula, who, as always, has been very supportive.

FOREWORD BY SIMON NYE

The best comedies are about the simplest things and there's nothing simpler than the set-up in *The Likely Lads*. The temptation for first-time writers pitching the same show to a TV commissioning editor today would be to suggest that Bob Ferris and Terry Collier run a dating agency together by day and solve crimes by night. If it were for American television, they'd have a talking dog.

Fortunately we were allowed to see Bob and Terry's lives unfolding more naturally and credibly, although, now I come to think about it, a talking dog might have been fun, too. Much as we all like a good gag, relentless wise-cracking is exhausting to watch because it's not the way life is, unless you're shacked up with a Northern Club comic. You can really *relax* into *The Likely Lads* or *Whatever Happened…?* without worrying that a character is going to come in the door and spoil it all with some duff quips.

There is greater pressure nowadays to make sitcoms more gag-heavy, probably in response to American sitcoms like *Cheers* and *Friends*.

When I started writing *Men Behaving Badly*, some fifteen years after Bob drove his wide lapels off into the sunset, I was advised always to get at least three jokes on a page, something I personally achieved by choosing a very small typeface.

It is customary in forewords to comedy-related books to make ludicrously overheated comparisons, for example likening *Are You Being Served?* to a Joe Orton play or – and this is always particularly unwise – comparing *Terry and June* to *Waiting for Godot*. So I won't fall into that trap.

But there is a decidedly Pinteresque quality to some scenes in *The Likely Lads*, as you will see from the extracts printed in this book. And, good though he was, Harold Pinter never came up with a line to match Bob's: 'English girls abroad with their peeling shoulders and flowery dresses, like wallpaper on the march.'

The success of a follow-up to *The Likely Lads* must have prompted hundreds of writers and producers to suggest sequels. I think we can generally agree that they are a bad idea, indeed viewers' answer to most TV Whatever Happened To's would be 'I don't actually give a toss'.

But *Whatever Happened to The Likely Lads?* is the gleaming exception. Why? Well, of all the men writing about men on TV Dick Clement and Ian La Frenais are probably the best at it.

This thoroughly researched book will at a stroke provide answers to the most trivial piece of trivia about *The Likely Lads*, as well as introducing you to a real person by the name of Horace Jeffcock. Have an enjoyable read, pet.

SIMON NYE *March 1999*

INTRODUCTION BY DICK CLEMENT

The Likely Lads has a very special place in my heart. How could it be otherwise? For one thing, it was the first professional work that Ian and I did together. That alone gave it a special adrenalin rush, together with a sense of disbelief. On top of that, when I was asked to direct the shows too, I had suddenly stumbled into the perfect situation that people strive for years to attain. I should have been terrified but I was protected by ignorance. Innocence, as Len Deighton once said, is knowing you can do something. Experience is knowing that you can't.

I was further cushioned by two other factors. First by Syd Lotterby, who was assigned as my Production Assistant. He was far more experienced than I was and many people in that situation would have 'come the old soldier', sat back and watched me flounder. On the contrary, he shielded me and helped me with extraordinary generosity. The second factor, in a perverse way, was neglect. The show was clearly a schedule filler. Nobody expected it to achieve anything and consequently nobody bothered us – quite literally. None of the top brass attended one of the rehearsals or recordings. At the time, we felt faintly hurt. In hindsight, it was infinitely preferable to the alternative – endless notes from the legions of Network Executives.

On the night of the first recording Ian was standing behind me in the 'gallery' as I stared glassy-eyed at the bank of screens. When we got our first laugh I turned round to share the moment with him – and missed about four shots. I was saved again by professionalism. Clive Doig, the vision mixer, kept cutting without me, as per script. I was a useless ornament for the rest of the show, my brain trying to catch up, but still dazzled by every reaction from the studio audence below.

It was extraordinary on-job training. It was almost impossible to edit tape in those days. If something went seriously wrong, you recorded a whole segment again. So it was very close to doing the shows 'live'. Plotting my camera script was the worst sort of homework, moving around pennies, to simulate cameras, on a floor plan of the sets, and trying not to get their cables tangled. Learning not to cut away too soon if a line got a laugh – if you did, the audience stopped laughing and got ready for something new. Learning not to make bad cuts where actors 'jump frame' – one moment they're on the left, the next on the right – which jars the eye. But generally, when I tried to commit this cardinal sin, Syd or the camera crew wouldn't let me.

The show's unexpected success made it even more piquant. We felt we'd done it on our own. We were probably unbearable at the time. We certainly thought we were fireproof. This was what you did – wrote a show and it became a hit. Fortunately for our egos our next, for ITV, was an abject failure and a miserable experience and balance was restored.

DICK CLEMENT *July 1999*

THE HISTORY OF *THE LIKELY LADS*

The Meeting

The Clement/La Frenais writing partnership was born in a London pub, back in 1961, three years before 'Entente Cordiale', the first episode of *The Likely Lads*, was transmitted. Instrumental in bringing them together that evening at the Uxbridge Arms in Notting Hill was Michael Burridge, a friend of both Dick and Ian.

'When you're in your early twenties, you meet lots of people; you're also introducing people to others, so I didn't have the slightest idea that by taking Ian along to the pub that evening I was helping form one of television's best writing partnerships,' he says.

Michael's not surprised they've achieved so much success. 'Ian and Dick can extract humour from virtually any situation, however routine; they always saw ordinary events in a slightly different way from the rest of us. Routines such as going to a pub, or the cinema, would become amusing. They share a certain perceptiveness, which is one reason they work so well together.'

Dick – who was employed as a studio manager at the BBC – and Ian – who'd done odd jobs, like working for a cleaning firm before moving into market research – remember their first meeting vividly.

'Mike was always pushing me to get a job that was more glamorous than the one I had,' says Ian. 'He kept saying I should be in PR; I didn't even know what it meant. That never happened, but he did introduce me to Dick. I went with him to this pub and got talking to several people. I remember Dick very well: he was tall and wore a long overcoat, just like he'd graduated from Oxford. He seemed well-informed, probably because of the *Guardian* stuffed in his pocket!'

They got on well and began socialising, as Dick explains. 'Several friends, including me, would go

Enjoying a few pints at the local pub was the focal point of Terry and Bob's early life.

round to Ian's flat at the weekend and play cards.' It wasn't long before their friendship progressed into a working relationship.

One of their drinking pals was Horace Jeffcock, who was sharing a flat with Ian when he met Dick. He noticed that as soon as they started writing sketches, some of which were used in that year's Ariel Players' Christmas performance, they were constantly on the lookout for story-lines.

'They would always talk about this story-line or that story-line, usually over a beer!' says Horace, who grew up with Ian in the North-East. 'Everything that happened was celebrated in a pub afterwards. They worked hard in the early days to achieve something, and were always astute in any decision they faced. They're very talented, imaginative guys. Ian's very funny and is always killing people with his humour; he has a natural acidic style, which shows in his writing.'

Someone who frequented the pubs with Dick was old school friend, Terry Taylor. 'We drank in a pub which had a game of pinball football; we used to have knockout tournaments – it was great fun. I began meeting Ian a lot. He's a very funny guy, and so is Dick, but they're completely different, which is, perhaps, why they get on so well.'

Bringing the Lads to Life

Ever since he tried writing an episode of the *Paul Temple* radio series as a boy, Dick Clement wanted to work in show business. While employed by the BBC, he tried keeping his aspirations alive by joining the Ariel Players, the BBC's amateur dramatics group. He began writing sketches for revues the Players performed; this provided the ideal vehicle for Dick and Ian's writing partnership to start in earnest.

'Ian shared a flat,' recalls Dick, 'and two of the guys – Brian Flint and Maurice Hardaker – had written and performed for Tyne Tees Television; Ian – who'd always wanted to be a writer – felt left out, so we decided to write something together. We went to a pub in the Old Brompton Road and wrote a sketch.'

Entitled 'Double Date', the sketch spotlighted one evening in the lives of two boys and two girls, examining the success of their double dates. Maurice Hardaker believes the scenario was based on a conversation Ian had overheard on a bus. 'A couple of girls sat behind Ian and were talking about their dates. They discussed how the boys had kissed, making all the sound effects. He told me about the conversation and it triggered the idea for a sketch.'

When it came to writing the Ariel Players' 1961 Christmas revue, *It's All Got to Stop*, Dick and Ian contributed several sketches, including 'Double Date'. Staged at the Lycée, between the 18 and 21 December, 23 sketches were performed, with Marion Gates, Jenny Thacker, Brian Hodgson and Dick appearing in 'Double Date'.

Dick played Terry, modelling his performance on Albert Finney's in the 1960 movie, *Saturday Night and Sunday Morning*. 'The sketch was cross-cutting

6d

IT'S ALL GOT TO Stop

Production:	John Stockbridge
Music:	John Baker
Design:	Tony Lightley

The Lycée
December 18 - 21
1961

The BBC Club presents the Ariel Players in a new revue

between two guys and two girls carrying out a post-mortem of their dates, with the male point of view being contrasted against the female's.'

The sketch was well received by the audience, which included Dick's friend, Terry Taylor. 'Dick was always good at inviting friends along to such events,' he says. '"Double Date" was of its time, when more realistic, northern drama and humour was emerging. With shows like *Coronation Street* and *Hancock* we were moving away from the surreal to a Northern, working-class style.'

Although tame by today's standards, it was regarded as outspoken in 1961, as Terry explains. 'We were talking about 1961, pre-Pill days, so when Jimmy turns to Bob and asks whether he "scored", it was seen as realistic and funny, but also daring.'

Brian Hodgson, who played Bob in the sketch, met Dick while training as a studio manager at Bush House, and was keen to get involved with the Ariel Players, and their many productions.

• • • • • IT'S ALL GOT TO STOP • • • • •

FIRST HALF

1. POINT COUNTER POINT (*Clement, La Frenais, Baker*) .... THE COMPANY
2. HOME ON THE MANGE (*Clement*) .... DICK, MARION
3. ~~PIANISSIMO (*Graham*)~~ .... ~~RODDY~~
4. YOUR LIFE IN THEIR HANDS (*Marshall*) ....DICK, MURRAY, RAY, BRIAN
5. KEEP THE HOME PYRES BURNING (*Gardner*) ....MURRAY, MARION
6. THE BEAT GENERATION (*Flint, Hardacre*) .... DICK, MURRAY, RAY
7. I KNOW WHAT I DON'T LIKE (*Clement, La Frenais*) .... RODDY
8. MORAL DISARMAMENT (*Clement, La Frenais, Baker*) ....BRENDA, JILL, DICK
9. ONE FOOT IN THE GRAVE (*Mills*) RAY, BRIAN, JENNY, MURRAY, RODDY, BRIGIT, JILL
10. TWO HEADS ARE BETTER THAN ONE (*Flint, Hardacre*) .... BRENDA, DICK
11. THE PERSUADERS' HIDEOUT (*Clement, La Frenais*) .... BRENDA, BRIAN, RODDY
12. WHEN DID YOU LAST SEE YOUR STOOL PIGEON ? (*Clement, Baker*) ....RAY, BRIAN, DICK, MURRAY

THERE WILL BE AN INTERVAL OF 20 MINUTES

THE CAST

THE MEN

DICK CLEMENT
RAY COLLEY
RODDY GRAHAM
BRIAN HODGSON
MURRAY MARSHALL

THE GIRLS

JILL CARTER
MARION GATES
BRENDA SHEPHERD
JENNY THACKER
BRIGIT WALTON

THE MUSIC

JOHN BAKER *piano*
JOHN LOFTIN *bass*
CARL FRANCIS *drums*

SECOND HALF

1. RESTORATION PIECE (*Brinsley Congreve*) ....JENNY, MARION, DICK, BRIAN
2. I'M IN THIS YEAR (*La Frenais*) .... RODDY
3. THE STRANGE CASE OF VINTRIX POLLBARTON (*Tilly, Flint, La Frenais*) .... DICK, BRIAN, MURRAY
4. MEN OF EXTINCTION (*Flint, Hardacre*) ....RAY, MURRAY, DICK
5. TIN PAN AISLE (*Clement, La Frenais*) RODDY, JENNY, BRIAN, MARION, MURRAY
6. A GIRL FOR ALL SEASONS (*Clement, La Frenais, Baker*) .... MURRAY, BRENDA, JILL
7. HIS MASTER'S VOICE (*Tilly*) ....BRIAN, RAY, DICK
8. ELF HELP (*Flint, Hardacre*) ...... BRENDA, JILL, JENNY, MARION
9. DOUBLE DATE (*Clement, La Frenais*) ....BRIAN, DICK, MARION, JENNY
10. BARGAIN BASEMENT (*Clement, La Frenais*) .... RODDY, JENNY
11. INSTANT CHRISTMAS (*Clement, La Frenais, Baker*) .... THE COMPANY

COFFEE WILL BE SERVED

(Above) The Lads come to life in a sketch from the Ariel Players' Christmas Show, 1961, with Dick Clement (opposite, bottom left) Playing Terry.

The Revue was written by
DICK CLEMENT and IAN LA FRENAIS, with BRIAN FLINT

Additional material by
MURRAY MARSHALL ANDREW GARDNER PAT TILLY
and ROGER MILLS

The music was specially composed by
JOHN BAKER and MAURICE HARDACRE
and arranged by JOHN BAKER

Dance numbers arranged by BRENDA SHEPHERD

Production Assistant MARY KENNEDY

Stage Director KEITH LANGDALE-BROWN

Assistants SARAH GREATOREX DIANA ADAMS LEO FEORD
ELIZABETH JONES NEIL MURRAY SUE VALLER
MICHAEL WAKEFIELD ELIZABETH RAYEN

Lighting NIGEL WRIGHT TONY HART

Sound PAMELA McNEIL

Wardrobe LESLEY HEATH

Assistants MAUREEN BEBB ELIZABETH SELLEY JOAN SCOTT

Front of House Manager MARY LEWIS

Settings Designed by TONY LIGHTLEY
and Built in the Ariel Players Workshops by
TONY LIGHTLEY, BRIAN HODGSON, LEO FEORD and
ELIZABETH FOSTER

Publicity NICHOLAS THORNELY

JAMES WAKEHAM & CO. LTD., (T.U.) KENSINGTON, W.8

'Dick was already in the Players when I joined. It was a lot of fun, but even though we had many laughs, we always took our work seriously. Our shows were certainly popular and most productions were packed.'

He's unsure why Dick picked him to play Bob in 'Double Date', but thinks it may have been his Northern roots. 'I did it with a Lancashire accent because I'm not very good at Geordie.'

Someone else who remembers the sketch well is Brenda Punshon (née Shepherd) who appeared in some sketches as well as arranging the revue's dance numbers. She auditioned for a part in 'Double Date', but was turned down. 'I wasn't very good at acting,' she admits, with a smile. 'But "Double Date" stood out from the rest of the sketches because it was so accurate. Like any good writers, Dick and Ian had this marvellous skill of observation.

'Times were changing; scriptwriters, both comedy and drama, who could observe everyday ordinary activities and react with their writing, were moving things on. Dick and Ian were there and very much part of it, sensitive to the atmosphere and not only running with it but leading the way with their humorous observations. When they were together they would spark each other off; they were on the same wavelength and a great inspiration to each other.'

The Ariel Players may have been an amateur outfit, but the standard of work was high. 'It wasn't like your typical amateur group, it was more like fringe theatre,' says Brenda. 'We had a tremendous time, but the work was always taken seriously and performed very professionally.'

The Players staged entertainment evenings in pubs around the city, but the highlight of the year was the Christmas revue, which was performed in a theatre, often the Lycée.

'Most of the sketches were written by Dick and Ian, who obviously had talent,' Brenda says. 'Dick stood out as a leading light: he pulled the production together, giving it the professional touch.'

Ian, meanwhile, always attended rehearsals. 'Scripts often needed changing during rehearsals, and he was always around to help amend the work.'

The 'Double Date' Sketch

This is the sketch that was performed during the 1961 Christmas show.

Dick Clement says…

'This sketch was called "Double Date" and we emphasized beforehand that we'd gone all out for naturalism in the writing, and the laughs should come by recognition more than anything else. It started with a couple of blokes, one of them swigging from a carton of milk. It wasn't in the least bit exaggerated, like one often finds in revue; it was meant to be realistic. By the use of lights, we kept cutting from the two boys at the end of the double date to the two girls; so every time a change of voice was heard, the lights would be directed away from the two boys to the two girls, and vice versa.'

BOB: You coming in?

TERRY: No, that's all right, mate, your folks will be in bed.

BOB: Oh, right. How are you going to get home, then?

TERRY: Oh, it's all right, the last bus doesn't leave till twenty past eleven.

BOB: Oh, good night, then.

TERRY: Oh, yeah.

BOB: They're all right those two.

TERRY: Oh, yeah.

BOB: They enjoyed themselves.

TERRY: Oh, yeah. I think they did.

BOB: Well I know Pat did, I mean she said so.

TERRY: Oh, Deirdre did, Deirdre did.

BOB: It was all right, wasn't it?

TERRY: Oh, yeah.

BOB: It was all right.

TERRY: Yeah. How d'you get on then?

BOB: All right, you know…you didn't seem to be doing too bad?

TERRY: Oh, well, she's all right, Deirdre, you know, I mean…she's all right.

BOB: She is all right.

(Pause)

TERRY: Did you score?

BOB: Come off it! Standing there next to a ruddy milk machine, did I score? Who d'you think I am, Mighty Mouse?

TERRY: You didn't, then?

BOB: Well did you?

TERRY: What? Oh, well, you know.

BOB: Yeah…still it was all right, mate.

TERRY: Oh, yeah.

(Next scene involves the two girls)

PAT: It was quite nice, wasn't it?

DEIRDRE: Oh, yeah, it was quite nice.

PAT: And I enjoyed it myself, like.

DEIRDRE: Oh, yeah, I did.

PAT: No, but they're nice boys.

DEIRDRE: Oh, yeah, Bob's a laugh, isn't he?

PAT: Oh yeah, he's all right – I like your Terry, mind.

DEIRDRE: What? Oh, yeah, he's all right.

PAT: Did he try anything? Mine did.

DEIRDRE: I don't see how, standing in front of that milk machine. We could see him from where we were.

PAT: Where were you, then?

DEIRDRE: Oh, in the launderette doorway.

PAT: And he didn't try anything?

DEIRDRE: I didn't say he didn't.

PAT: Well it wouldn't surprise me if you let him, you had enough to drink.

DEIRDRE: Don't be silly, a couple of lager and limes and a Tia Maria. Anyway, you can talk.

PAT: I only had three Babychams.

DEIRDRE: And a sweet stout!

PAT: Anyway, who's counting? It didn't affect me. Still, was a nice night, though.

PAT: Oh, yeah. Oh, yeah.

(Back to the Lads)

BOB: Mind you, it was a bit slow to start with.

TERRY: Well, it always is, isn't it?

BOB: When we first went in that pub and just sat there not saying owt.

TERRY: Oh, yeah, well mind you, they were all at us after a couple of drinks, though, weren't they?

BOB: Yeah, mine was drinking Babycham. *(laughs)* Well she wanted bitter lemon to start with; eh, what did yours have, lager?

TERRY: Yeah, but later on I got her on to Tia Maria.

BOB: Oh. Are they strong, like?

TERRY: Strong? A couple of those, mate, and you'd be standing in a bucket of sand singing 'The Desert Song'.

BOB: In that case you should've given her a few more before you told her that joke.

TERRY: No, it didn't go down so well, did it?

BOB: Not surprising, mate.

TERRY: Mind you, I reckon she'd have laughed if the other one hadn't been there.

BOB: Oh, I dunno.

TERRY: Well they both got it.

BOB: Yeah, but it's a bit crude, though.

TERRY: Oh, I dunno.

(Back to the girls)

DEIRDRE: Have you not heard that one before?

PAT: It was funny.

DEIRDRE: Yeah.

PAT: Can you image it, an elephant?

(They both laugh)

DEIRDRE: Mind, you didn't laugh much when he told it, though, did you?

PAT: Well, nor did you.

DEIRDRE: Well I'd already heard it.

PAT: Oh, go on.

(Deirdre looks down and spots a ladder in her stocking)

DEIRDRE: 'Ere, look at that.

PAT: How d'you do that?

DEIRDRE: Getting into that taxi.

(looking at other stocking) Oh, and I don't know where this one went.

PAT: Oh, anyway, you can wear them under your jeans.

DEIRDRE: Oh, yeah.

PAT: You know, that taxi must have cost something.

DEIRDRE: Oh, they didn't seem to mind how much they spent – I will say that for them.

PAT: And that Chinese restaurant is not cheap.

DEIRDRE: Oh, no, no, no, I will say that for them.

PAT: They didn't seem to mind *how* much they spent.

DEIRDRE: No, they didn't seem to mind what we had.

(Back to the Lads)

TERRY: I haven't half spent some bloody money, tonight!

BOB: I must have spent nearly two quid.

TERRY: I spent three.

BOB: Well you would get that taxi.

TERRY: Oh, well, you know.

BOB: Oh, what's a matter with the bus?

TERRY: Oh, well, you know.

BOB: Eh! I've nearly spent three, too. I got that last round.

TERRY: What, the one in that cocktail lounge? Cocktail lounge, no draught beer and two bob for one Double Diamond.

BOB: Two bob?

TERRY: Two bob. By, they must be making something there.

BOB: Still it's a change though, ain't it?

TERRY: Oh, yeah, suppose so.

BOB: Oh, yeah. And that Chinese place.

TERRY: Oh, yeah, suppose so.

BOB: Mind, it wasn't much of a change for you, though, was it? Sausage, egg and chips.

TERRY: Well, you know, at least you know what you're getting. God knows what it was you were eating.

BOB: What d'you mean? I had chicken chow mein.

TERRY: Chicken chow mein, probably more like Chick-e-Kat, enriched with nourishing marrow bone jelly.

BOB: Eh, you know that Pat? She's all right, you know.

TERRY: Oh she's all right.

BOB: No, she's all right.

TERRY: I dunno, I thought she seemed a bit…young.

BOB: Oh, no, no, she's all right, we had a good time.

TERRY: It's just an impression I got, you know.

BOB: Oh no, no, she's all right.

(Over to the girls)

DEIRDRE: 'Ere, look at that?

PAT: What is it?

DEIRDRE: A love bite, what do you think? I'll have to wear a scarf in the morning.

PAT: Deirdre…you know that Bob?

DEIRDRE: Yeah?

PAT: Well …he kisses with his mouth open.

DEIRDRE: Well?

PAT: Do you?

DEIRDRE: Well, yeah.

PAT: No, but I mean not just like that *(opens her mouth a little)*, but wide, like that. *(opens her mouth wide)*

DEIRDRE: *(opening her mouth wide as well)* Like that?

PAT: Um, like that.

DEIRDRE: No, I don't. Not like that.

PAT: Well, he does. Like that *(opens her mouth wide again)*

DEIRDRE: It's a wonder he doesn't bloody choke himself.

PAT: Want a fag?

DEIRDRE: Oh, no, thanks.

PAT: Do you think they'll ask us out again?

DEIRDRE: Oh, I don't know, they might. He seemed quite keen on you.

PAT: Do you think so? Do you know, he gave me all his luncheon vouchers for next week.

DEIRDRE: Did he?

PAT: Yeah, ever so nice of him.

DEIRDRE: Um, yes.

PAT: Mind, I think Terry liked you, you know.

DEIRDRE: Oh, maybe he did, maybe he didn't.

PAT: Oh, I reckon he did. Still, hope we do see them again, don't you?

DEIRDRE: Oh, yes.

PAT: Oh, I do.

(Back to the Lads)

TERRY: You gave her all your luncheon vouchers?

BOB: Oh, well, you know.

TERRY: What's a matter with you, are you some kind of nut? What are you going to live on next week, Wimpys?

BOB: Oh, well, you know.

TERRY: Anyhow, I've got to be off then, mate.

BOB: Yeah.

TERRY: You got half a crown for the machine?

BOB: No, why?

TERRY: I had a full packet when we left that pub.

BOB: Yeah?

TERRY: Yeah. Oh, tarra then.

BOB: Yeah, tarra.

TERRY: See ya.

BOB: Yeah…d'you reckon you'll see her again?

TERRY: Maybe, maybe not. What about you, then?

BOB: No, I dunno.

TERRY: *(teasing him)* Eh!

BOB:*(raising his voice)* I dunno!

TERRY: Eh!

BOB: Oh, get on with ya.

TERRY: Aye, cheerio then, mate.

BOB: Yeah, cheerio.

TERRY: See ya.

BOB: Yeah, you know what, though?

TERRY: What?

BOB: She's all right.

TERRY: Oh, yeah.

THE END

(Left to right) Laurie Asprey, Coral Atkins, Valerie Varnam and Brian Miller appeared in the BBC sketch.

It wasn't long after the Christmas Show that Dick received some good news: he'd been accepted for a three-week BBC directors' course. 'It was a great course. I remember Huw Wheldon giving a wonderful lecture: he explained that no one could be taught how to direct; it was like theorizing how to ride a bike, eventually you have to get out and see if you can do it.'

The course culminated in students being thrown in at the deep end: with a paltry £100 budget, a studio and a small crew for the day, they were expected to make their own show reel, which would be judged by the instructors.

Recording a piece of work on film – even if it was only closed-circuit – was an opportunity Dick relished, and after discussing matters with Ian, he dug out their old sketch, 'Double Date'. 'We polished it and wrote a preamble, which included details of the guys picking up the girls, and a little of the date, even though it was the post-mortem that took most of the allotted time.'

The BBC had a special arrangement with Equity whereby actors appeared in such training films for a nominal fee. The foursome recruited for the recording consisted of Laurie Asprey, Brian Miller, Coral Atkins and Valerie Varnam.

The shoestring budget, and the restrictions it caused, certainly made the students prove their mettle. Dick wanted to create a short film that was as entertaining and professional-looking as possible, but knew he had to watch the pennies. One money-saving idea included using a photo montage to show scenes from the date, a method Clement later adopted in the actual TV episode, 'Double Date'.

Actor Brian Miller felt the use of photos – taken in a pub and a Wimpy restaurant – worked well. 'Dick couldn't afford to film the date, so we all met at his house one Sunday before going out and taking the photos.'

After rehearsing during the week, the recording took place at the Riverside Studios on 21 November 1963. Brian – who later appeared in two episodes of Clement and La Frenais' 1992 sitcom, *Old Boy Network* – enjoyed making the mini-film, although the

pay was nothing to write home about! 'We got a small payment, but it was good fun.'

Brian, who has recently appeared in *EastEnders* as a TA officer, a children's series *Number Time*, and an episode of the BBC sitcom, *The Last Salute*, has Bernard Hepton, who attended the same directors' course as Dick, to thank for the part. 'I'd known Bernard a few years. Not only had I worked for him as a student at Birmingham Rep, but had just finished a season for him at the Liverpool Playhouse. After moving to London to understudy in the West End, I got a phone call from Dick. I lived at Chalk Farm in London at the time, and Dick came to see me. I read for him and was offered the part.'

Unlike the Ariel Players' sketch, and subsequent TV series, which were both set in the North-East, Dick's training film was played with Liverpudlian accents. 'It was the era of the Beatles and the Mersey sounds,' says Brian, 'which I think was the main reason Dick opted for Liverpool.'

Laurie Asprey, who gave up acting to become a full-time photographer, viewed the training film as a possible future investment, because there was always a chance it would develop into a series. Even though he never auditioned for the TV series – by then he'd begun a two-year stint with the RSC – Laurie still enjoyed working with Dick. 'The film was very good, even if there wasn't much time to rehearse. Dick was also happy with the result, I remember him telling us that he was.'

Dick Clement wasn't the only one impressed with the film: the BBC hierarchy was, too. He couldn't have chosen a more propitious time to attend the directors' course because the BBC was soon to launch the third TV channel. BBC2 began transmitting in April 1964, offering a wider choice of viewing to the British public. However, its coverage of the country was gradual, with the London area first to welcome the station. Even if you lived in an area that received the signal, it didn't guarantee you would receive the channel, because a new style aerial and television were required. But there was enormous excitement within the BBC, as Michael Peacock, in his capacity as the station's first Chief of Programmes, explains.

'Everyone was pleased because it meant the straitjacket of having only one channel, which had to cater for all tastes, would finally be removed. It took a while before the whole country could receive the channel, but by the first summer we were attracting ten per cent of the London audience, which was very pleasing.'

Another station meant plenty of space in the programming schedules, so everyone was on the lookout for promising material. Bill Cotton, who was in charge of the directors' course, spotted potential in Dick's training film, and didn't waste time speaking to Michael Peacock. 'I thought it had great comedy potential,' says Bill. 'Knowing Michael was looking for programmes, I suggested he watched it.'

Michael remembers the day Bill rushed into his office. 'He was very excited and wanted me to see a film in his office. He had a 16mm projector and was projecting it onto the wall.' Michael was suitably impressed. 'Here was a show that was clearly chock-a-block with promise. I immediately told Bill we should go for a series, and we did.'

Dick was aware of the positive vibes the film generated. 'Several people saw it, including Dennis Main Wilson – a great enthusiast – and Marty Feldman.' Dick sat at the back of the room when Feldman was watching. 'Knowing I was present Feldman remarked: "'They're good writers, keep them down!"'

Awaiting a decision regarding the series being commissioned was agonizing, as Dick pointed out in a letter he wrote to Brian Miller in January, 1964.

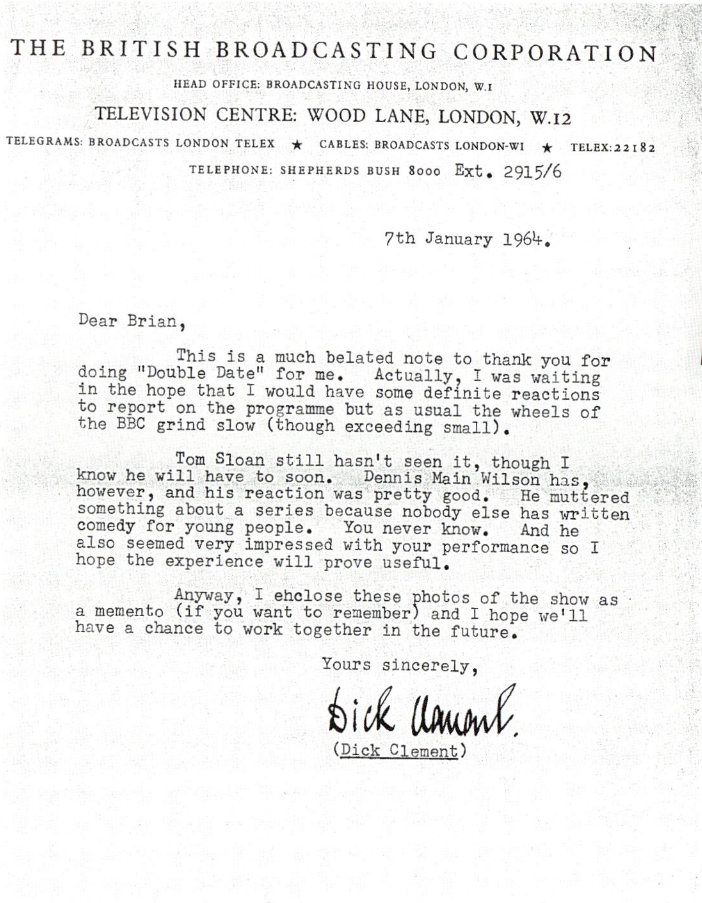

THE BRITISH BROADCASTING CORPORATION

HEAD OFFICE: BROADCASTING HOUSE, LONDON, W.1

TELEVISION CENTRE: WOOD LANE, LONDON, W.12

TELEGRAMS: BROADCASTS LONDON TELEX ★ CABLES: BROADCASTS LONDON-W1 ★ TELEX: 22182

TELEPHONE: SHEPHERDS BUSH 8000 Ext. 2915/6

7th January 1964.

Dear Brian,

This is a much belated note to thank you for doing "Double Date" for me. Actually, I was waiting in the hope that I would have some definite reactions to report on the programme but as usual the wheels of the BBC grind slow (though exceeding small).

Tom Sloan still hasn't seen it, though I know he will have to soon. Dennis Main Wilson has, however, and his reaction was pretty good. He muttered something about a series because nobody else has written comedy for young people. You never know. And he also seemed very impressed with your performance so I hope the experience will prove useful.

Anyway, I enclose these photos of the show as a memento (if you want to remember) and I hope we'll have a chance to work together in the future.

Yours sincerely,

Dick Clement

(Dick Clement)

Dick Clement boating on the Norfolk Broads (above) and the Thames (below).

When Dick and Ian were eventually invited to Michael Peacock's office to learn the fate of 'Double Date', it was early May, and Dick was holidaying on the Norfolk Broads with his wife, Jenny, and friends Terry and Mary Taylor. 'We hired this motor launch, not that any of us knew the slightest thing about sailing,' says Terry, who'll never forget the first night. 'We tied the boat to a tree, and at three in the morning, Mary nudged me and said worryingly: "The boat is capsizing." I told her I hadn't noticed, and she replied: "I've fallen out of bed three times!" We all got off the boat to find it keeled over at a 60-degree angle. There we were, walking around at three in the morning, hoping someone could help us. We didn't know the Broads were tidal, until we noticed that twigs, which had been travelling one way, were now coming back: the tide was on the way in. All we could do was wait.'

Dick knew he'd have to interrupt his holiday and return to London for a make-or-break meeting with Peacock. 'Michael asked Ian and me if we felt the idea was strong enough for a series,' recalls Dick. 'We replied immediately: "Oh yes, we always saw it as a series," which was a lie because we'd never thought of it beyond what it was: a revue sketch that had been made into a small film.'

To Dick and Ian's amazement, three episodes were commissioned, with an option for a further three. 'It was a fantastic day, I was incredibly excited. I'm glad I didn't have to pitch the idea, because describing it as a show about two young blokes who drink beer and chase girls is totally nebulous – but then a lot of ideas are the same.'

When Dick arrived back at Norwich train station he ran all along the platform, jubilant, and was met by Jenny, Terry and Mary. 'He was smiling all over his face,' recalls Terry, 'and told us he'd been asked to write six episodes. It was exciting for all of us because this was Dick's big break. We were pleased for him.'

Ian, meanwhile, was full of elation when he heard the decision, but the feeling was short-lived. 'It was extraordinary because the joy quickly turned to apprehension.' Suddenly they were professional writers and had to deliver six scripts.

The Concept

Although Clement and La Frenais didn't consciously sit down and list meticulously all the themes and attitudes they wanted to explore in *The Likely Lads*, their drive to maintain naturalism in their writing saw them create a social document reflecting the general attitudes and behaviour of many young men of the period. And because the sitcom focused on subjects that are timeless, such as the opposite sex and socializing, the programme's appeal has never waned; its careful and affectionate study of proletarian life is just as accessible today as when it was made, 35 years ago.

Bob and Terry's friendship is armour-plated; a solidarity exists that quickly expunges any annoyances beyond the disagreements and petty arguments that affect all friendships. But one of the greatest differences in the Lads' make-up is their attitudes towards relationships. Although they both appear to be dating a new girl every episode, Bob and Terry's views on love are as different as chalk and cheese. Whilst Terry's hard-edged 'life's too short' attitude means he is an exponent of playing the field, even if it leaves broken hearts in his wake, Bob is inclined to fall in love after the first date, particularly if he is the recipient of love letters like the one Veronica Holmes, whom he dated at school, sends him.

My darling Bobby,

Vin Welsh has told me that you told him to tell me that you want to go with me. I was so surprised when he told me because I did not think that you had even noticed me, and in fact I thought that you loved Nancy Ridley? – I dunno where she got that idea from.

I, myself, personally, needless to say – would love to go out with you. I have always liked you, Bobby, and have told Janet, my best friend, so…even though she thinks that you will get into trouble if you go on knocking around with that rough Terry Collier.

I will meet you on Saturday, if it is convenient, near the swings at Priory Park at 2 o'clock. If not, let Vin know and he will tell me. Will you be wearing your new drainpipe trousers? I think they are dead good, even though Janet says they are common.

Finally, I would only like to say, in conclusion, that if you really do want to go out with me I will always be true and go out with nobody else. I say this because I know in my heart that you, and only you will be the only one that I will ever care for – always.

All my love – yours truly

Veronica.

Clement and La Frenais specialize in depicting life for people on the bottom rung of the social ladder, characters who appeal to the general public, who sympathize, or even empathize, with their trials and tribulations. Bob Ferris and Terry Collier work in a maintenance shop at Ellison's, a North-Eastern factory, in the days of militant trade unions and great divides between the browbeaten blue-collar workers, and management.

This is beautifully highlighted in the episode, 'The Razor's Edge', when Terry classes the management's demands for Bob to shave off his beard as sheer victimization. There was a distinction, at the time, between people who wore ties, and those who didn't.

For Peter Fairley, a journalist on Newcastle's *Evening Chronicle*, the sitcom encapsulated much of the down-to-earth, open manner of the people from the North-East. 'The programme always struck a chord, and everyone took to it straight away. There's a heavy thread of nostalgia running through the show, visually as well. That macho 'lads together' approach still exists, but it's very different now: it's all high gloss and designer beer, rather than a pint down the pub where your father went, and his father before him.'

For the first time, *The Likely Lads* gave a voice to the people from the North-East, as Clement and La Frenais came up with a style of humour that was gentle and nostalgic, yet had a marked edge to it. Tensions had their origins in the social changes taking place, whether in the workplace, regional culture or relationships, and were appreciated by viewers across Britain, who became very fond of their 'Likely Lads'.

The Scripts

With Dick and Ian both having full-time jobs, the only time free to write the first series of *The Likely Lads* was evenings. They'd meet at Dick's house in London's Kentish Town and, as Jenny Clement recalls, would work at the kitchen table or in the dining room. 'Dick would sit and write the scripts out longhand, while Ian paced around – both speaking lines in character as they went along.'

'Dick's got better handwriting than me; that's why he did all the writing,' laughs Ian. 'When *Whatever Happened to…?* came along, we actually had an office at the BBC, with secretarial help, everything – it was wonderful. But for *The Likely Lads* we usually met at Dick's, with a baby crying in the background. Always working at his house was a pattern we established, and is something we still do, after all these years.'

Deciding on a title is never easy, as Dick and Ian found out. 'We decided to follow the guys rather than the girls, so that obviously influenced the title, but it was a while before we opted for *The Likely Lads*,' says Dick. Promotional material they wrote before the series was launched helps explain the origin. It states: 'In the North the old men in factories…shake their heads watching the younger lads, the apprentices, and they might say of some of them: "There's a likely 'un'." They say it with affection or malice, because "likely" could qualify for anything – good or bad. But there's a rueful respect in the observation, because the lads must have something even if it's just the fact that they stand out.'

MEMORABLE SCENES

EPISODE

Other Side of the Fence

(The hooter sounds, signifying the end of another day's work. Cloughy disappears at speed, and Terry plans to meet Bob, who's been seconded to a white-collar job.)

TERRY: *(pretending to time Cloughy)* Seven point nine. He's slipping.

JACK: Well, he had a heavy dinner, didn't he?

TERRY: And he's never his best on Mondays.

JACK: You coming?

TERRY: No, I'm gonna go over and wait for Bob. Watch the girls comin' out.

JACK: Aye. You want to watch yourself, you know. They never get to see a factory lad. They'll probably tear all your clothes off.

TERRY: You reckon? Eh, I wish I'd changed me underwear.

The phrase was commonly used in the North-East, but, in addition, had a wider usage, as Dick explains. 'I thought it was an English phrase, but if you listen to the soliloquy in *Carousel*, you'll find Oscar Hammerstein used it, which I wasn't conscious of until later, so it must have been in parlance both sides of the Atlantic.'

Not everybody liked their choice of title. 'We weren't sure about it for some time,' admits Ian, 'but once we'd decided, we had to go with it.'

Dick remembers telling his first wife, Jenny, and their friends, while on their Norfolk holiday. 'Jenny didn't like it at all, but we never came up with anything better, so ran with it.'

Someone else who wasn't keen on the title was Rodney Bewes. 'I've never been very good with titles, and when I first saw *The Likely Lads* written on the scripts, I thought it was terrible – but then I didn't think the Beatles was a very good name! It was only later that I began realizing just how appropriate it was.'

The process for crafting an episode always followed a similar path: the plot would be discussed, they would map out what was going to happen and jot down some lines of dialogue. 'Dick writing everything down gave me more time to walk around, which helped my thinking process,' says Ian. 'In the beginning, we depended on each other so much, we'd have been terrified to face a few hours on our own, with just a piece of blank paper!'

Whilst drafting their scripts, Dick and Ian read them aloud. Ian feels that if you're intending to create comedy from natural speech, it's wise to hear the words. 'You need to when you're writing for the spoken word; that way you can ensure it sounds like everyday dialogue.'

All along Dick and Ian found the thought of writing three scripts daunting, so they were over the moon when they eventually submitted them and received a favourable response from the BBC.

A revised version of 'Double Date', 'Entente Cordiale' and 'Older Women Are More Experienced' were the first written. In a memo to Tom Sloan – Head of Light Entertainment at the time – dated 8 July 1964, Duncan Wood confirmed the scripts had arrived, and a decision was required, since the 'authors are willing and anxious to commence work on the next script.'

After assessing the work, he sent a further memo, six days later, stating: 'On the quality of the writing

Duncan Wood, 4146 T.C.

"THE LIKELY LADS"

8th July 1964

H.L.E.G.(Tel.) Copy to: Mr. John Law

We have now received from Dick Clement and Ian La Frenais two original scripts and the re-written version of the pilot, "Double Date". None of these scripts has as yet been formally accepted. However, we must now assess this material, since the time has come to take up our option for a further three or otherwise.

Thinking in terms of a series of six programmes, the present situation is as under:-

1. "Entente Cordiale". Written. The ending needs some slight adjustment but basically this is a good and funny script. Copy attached.

2. "Double Date". This is also written. It is at No. 2 in the series since the action is a direct follow-up to "Entente Cordiale" and takes place one week later. This is of course the re-written version of the pilot and with some slight adjustments is by and large acceptable. The script is at the moment being duplicated - copy will follow.

3. "Hero Worship". This story line has been discussed and agreed and a short synopsis is in existence. On our taking up the option, this will be the next one to be written.

4. "Older Women are more Experienced". Written. Again the ending needs a slight re-write which has been discussed and agreed. Copy of the script attached.

5. To be decided.

6. "The Emigrant". Again the basic story line has been discussed and agreed, and a short synopsis is in existence.

I would appreciate a decision on our option rights as soon as possible, since the authors are willing and anxious to commence work on the next script.

(Duncan Wood)

EC

so far I think there is no question other than we should take up the option [for the authors to provide a further three scripts] forthwith.'

Wood's request was accepted and Dick and Ian were commissioned to complete the final three scripts: the working titles 'Hero Worship' and 'The Emigrant' were dropped and 'The Other Side of the Fence', 'Chance of a Lifetime' and 'The Suitor' were written.

Initially they found the process of scriptwriting slow, but as they began understanding their characters and establishing an ethos, they gradually found their feet. 'We were slow at first because we were also learning how to write plots,' says Ian 'But we got faster, and wrote "The Suitor" – the last of the first series – very quickly. Funnily enough, it got the best ratings. Once we had a plot, the dialogue was fairly easy; by then we were doing one a week, but I'll never forget that first script. We didn't finish until two in the morning!'

As Dick and Ian's writing matured they would always create the plot first, but in the early days this wasn't necessarily the case. Occasionally they'd start a script without knowing how the episode would develop, writing themselves, more times than not, into a corner, as Dick recalls. 'When we wrote "Brief Encounter", one of my favourite episodes, where the Lads go out with the same girl, we were planning they'd discover this halfway through. We then asked ourselves: "What would happen if they don't find out it's the same girl until the last frame of the show, could we get away with it?" We tried and it worked beautifully, but changing the plot halfway through isn't ideal; it's far better knowing how things will pan out.'

One way of distinguishing good scriptwriters from the pack is to consider how much their scripts have to be rewritten before filming can begin. It's not unusual for lines to be reworked before recording the show, but with Dick Clement and Ian La Frenais' scripts, nothing was required. As Rodney Bewes points out, 'We didn't even alter a comma.'

The Setting

When it came to placing the series geographically, Dick and Ian returned to their original North-Eastern setting. Although they felt the idea of following the lives of two lads-about-town wasn't particularly original, they broke new ground in other ways, as Dick points out. 'Nobody had portrayed the North or the working-classes in situation comedy. We had been influenced by all those British black and white films of the period: *Saturday Night and Sunday Morning*, *Billy Liar*, *A Kind of Loving* and *The Loneliness of the Long-Distance Runner*, all bringing a breath of fresh air to the British Cinema.' Dick and Ian wanted to do the same for TV.

Ian La Frenais, who grew up in the region, agreed the North-East was the ideal spot. 'Nothing had been based there before, so it seemed right. But it was set in no man's land initially: we didn't specify whether it was Teeside or Tyneside, although by the time *Whatever Happened to …?* came along, we'd settled for Tyneside.'

'Another reason we changed back to the North-East was to accommodate Jimmy Bolam's accent,' explains Dick. At first, the writers resisted placing the series in any specific town or city. 'Jimmy Bolam was from Sunderland, Ian from Whitley Bay, so that nudged the show towards the North-East. But in those days there weren't enough actors who could do a decent North-East accent, so it was far too adventurous to try and specify exactly where the show was set.'

Rodney Bewes liked the fact that no actual locale

was mentioned in the early episodes. 'I remember Dick getting a map and drawing a line between Sunderland, where Jimmy was born, and Bingley, just outside Bradford, where I was born. At the middle of the line was Middlesbrough, so we started off telling ourselves this was the setting as a sort of compromise.'

Dick's liking for the region played its part, too. Even though he was an Essex lad, Jenny Clement felt Dick would have loved to have felt there had been a mix-up at birth, and he'd actually been born in the North-East. 'He had a great affinity for the area, and the people's sense of humour – he wasn't really an Essex lad,' she says.

In hindsight, Dick feels that if they'd opted for another region in which to base their sitcom, it wouldn't have worked. 'The setting was so important: it gave the show a freshness.'

However, the production wallet for *The Likely Lads* was far from bulging, so location work was kept to a minimum, and whenever the need arose, selecting locations within close proximity to Television Centre proved adequate.

Rodney Bewes recalls one such spot, just minutes from the BBC, that worked wonders. 'We found a street in Willesden Junction where most of the location shooting took place. Two rows of proper back-to-back houses, with little brick loos at the end of the gardens, became the North – you couldn't have recreated anything better. We didn't need to go and film in Newcastle. I always adored location filming at Willesden Junction, and it made me smile to think we were so close to Television Centre.'

But when it came to filming 'Anchors Aweigh' – which was set on the Norfolk Broads – in the third series, it was decided to venture further afield. After recording, Dick, Ian and Jimmy would eat at an Italian restaurant in the Fulham Road, and it was during one such occasion that a decision was taken to go on location properly.

'This episode was one of my favourites,' claims Rodney. 'It's such a shame there are so few of the old black and whites left in the archives because they were so good, and it's sad to think they may never be seen again.'

The public enjoyed 'Anchors Aweigh', and so did Rodney. 'There was a fantastic atmosphere throughout the series, and it was good to find the landlord of the pub in which we were staying liked the show, too. He was so pleased to have us staying; I remember him saying to me: "The crew are drinking a lot, aren't they?" I replied: "They do, it's the first day and we're not doing anything tomorrow."

'I told him I was slimming and that I was only

drinking red wine. When I asked him to put by a bottle, he enthused: "I've got a wonderful red wine in the cellar. I'll tell you what, Rodney, I'll put a bottle behind the counter and you can have it for the week – I'll write 'Rodney's bottle' on it." That lunchtime we drunk 27 bottles of it!'

The Characters

Over the years, people have wondered whether Dick Clement and Ian La Frenais were looking in a mirror when they wrote *The Likely Lads* and the Seventies' sequel. Even though the writers dismiss the idea of them being Bob and Terry, several of their old friends aren't so sure. 'I think Dick and Ian were the two characters,' says Terry Taylor. 'Terry, with his anarchic, slightly angst-ridden humour was Ian,

MEMORABLE SCENES

EPISODE

Baby, It's Cold Outside

(Terry and Bob, who've agreed to look after their friends' kids while they go out, bring two girls back pretending it's their pad.)

TERRY: It's all right, Bob, don't you worry. I've fixed the kids, there's nothing more to worry about. They don't suspect a thing.

(June re-enters)

JUNE: All right, what's going on?

BOB: What d'you mean?

JUNE: Well it's the first bachelor flat I've ever known where I've come across one of these. *(She produces a yellow plastic potty)*

and Bob, slightly more pompous and serious, was, perhaps, more like Dick. There's a nice contrast between Dick and Ian and this comes across whenever you watch Bob and Terry.'

When the episodes were transmitted, Horace Jeffcock, who grew up with Ian in Whitley Bay, noticed grains of truth in many of the stories. 'I'm sure lots of the stories were founded on Ian's early life. In several of the early episodes, I recognized events that had happened in my time with him.'

David Hallwood, another of Ian's friends, also spotted such events. 'One of the many "Likely Lad" adventures which was based on fact was the Rupert Bear quiz when Bob and Terry quizzed each other on these famous annuals – I remember such a thing really happening.'

Inevitably, Ian's life growing up in Whitley Bay influenced the show, but *The Likely Lads* isn't entirely based on it. 'I never worked in a factory for a start,' he says. 'But I used to hang out at seaside arcades, and tried getting to know the guys there, who wore drape jackets. They were all apprentices working in the factories, which is what we decided to make Terry and Bob.'

Dick Clement acknowledges parallels have been drawn, but feels they were always a bit 'glib'. When the series started, Dick was enjoying a life of domesticity while Ian was savouring his days as a bachelor. 'I was much more Bob-like, being married with kids, and Ian was like Terry; but it would be pushing it to strike too many similarities. We may have picked up on emotions within ourselves, but we weren't looking back at our lives. When we were writing the episodes, we never thought my responsibilities were

to Bob, and Ian's to Terry: we were simply trying to find a story with a beginning, middle and end.'

From the outset, the central characters were strong and sharp, so it's surprising to hear the writers spent little time on character profiles before launching into those early episodes. 'Bob and Terry just evolved,' says Dick. 'We didn't sit down and decide what they would do and be like – we were too green for that!'

Slowly it became clear that one of them was more disreputable, and while one was more conservative, the other was a tearaway.

'When we cast the roles, the actors brought their own personalities to the characters. It's at that point that you start writing towards the actual actors' strengths.'

Bob and Terry are working-class lads, serving apprenticeships in one of the region's big factories. 'When we were thinking about the setting, we knew it would be impossible to have a whole factory floor with thousands of extras slaving away in the background, so we put the Lads in the maintenance shop, which was controllable,' says Dick. 'The fact only four people worked there meant it was a manageable set that could be used time and again, while still having a sense of the factory floor not far away.'

Bob is easily led by Terry, and is more idealistic. He has yearnings, whether it be to go abroad or in the army, whereas Terry is content to stay put. Ironically, it is Terry who ends up in the Forces, thanks to Bob. 'This amused us enormously,' says Ian, 'and we were pleased with the way we wrote them out of our lives. It also gave us a great way to start the new series when we brought them back.'

Some people view Terry as a loser, particularly during the sequel, when he leads a life devoid of hope and prosperity. He despises pretentiousness, and clings to the belief that progression might be construed as abandoning his roots, a charge he fires at Bob. In reality, it could be a ruse to shield himself from the true facts: he's struggling to adjust to life back in his home town.

Dr. Les Gofton, a lecturer in behavioural science

Clement and La Frenais' classic sitcom was influenced by films like *Saturday Night, Sunday Morning* and *A Kind of Loving*, all depicting working class life.

at the University of Newcastle, and a fan of the show, doesn't feel it's all doom and gloom as far as Terry Collier is concerned. 'Terry also represents the kind of toughness of the North-East, which is such an important quality. I don't think Terry is a loser at all; he's not a pathetic or sad figure. He represents parts of the North-East character which people are most proud of: the sharp, incisive intelligence, the fact that he can't be fooled. People can try to look down on him, or try patronizing him, but actually he's a smart cookie. What he sees is the reality; he's not going to be fooled by any rubbish from politicians or anyone else.'

The interplay between the two central characters is beautifully worked, even though both Rodney Bewes and James Bolam were still getting to know their characters. They may not always agree with each other's point of view, and argue vehemently, but there is obviously a strong bond between the lads.

Casting

The success of so many shows is determined by the casting. Offer a central role to the wrong person, and the odds on failure rocket. Even veteran producers occasionally get it wrong, which makes Dick Clement's achievement even more outstanding, bearing in mind he was only a cub producer. Rodney Bewes and James Bolam were perfect for the roles. 'They certainly auditioned the best,' says Dick, who was responsible for all the casting. 'They were both first choice, loved the scripts and were very supportive.'

Even though Dick felt Bewes and Bolam auditioned the best, casting the main roles was difficult, particularly as he'd cast the roles once before, for the film he made during his directors' course. Now a series had been commissioned, it was only right he considered Brian Miller and Laurie Asprey, who had played Bob and Terry respectively.

By the time it came to the auditions, Laurie Asprey was busy working with the RSC and wasn't free, but Brian Miller was keen to be considered. He was working in Glasgow when he received a call from Dick Clement's office, inviting him to travel down for a reading with another actor. At first, Brian was optimistic about his chances of landing the part of Bob. 'I'd been told that the film we'd made for the training course had been shown to various people at the BBC, and everyone liked my performance. So things sounded hopeful.'

Brian ended up reading with Jimmy Bolam, but as soon as he'd completed the audition, he knew he hadn't got the job. 'When Dick said he'd let me know later that week, I realized I wasn't going to get it.'

'Brian Miller was very close to getting the part,' says Dick. 'I knew Jimmy was right from the start, but it was close between Brian and Rodney. In the end it was a very good day's casting, and everything slotted nicely into place.'

Understandably, Brian was sad, but now believes Dick made the right choice. 'I was disappointed at the time because it was a television series and they didn't come along every day. But as it turned out, Rodney Bewes was perfect casting, much better than I would have been. Anyway, I wouldn't have been the right combination physically. I was too similar to Jimmy Bolam.'

Brian enjoyed watching the series. 'It was quality stuff: the writing and playing was perfect; there was a certain chemistry between the entire cast. I thought Brigit Forsyth's portrayal of Thelma in the sequel was almost as vivid as Basil Fawlty's wife.'

Whenever he was casting, Dick would often flick through *Spotlight* (the actors' directory) to see if any of the smiling faces caught his eye. 'Sometimes I'd look at an actor and say: "He looks like he has a sense of humour." As crazy as it sounds, you can sometimes sense the people who have a funny bone, simply from looking at a picture; you can also tell actors who haven't. They may hate me for saying it, but I think there's some truth in it.'

But that wasn't the method used to find Bewes

MEMORABLE SCENES

EPISODE

The Suitor

(Terry is at home having tea with his family and Mario, Audrey's new boyfriend. He's just found out that another barber cuts Mario's hair.)

TERRY: I've often wondered about that myself, you know. It's like doctors. I mean, do they examine themselves like. *(pause)* I once heard about a French doctor. Took his own appendix out. I dunno how he managed it though. I don't know how he could do it.

MRS COLLIER: Something else, Mario? Don't be shy, love, help yourself.

AUDREY: Yes, a bit of swiss roll or Mum's fruit cake?

MARIO: I'll have another scone, thank you.

TERRY: I suppose he must have managed it somehow – I don't see how he could see though.

AUDREY: Excuse my brother – he's always taking his appendix out at the tea table.

and Bolam: both actors were recommended. 'A friend of mine, who's not in the business, said I should take a look at James Bolam, who was at the Royal Court at the time. As soon as I saw Jimmy I knew he was right.'

Rodney, meanwhile, was suggested by Sydney Lotterby, Dick's production assistant. Both actors had already gained plenty of stage experience, and had appeared in films: Bewes had recently made *Billy Liar*, while Bolam was seen in *A Kind of Loving* and *The Loneliness of the Long-Distance Runner.*

Another important role was Terry Collier's sister, Audrey, for which Sheila Fearn was recruited. 'I saw a lot of people for that role,' says Dick. 'I'd never seen Sheila before, but liked her immediately. She went on to play the part beautifully.'

Rodney Bewes also enjoyed working with Sheila. 'She was wonderful, a great foil as Terry's sister. Although she didn't always have a great look-in as far as dialogue was concerned, she was very good.'

When it came to casting characters like Cloughy, Jack and Blakey – played by Bartlett Mullins, Donald McKillop and Richard Moore respectively – Dick relied on his trusty *Spotlight* directory, after carrying out some research locally. 'I went round some factories on a trading estate not far from White City. I'd never

worked in a factory, so wanted to appreciate what it must have been like, and the sort of people who worked there. I wanted some working-class credibility when it came to Bob and Terry's work colleagues, and Bartlett, Donald and Richard played the parts well.'

Working Behind the Scenes

There are many components to a successful TV show, such as having a skilled production team beavering away behind the scenes. Often denied their rightful credit, the people in charge of all the

cameras, sound equipment, make-up, costumes, design and myriad of other jobs involved in making a programme, are key to the whole enterprise.

Having a novice, like Dick Clement was back in 1964, not only write a new sitcom, but produce and direct it too, was, arguably, an unprecedented event. 'It was extraordinary, a once-in-a-lifetime opportunity. I knew that if I didn't accept the challenge, I'd never get the chance again.'

But it was a series of unforeseen circumstances which led to Dick being offered the job in the first place, as he explains. 'A veteran producer called Harry Carlisle was assigned to the show, but was unable to do it. So Duncan Wood – who was the doyen of BBC producers – was asked, but turned it down. However, he suggested I produced the show because he felt I'd done a good job with my training course film.'

To Dick's amazement, he was offered the chance to produce the sitcom. 'In one way I was too inexperienced to fully understand what I was taking on, but it was an incredible opportunity.'

To help, Sydney Lotterby – already an experienced producer in his own right – was drafted in as Dick's right-hand man, providing valuable support, if required. But as Sydney points out, he didn't need too much guidance. 'Dick was a very quick learner and was able to jump straight into the job without any problem; he didn't need much help from me. He did terribly well, and nothing ever seemed to go wrong – I was amazed.'

Sydney didn't mind being Dick's production assistant. 'It was rather flattering that they should ask me.

MEMORABLE SCENES

EPISODE

Faraway Places

(Bob and Terry are planning their hols. Bob wants to go abroad, even though money is tight.)

BOB: We're twenty-two next birthday. We might never get another chance to go abroad again.

TERRY: You're not engaged again, are you?

BOB: No, don't be stupid. But for all we know I might be a year from now! And so might you. And we'll look back and see we've never been to France, or the Riviera or – or – or the Canary Islands.

TERRY: We never been to a holiday camp either.

I was also pleased because I'd been a producer before giving it all up, and this enabled me to start all over again.'

One thing he remembers fondly from those days was playing table tennis. 'I encouraged Dick to finish rehearsals as quickly as possible, so we could have a game of table tennis. He was very good and would beat us all, but it was great fun.'

Sydney enjoyed his time on *The Likely Lads*. 'It was an excellent idea. Before that we hadn't really had any comedy about two young lads, and it was bright, new and fresh.' He understands why people liked the show. 'We've all been through those days when we were younger; it was true to life and very innovative. If it had been made today, it would have much more punch, but back in 1964, it was just right.'

Having Sydney to discuss ideas and thoughts with was important to Dick. 'He was a great help, and I'll be eternally grateful to him for using his experience to help someone like me, who was so green.'

Once a second series of *The Likely Lads* had been commissioned, Dick and Ian were given an office on the seventh floor of Television Centre, in which to work. Assigned to the team, as production secretary, was Ann Milford, who had worked on numerous other shows, including *This Is Your Life*. 'I found it all very exciting,' says Ann, whose responsibilities involved organizing studios, film locations and also many of the administrative tasks. 'Dick and Ian were lovely people to work for. Sometimes it was so much fun, it didn't feel like work.'

Ann and the rest of the team worked hard. 'Getting all the paperwork sorted out took a lot of time, and I'd spend several late nights doing old-fashioned things like completing camera cards. Dick would mark up the script with all the camera shots, which then had to be typed on cards. The cards would hang on the cameras, because every shot had its own individual number and a camera allocated to film it.'

Ann, who left the BBC 28 years ago when her first child was born, feels *The Likely Lads* was one of her favourite shows. 'It made everyone working on it laugh, which was always a good sign regarding its general appeal. It was such a funny show.'

Dick Chamberlain, who was in charge of sound recording for the first two series, agrees with Ann. 'It was a brilliant show; everyone seemed to enjoy working on it.' To the sound department *The Likely Lads* was a challenge, because it was made at a time when the fine tuning that now takes place after the recording wasn't possible. 'In those days, you had to get everything right first time. If, like *The Likely Lads*, you were recording a show in front of a live audience, you avoided retakes as much as possible. Jokes aren't as funny second time around, and this would show in the audience's reaction. Nowadays, if you do a retake and the audience reaction isn't as good, you can overdub laughter afterwards.'

One piece of equipment that has advanced considerably since *The Likely Lads* was recorded is the microphone. 'Today, when you use radio mikes, the transistor is so small it's easily concealed on the person. They're so advanced they no longer crackle, whereas the type we had were substantial in size, and crackled a lot.'

Another problem facing Dick Chamberlain and his colleagues involved getting the mikes close enough to the actors to pick up the sound properly. 'They were just above the picture line, which made camera operation and boom operating very difficult. If you weren't careful you'd cause problems with lights reflecting off the microphone booms, casting shadows on the set. It was certainly a challenge!'

Responsible for designing the opening titles was Colin Cheeseman, who didn't have computer graphics or other modes of advanced technology to help. Back in 1964, he relied on still photography.

'I designed a sequence that showed a dartboard with darts flying into it. Photographs were shot and then filmed, before editing it to the soundtrack – there was nothing elaborate about it!'

When it came to the opening and closing credits, it was the graphic designer's responsibility to come up with ideas for how the title sequences would look. After reading the scripts, a storyboard would be drawn up before meeting the director to discuss ideas.

'Then you had to agree the typography and listen to the music in order to work out how long each shot would have to be held on screen. That way, the music and titles complemented each other.'

Overall, Colin was pleased with his work, and felt it matched the style of sitcom. 'Dick was keen to present a realistic feel to the programme and, I felt, the titles were appropriate for that sort of show.'

Each episode usually required five sets, and one of the designers who worked on many of the early episodes was Geoff Kirkland.

'Geoff was responsible for all the sets, and came to me one week to show me the plans,' says Dick. 'Just as he was going, I said: "Wait a minute, where's the pub?" He looked at his plans and replied: "D'you know, I've forgotten all about it." Almost every week we had a pub, but he'd left it out, which meant changing the structure of all his sets to squeeze another one in.'

The pubs were important to the series, indicative of a social order where men went out while their wives stayed at home – a bastion of so-called male dominance and independence.

'Although we had a regular pub that Terry and Bob used, we knew that lads of that age were always trying out new places, or would go on pub-crawls,' says Dick. 'One of our favourite names was the Fat Ox. Sometimes we'd have a really big pub, and other times we'd opt for a snug bar inside a little corner pub. But they all looked so accurate and realistic, thanks to people like Geoff.'

Hitting Our Screens

Terry Collier and Bob Ferris' small screen life began on the evening of 16 December 1964. BBC2's first sitcom was transmitted at 9.55 p.m., when viewers – albeit those who were prepared, or could afford, to invest in a new set and aerial – were treated to the first glimpse of what would become a television classic, thanks mainly to the on-screen rapport that developed between Bewes and Bolam, and some sparkling scripts by Clement and La Frenais. It was the latter ingredient that convinced Michael Peacock the sitcom would be a sure-fire ratings winner. 'They were refreshingly sharp and contemporary. *The Likely Lads* stood out from other situation comedies we were looking at,' says Michael, who received no resistance within the BBC towards the show. 'When you're starting with nothing in your schedule it's terrific finding something you reckon will be a hit.'

Peacock enjoyed the show so much that when he later transferred to BBC1, he convinced David Attenborough, who took over as Controller of BBC2, to let him repeat the shows on BBC1. 'I wanted to transmit them as part of my comedy-scheduling plan. I had comedies on five nights of the week in an attempt to pull audiences across from ITV, and I thought *The Likely Lads* would help to achieve that.'

The first episode was well received. An audience survey conducted by the BBC produced promising

THE LIKELY LADS

A new series based on the lives of two young Northerners.

(2) 9.25 p.m.

In the North the old men in factories chew their plug tobacco and shake their heads watching the younger lads, the apprentices, and they might say of some of them - 'there's a likely'un'. They say it with affection or malice, because 'likely' could qualify for anything - good or bad. But there's a rueful respect in the observation, because the lads must have something even if it is just the fact that they stand out.

And there are hundreds of them. Lads like Bob Ferris and Terry Collier whose lives we follow in 'The Likely Lads'. Probably around twenty one with twelve or fourteen pounds a week coming in; four to your mother and the rest to yourself minus the H.P. on the 'bike. Most things happen at the weekends, best of all Saturday. In the winter there's football and the dance, in the summer you might take a girl to the coast for the day - or go with the boys and pick one up. But you're happiest in the town, with what's familiar. You know every back street pub and club, and how to get in the Palais without a pass-out. Everything's happening now and most of it's good; the future's something that comes along after you're twenty five.

Bob and Terry are lads like this. Acquisitive, irreverent, they don't miss much. At their age naturally they're idealists - but injected with a strong shot of northern commonsense.

The 'Likely Lads' is B.B.C. 2's first situation comedy series, and it is a 'first' in many respects for the team behind it. The series is devised and written by two young writers DICK CLEMENT and IAN LA FRENAIS, and developed from a ~~revue sketch written by them some time ago and subsequently used in a~~ script they wrote during a television training course ~~exercise~~ undertaken by Dick Clement when he was with Sound Broadcasting. Dick Clement also produces and directs the series - his first for television. A first series, too, for the two talented actors who play the lads; although JAMES BOLAM, who plays Terry, and RODNEY ~~BUES~~ BREWES, Bob, have already established themselves on television, the stage and in films. Oddly enough both played supporting roles, respectively, to Tom Courtenay in the films 'The Loneliness of the Long Distance Runner' and 'Billy Liar'. Both are northerners themselves; James Bolam is from Sunderland and Rodney Brewes from Bingley in Yorks, while writer Ian La Frenais is from Newcastle. Producer Dick Clement is in fact a southerner but has been granted honorary northern citizenship by the other three.

Talking of the series the writers said: "We have attempted to make what happens to the boys as naturalistic and as honest as possible, for so often writing about young people is terribly unreal. [~~This is partly why the setting is in the North, where the cult of the teenager is much less pronounced~~".]

In tonights episode the boys have returned home from their first holiday abroad.

(posted - 500 WORDS)

But neither of the boys can be posted in any of the currently convenient pigeonholes. They are neither mods, nor rockers, ~~for example~~ things or intellectuals. What we do hope is that what happens to them is funny.

results. The show was described as 'amusing, entertaining, enjoyable'. The audience liked the sitcom's working-class focus, and its 'homely' feel. Many of the people contributing to the sample praised the show's naturalness, with comments such as: 'natural comedy at its simple best', 'very good and down to earth – just the way two boys would talk to each other' and 'situation very true to life…'

Dick Clement and Ian La Frenais had achieved one of the goals they set themselves when writing *The Likely Lads*. They wanted to create a sitcom that didn't rely on an endless stream of gags, concentrating, instead, on establishing character in plausible situations, with a down-to-earth grittiness reflecting real life.

As Dick says: 'We wanted to get away from the sort of comedy seen in the *Doctor* films: Donald Sinden and Kenneth More wearing cravats as upper-class characters. We wanted to get back to a grainier reality.'

The general reaction from the audience sampled by the BBC, and the opinions of the national press, proved that the writers were well on their way to achieving their aim. As the sitcom progressed, journalists applauded the show. Maurice Wiggin wrote in the *Sunday Times*: 'Ian La Frenais and Dick Clement have created a pair who are not only credible, but precisely complementary…The happy fact is that they are rooted in life, true to life and to themselves.'

Stewart Lane, meanwhile, felt the series was one

"THE LIKELY LADS"

No. 1: 'ENTENTE CORDIALE' (11/2/4/0168)

13th October 1964

SHOOTING SCRIPT

SHOT NO.	SLATE NO.	CUTTING SCRIPT NO.	BASIC SET-UP	DESCRIPTION
1	1 Print 2	2	MAIDENHEAD	HIGH SHOT of the boys running across the station courtyard. PAN them right as they go into the station.
2	2 Print 2	4	"	LS of the boys thundering down a corridor towards us, past the two passengers. PAN them right and up as they turn the corner to run up the stairs.
3	3 Print 1	6	"	MID SHOT of the boys standing at the ticket collector's grille, looking through it at Louise. They speak from "Look at that .... to... It's me she's waving at." TERRY waves.
	4 Print 2	8		The boys as before. Dialogue from: "All right..... to .... pay him for two platform tickets." TERRY walks through the gate and out of shot left of frame. BOB is left fumbling in his pocket for the money for two platform tickets.
4	5 Print 1.	1	GREENFORD	LS train standing in station; the two girls are standing on the platform looking uncertain; two other passengers are coming towards us and walk out of frame R.
5	6 Print 1 (all).	3	"	MID SHOT of the girls with the train now in middle distance. Colette has her back to us and is checking her make-up. she looks up and sees the sign 'Ladies' says something to Louise and walks into the 'Ladies',right.

Continued...../

- 1 -

RECORDED

"THE LIKELY LADS" (No. 1) RECORDING 24th October 1964

T.C. 4 RECORDING 20.00 20.25

VT/6T/24821

11/2/4/0168. DICK CLEMENT.

Terry.	JAMES BOLAM	£ 105. 0. 0.
Bob.	RODNEY BEWES	73. 10. 0.
Cloughy.	BARTLETT MULLINS	52. 10. 0.
Jack.	Donald McKillop	52. 10. 0.
Mrs. Collier.	OLIVE MILBOURNE	68. 5. 0.
Audrey.	SHEILA FEARN	42. 0. 0.
Colette.	BETTINE LE BEAU	42. 0. 0.
Louise.	CHRISTINE COLLINS	36. 15. 0.
Waitress.	JOAN PICKERING	36. 15. 0.

(JAMES BOLAM – Photo Calls 4. 4. 0.
& RODNEY BEWES – Photo Calls) 4. 4. 0.)

Terry.	JAMES BOLAM	£ 10. 10. 0.
Bob.	RODNEY BEWES	10. 0. 0.
Colette.	BETTINE LE BEAU	10. 0. 0.
Louise.	CHRISTINE COLLINS	10. 0. 0.
Walk-on.	GERALD HARDRISTY	6. 6. 0.
"	BOB LANE	6. 6. 0.
music	RONNIE HASLEHURST ORCH. (10).	135. 0. 0.

Script	Ian La Frenais Dick Clement
Orchestrations	Ronnie Hazlehurst
Make Up and Wardrobe	BBC
Design	BBC
Facilities fee for use of Maidenhead and Greenford Railway Stations.	B.R. (Western)

of the 'best of its kind'. In the *Morning Star* he wrote: 'The two main characters have an acceptable working-class background, are credible, and become involved in easily recognizable situations.'

But Virginia Ironside, writing in the *Daily Mail*, back in 1967, summed up the essence of the sitcom beautifully, when she commented: 'What's nice about *The Likely Lads* is the dour drabness of the humour. Comedy situations in *The Likely Lads* involve hanging around for girls who don't turn up, rain, bad beer, being conned, greasy sausages, hangovers. Sheer desperate gloom is always funny, because unfortunately we have all experienced it.'

Watching the first episode being transmitted was an exciting time for Dick and Ian. 'I felt so nervous I had to take a lot of pills that day to control my nerves,' laughs Ian. 'And that was only the afternoon when they were doing the technical run!'

But the first series was also frustrating for Ian, who remained employed in market research throughout that time. Whenever possible, he'd hare over to the rehearsal room during his lunch break. 'I was terribly frustrated not being able to get more involved. It was exciting being in the church hall with all these actors reading your lines, moving around, acting out what Dick and I had created. Eventually I gave up my job and became a full-time writer – I just wish I'd been able to do it earlier.'

Dick was also thrilled to see their script come alive on the screen. 'It was unforgettable. It's enormously

MEMORABLE SCENES

EPISODE

Outward Bound

(Bob, Terry, Jack and Cloughy sunbathe on the factory rooftop)

TERRY: That's the trouble with the sun, isn't it – peeling. You can never leave it alone. You always want to pull a bit more off.

BOB: D'you mind?

(Jack comes out from under his newspaper. He looks at Terry)

JACK: I can't imagine you sunburned. Little shrivelled brown thing. You'll look like a chipolata.

(They all laugh except Terry)

BOB: He doesn't give himself much chance, does he? (*He looks at Terry still in his overalls, buttoned up to the throat*) Look at you – all buttoned up. He hasn't had his vest off since secondary modern. Let the sun get at you.

TERRY: I feel the cold.

British Broadcasting Corporation — Confidential

AN AUDIENCE RESEARCH REPORT

(Week 51) — LE VR/64/664

THE LIKELY LADS

Entente Cordiale

Written by Dick Clement and Ian La Frenais

Designer: Richard Hunt

Produced by Dick Clement

Wednesday, 16th December, 1964. 9.55-10.20 pm, BBC 2

1. Reaction of audience (based on questionnaires completed by a sample of the audience. This sample, 103 in number, is the 15% of BBC 2 Viewing Panel who saw all or most of the broadcast.)

The reactions of this sample of the audience were distributed as follows:-

A+	A	B	C	C-
%	%	%	%	%
19	45	30	4	2

giving a REACTION INDEX of 69. The current average for television light entertainment programmes is 64.

2. 'Amusing, entertaining, enjoyable' said one viewer in the sample, putting together the descriptions of praise that were most frequently used about this first part of The Likely Lads. The great majority of reporting viewers seem in fact to have liked it very much. They liked the Midland setting (working class and 'homely'), the characters (likeable and with two well-contrasted main ones in the boys, Bob and Terry), the dialogue (both witty and accurate), and the story (well shaped with a firm ending). Evidently all this added up to an episode that was refreshingly simple, down-to-earth and yet light in tone: 'A good working class story without the kitchen sink'; 'Natural comedy at its simple best'; 'Very good and down to earth - just the way two boys would talk to each other'; 'Situation very true to life and down-to-earth'; 'Typical of the lads who meet girls when on the continent for a holiday and are surprised when they actually meet them in this country'.

3. There were two main complaints, made, however, by only a very small minority. Several reporting viewers thought both story and characters unoriginal. 'A couple of grown up Clitheroe Kids in a stock situation with the corniest of scripts', was how one described it. The end was predictable, it was said, and the dialogue full of clichés. A few regretted, too, that the story took a long time to get going 'while the characters were being established'. All the same the main feeling amongst the sample was obviously that this was a good start to a series that promised to be amusing and enjoyable in a pleasantly light and uncomplicated and down-to-earth way.

4. The acting was highly praised as well. James Bolam (Terry) and Rodney Bewes (Bob) were perfectly cast, it was said, and played with absolute naturalness, and several viewers especially liked Sheila Fearn, who played Audrey, Terry's sister. But everyone in the cast, it was evidently mainly thought, played the 'likeable and amusing characters' very well and convincingly. If a few thought some of the sets lacked realism, especially the very empty-looking station buffet, the general feeling about the production seems to have been that it was satisfactory, with a good fast pace and on the whole 'typical' sets.

Copyright of the BBC
NE/BML

Audience Research Department
30th December, 1964.

gratifying that there are still people who like the series and want to talk about it, especially as one of the reasons we wrote it in the first place was to connect with people.'

Although everyone at Television Centre was pleased with the interest *The Likely Lads* generated, its big break came with the screening of a five-minute sketch about Rupert the Bear annuals on Christmas Day, 1964, in *Christmas Night with the Stars.* With nearly 19 million viewers watching on BBC1, it introduced the Lads to a much wider audience, many of whom hadn't been able to watch the start of the series on BBC2. 'That little sketch really started everything off,' admits Ian. 'It was as if people suddenly said: "What's this?" From then on we started getting some decent notices.'

But Ian feels it wasn't until much later that Bob and Terry made a real impact. '*Whatever Happened to…?* is when it really established itself, and started attracting good-sized audiences. We also won a Writers' Guild award for that series, which drew a great deal of attention.'

As with most successful shows, publicity and interest from the media and the public escalated as the sitcom evolved. Although it was well received on its original screening on BBC2, it wasn't until the series was repeated on BBC1, three months later, in the prime slot of 8 p.m., that it really took off. By the end of its run with the episode, 'The Suitor', on Friday, 9 April 1965, ten million people were watching the show.

'We got some great reviews from day one,' says Dick, 'even though, at first, it went out to a tiny audience. We were delighted when they repeated it on BBC1, because we got a wonderful response, and things really took off.'

But Dick was unhappy with the lack of publicity the show's launch on BBC2 received. He felt it was 'inadequate for the start of a new series' and wrote

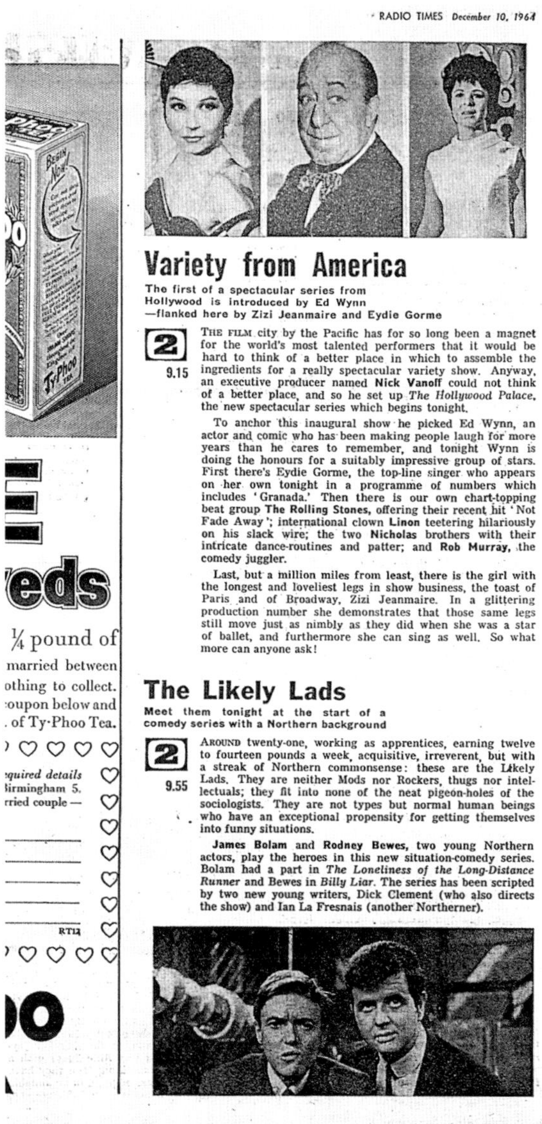

RADIO TIMES December 10, 1964

Variety from America

The first of a spectacular series from Hollywood is introduced by Ed Wynn —flanked here by Zizi Jeanmaire and Eydie Gorme

2 9.15 THE FILM city by the Pacific has for so long been a magnet for the world's most talented performers that it would be hard to think of a better place in which to assemble the ingredients for a really spectacular variety show. Anyway, an executive producer named **Nick Vanoff** could not think of a better place, and so he set up *The Hollywood Palace*, the new spectacular series which begins tonight.

To anchor this inaugural show he picked Ed Wynn, an actor and comic who has been making people laugh for more years than he cares to remember, and tonight Wynn is doing the honours for a suitably impressive group of stars. First there's Eydie Gorme, the top-line singer who appears on her own tonight in a programme of numbers which includes 'Granada.' Then there is our own chart-topping beat group **The Rolling Stones,** offering their recent hit 'Not Fade Away'; international clown **Linon** teetering hilariously on his slack wire; the two **Nicholas** brothers with their intricate dance-routines and patter; and **Rob Murray,** the comedy juggler.

Last, but a million miles from least, there is the girl with the longest and loveliest legs in show business, the toast of Paris and of Broadway, Zizi Jeanmaire. In a glittering production number she demonstrates that those same legs still move just as nimbly as they did when she was a star of ballet, and furthermore she can sing as well. So what more can anyone ask!

The Likely Lads

Meet them tonight at the start of a comedy series with a Northern background

2 9.55 AROUND twenty-one, working as apprentices, earning twelve to fourteen pounds a week, acquisitive, irreverent, but with a streak of Northern commonsense: these are the Likely Lads. They are neither Mods nor Rockers, thugs nor intellectuals; they fit into none of the neat pigeon-holes of the sociologists. They are not types but normal human beings who have an exceptional propensity for getting themselves into funny situations.

James Bolam and **Rodney Bewes,** two young Northern actors, play the heroes in this new situation-comedy series. Bolam had a part in *The Loneliness of the Long-Distance Runner* and Bewes in *Billy Liar*. The series has been scripted by two new young writers, Dick Clement (who also directs the show) and Ian La Fresnais (another Northerner).

From: Dick Clement, L.Ent., 4005 T.C. PABX 2783/4

Subject: "THE LIKELY LADS" 9th December 1964

To: Ch.P.(BBC 2), through H.L.E.G.(Tel.) Copy to: C.A.(Gen.)L.E.
Editor, Radio Times.

I would like to register a strong protest at the Radio Times coverage of "The Likely Lads" (Week 51).

On Friday, 27th November, I was shown the proof of the promotion material for this edition and immediately expressed my opinion that it was inadequate for the start of a new series. My main point was that the amount of information about the stars, James Bolam and Rodney Bewes, was scanty to the point of being downright insulting.

In fact they are victims of ill-informed, unintelligent, sub-editing. My co-writer and I wrote some promotion material several weeks ago in which we mentioned in passing that both the actors had co-starred with Tom Courtenay and named the relevant films. This was reduced by the Radio Times to "Bolam had a part in 'The Loneliness of the Long Distance Runner' and Bewes in 'Billy Liar' ", which demoted them to the level of walk-ons. When one considers that James Bolam, for example, has appeared in the West End with Olivier; as Christ at The Mermaid; and in important parts in films such as "A Kind of Loving" and "Murder Most Foul", recently, the inadequacy of the promotion becomes quite apparent.

I expressed this opinion to Bill Cotton who agreed with my view, and suggested that I rewrote the second paragraph. Accordingly, I went to John Humphreys (C.A.(Gen.)L.E.) who reiterated my views on the telephone to someone in Radio Times. It was pointed out that there was some difficulty in promoting two new shows on the same night (mine and 'Hollywood Palace'). However, we were promised space for an extra two lines which would give more adequate description of the stars of the show. I rewrote the second paragraph immediately and handed it to John Humphreys later that day. At the same time I pointed out that two of the four names in the copy were mispelt, (James Bolan and Ian La Fregnais) which seemed a remarkably high average. When one adds that Rodney Bewes has become Rodney Bgwes in the current BBC 2 Press Information handout and that I myself was described earlier this year as Dick Tennant, the general talent for mispelling in the Corporation is seen to amount to nothing less than genius.

/Continued....

- 2 -

Today I have been handed a copy of the Radio Times for Week 51. James Bolam is now correctly spelt. Ian La Frenais, alas, is not. Nor has anything else been either added or subtracted. The promotion remains lamentably inadequate. Even if it had been impossible to provide more space, at least some rephrasing would have avoided offending the two artists involved.

I would agree that it is better to undersell this series than to give it too large a build-up. I think however that at the very least, a proper respect to artists should be shown and would suggest that better coverage should be given them as soon as possible.

(Dick Clement)

AJM
9.12.64.

to Michael Peacock on 9 December 1964, prior to the first episode being screened, to complain.

Dick felt strongly about the *Radio Times* coverage given to *The Likely Lads* in the edition dated 10 December 1964, particularly the amount of space given to detail about Bolam and Bewes. He felt it was 'scanty to the point of being downright insulting', and that their careers warranted much more information. To make matters worse, Ian La Frenais was misspelt in the article.

Clement's memo was answered by the *Radio Times'* television editor, who pointed out that with half a page to cover BBC2's coverage for the day, and with two new series to publicize, the available space was divided. However, the editor mentioned that the other new series, *The Hollywood Palace,* was judged to be 'more important', so it got top position and more space than *The Likely Lads.*

Although Bewes and Bolam had already appeared in films and stage shows, their TV careers were just beginning. The television editor pointed out that 'neither Bewes nor Bolam is at all widely known', before adding: 'You may remember that at the promotion meeting at which you told us about this series not a single person of all the various experts present could recall who they were.' How things were to change!

The Success

Like other shows from the era, many of *The Likely Lads* episodes were victims of the BBC's retention policy. Made before videotape slashed the cost involved in storing programmes, thirteen episodes were wiped. Only a handful of instalments ('Entente Cordiale', 'Double Date', 'Older Women Are More Experienced', 'The Other Side of the Fence', 'The Suitor', 'Rocker', 'Goodbye to All That' and a 'Christmas Night with the Stars' sketch) survived the hatchet man.

Although their screening is rare, episodes of *The Likely Lads* have always received a favourable response from viewers, proving their comedic appeal is timeless. The show's success and accessibility reveal the writers homed in on issues and emotions that transcend the boundaries of time. Although, just as in the sequel, the fashions have dated, the themes running throughout the twenty episodes will always be relevant, as the writer and broadcaster, Barry Took, affirms.

'People are still growing up into the situation Bob and Terry found themselves in. You have a constant stream of people leaving school, getting jobs and beginning to realize what adult life is all about, and that's the area *The Likely Lads* explored.'

Took is a long-time admirer of Clement and La Frenais' work. 'They are one of the best writing teams ever on television. When *The Likely Lads* was written, there was great competition in scriptwriting, with people like Galton and Simpson, Esmonde and Larby, Feldman and myself – everyone was writing good stuff. Dick and Ian came into that melting pot, held their own and eventually came up with *Porridge*, probably the best sitcom of all.

'But I've always enjoyed *The Likely Lads*. Bolam and Bewes were perfect, and the whole concept was right, with interesting characters emerging from their chrysalis and becoming involved in the mainstream of life. It was also nice having a North-Eastern comedy, because people didn't think of that region being a fountain of humour.'

Looking back over the twenty episodes, Dick and Ian have their favourites, as well as those they feel didn't reach the mark. One episode they were disappointed with is 'Double Date', which is strange when you think it was on the strength of this plot that the series was commissioned. While Ian admits he doesn't like it, Dick says, 'It was the weakest episode in the first series; it didn't have the same drive as the others. Perhaps it was because we'd done it before, and recreating it wasn't madly exciting.'

'I'm very fond of one that doesn't exist anymore: "Where Have All the Flowers Gone?",' says Ian, 'but "Goodbye to All That" and "Older Women Are More Experienced" had excellent story-lines, too.'

Dick enjoyed the experience of producing the three series. 'I was very happy with everything,' he says. 'Inevitably there were mistakes, because I was learning. But these were normally where I was over-cutting like crazy, something I can spot now. I feel I could have shot the characters better: there's a rawness, but it's of its time, one has to accept that.

From: Television Editor, RADIO TIMES 310, 35 MHS PABX 4264

Subject: 'THE LIKELY LADS' 16th December 1964

To: Mr. Dick Clement Copies to: Ch.P.(BBC-2) H.L.E.G.(Tel.) C.A.(Gen.)L.E.

I should like to apologise for the mispelling of La Frenais in our article for week 51. This was a Christmas catch-up week - we went to press in four days instead of five. It was also the week in which we increased our pages yet again to accommodate extra radio programmes. There was an unusual strain on our subs and readers who normally check names in articles against names in billings.

Incidentally the action you took on the proof you saw is rather irrelevant to this procedure. We send producers the first proof we get back from the printers - an 'unread' galley proof which is often full of spelling mistakes and literals perpetrated by the typesetters. (These get checked and corrected in due course). All we intend to convey to producers is the general content and tone of an article and to get their reactions to them as quickly as possible.

We are not of course responsible for Press Information.

Now we come to your main complaint: inadequate promotion. We mentioned 'The Likely Lads' on the cover - a signal distinction. Inside we had half a page to cover BBC-2 that day and it had to be split with another new series, judged to be more important. So 'Hollywood Palace' got the top position and slightly more space than 'Likely Lads'. It is true that we promised to <u>consider</u> adding two lines to the latter, but it proved impossible, and anyway I doubt whether it would have had much effect.

The fact is neither Bewes nor Bolam is at all widely known. You may remember that at the Promotion Meeting at which you told us about this series not a single person of all the various experts present could recall who they were.

Please turn over

TOP

By quoting the two film titles we merely meant to give readers a clue to the kind of actors they were, not to their relative size. If they are going to establish themselves with a wide audience this series is their best chance so far, and we intend to carry follow-up articles on each of them after the first couple of episodes have enabled them to register with viewers. This, by the way, is our normal procedure in covering a new series with untried actors: present the main idea and outline facts in a launching article, and follow up with more details of important actors after the third instalment which, we find, is about the time when people are starting to ask questions about them.

May I say, finally, that it is a pity that your complaints were not made to us first on the telephone so that we could dispose of irrelevancies and so avoid having to write long memos of detailed explanation which consume everybody's valuable time.

D. Flessati

(D.P. FLESSATI)

pam

Nothing to be written or typed in t margin

'One thing I'm proud of is that the episodes had tremendous pace, especially "The Suitor" and "Rocker". Everybody just got on with their job; we filmed in chunks and tried not to have to retake, because that meant doing the whole chunk again. There was no videotape editing in those days.

'Occasionally you'd spot things like a camera appear in the picture. If you look closely at "Older Women Are More Experienced" there are a couple of camera lenses in shot. I was shooting in the canteen around a table, and had to have lots of room for different angled shots; it was all a bit hairy!' says Dick.

His least favourite episode is 'The Last of the Big Spenders' [in which Terry and Bob date a couple of in-store demonstrators]. 'Whenever you write a series there will be a couple of scripts that are potboilers. This one was the worst we ever wrote. I ended up shooting at Runnymede on the day a big celebration was taking place. It was unbelievably crowded, and the whole thing just didn't feel right.'

Dick's favourites include 'Goodbye to All That'. When Bob said goodbye to Terry, the audience was suddenly quite choked. It was gratifying to know you could affect an audience emotionally as well as humorously. It gave the show another dimension.

'I also liked "Where Have All the Flowers Gone?" The Lads were at a wedding and everyone was telling them they'd be next. Terry and Bob got nostalgic about how time was slipping by although they were only in their early twenties.'

Nostalgia has a fundamental role in *Whatever Happened to…?*, but it's a theme spotted in *The Likely Lads*, too. 'I've often been aware of the sense of change, which came out in the scripts,' says Ian. 'Even when the Lads were young we'd give them speeches about loss: they were only 22 but were being nostalgic about when they were 15.'

The episode 'Brief Encounter' is another of Dick's favourites. 'It's a very good story, and there's nothing to beat a really good plot. I enjoyed "The Suitor" and "The Rocker", which had the scene where Terry steps out in front of the scooter and gets knocked down, which came from a true story I'd heard. It was a very exciting time in our lives.'

Bringing the Curtain Down

Bob and Terry walked off into the small screen sunset after 'Goodbye to All That' was transmitted on BBC2, on 23 July 1966. Although the whole third series was repeated on BBC1 later that year, it was the last time the Lads were seen as twentysomethings. When they reappeared in *Whatever Happened to…?*, they'd be approaching middle age.

As far as Dick and Ian were concerned, it was time to move on. 'We were getting offers in other directions,' says Dick. 'We thought three series was enough, and so did the actors.'

Ian agrees the show had run its course. 'I could have probably done another series, but the boys were talking about film careers, as if doing seven or eight episodes of *The Likely Lads* affected things. It was a time when television was building an audience, as well as TV stars, and with that came the worry for actors that if they did too much television work, they'd never be offered anything else.'

But that wasn't the end of Terry and Bob: another chapter in their lives would soon be explored.

MEMORABLE SCENES

EPISODE

Goodbye To All That

(Terry and Bob discuss how the army has changed George.)

TERRY: That's what amazes me about the Forces.

BOB: What d'you mean?

TERRY: You go in as one thing and you come out as another. I mean, who decided George Murray should be a cook? He's a corporal cook, now. What was he when he went in?

BOB: Uh…plasterer.

TERRY: Exactly…stupid.

BOB: Still, I suppose it comes in handy when you're buttering bread!

Dick Clement

Even as a young boy, Dick Clement aspired to making people laugh. The youngest of five children, he admired his elder brother's ability to have the rest of the family in stitches. 'I saw how much Arthur got away with and knew I wanted to emulate him. I've always liked the feeling of making people laugh, and when the family did for the first time, in response to one of my jokes, it was very satisfying,' recalls Dick, who also tried his hand at writing from an early age.

Even as a schoolboy (right, taken in 1953), Dick enjoyed making people laugh, and an early ambition was to become an actor.

His attempt to pen a radio show fell short of requirements, but the seed had been sown for what would become a glittering career. 'I was about eight at the time, and one of the first things I wrote was a *Paul Temple* episode, except it only lasted three minutes instead of 30!'

'I was always keen on writing dialogue rather than prose, but it was one of those things I put to the back of my mind.' Eventually, it dawned on Dick that he'd have to make a living, and writing didn't seem a viable option. It was only later, whilst working for the BBC, that he rekindled his interest. 'It's strange that it was only then that I remembered that I had tried writing at a young age; I'd forgotten all about it.'

Born in Westcliff-on-Sea, Essex, in 1937, Dick savoured a happy childhood by the sea. 'One of the things Ian and I have in common is that we both grew up in seaside towns. It was fun having the sea nearby. I remember the immediate postwar years, when mines were slowly being removed from the beaches, and exploring bombed-out houses with other kids.'

Dick's father had established a successful milk business, and his two brothers followed in their father's footsteps upon leaving school. But Dick was determined to pursue a different path.

'Father had a chain of shops, and was doing very

well. My brothers went into the business, but because I felt I would never be able to catch up with them, I decided to do something very different.'

Dick's sense of inferiority affected his life in more ways than one. 'For a long time I didn't drive a car because I couldn't do it very well. My brothers went sailing, and occasionally I'd go with them, but whenever I did anything wrong, they'd shout at me, so, as far as I was concerned, that was a failing. We got on very well, but at that age I didn't want to be the last in line to join the family business.'

Although keen on writing, Dick's early ambition was to become an actor. 'The most important thing I did at school was act in school plays – I took it very seriously. I don't know whether I would have made a very good actor, but the exposure was valuable later when I began directing and writing: the experience I'd gained on stage, like getting people on and off, using dialogue and, basically, how it felt to act, helped greatly. There's an enormous overlap between the skills of acting and directing or producing, so the more you understand everyone else's problems, the better you'll understand the business as a whole.'

Someone who encountered Dick's bent for acting is old school friend Terry Taylor. They met at Bishop's Stortford College while in their early teens.

'Dick was in the dramatic society, and we were both in a puppet club as well,' remembers Terry. 'I don't know why we joined, but we ended up doing a few puppet shows.' With the help of some rudimentary tape recorders they visited local schools. 'We'd use string puppets, and Dick was always good with the voices on the tape recorder.

'Culturally, he was a big influence on me,' says Terry. 'He was always first into things, like Hemingway and other authors of the day. One day he asked whether I listened to *The Goon Show.* I didn't, but made sure I did the following Wednesday. When we met next day, we did Bluebottle, Eccles and all the other voices.' Terry also recalls putting their Saturday morning study periods to good use. 'We'd creep off and listen to the repeat; it was a joy hearing it all over again,' he enthuses.

'Dick was a boarder and I was a day-boy; I don't know how we chummed up, I think we used to laugh at each other's jokes, and consequently became good friends.' Terry remembers them breaking some of the school rules. 'We were a bit naughty: there were rules about not going out with girls and not going to the pictures, but we broke both of these. I'm sure that some of the girls' names that cropped up in *The Likely Lads* came from girls attending the local schools. The teachers were always suspicious, and whenever there was a school dance, the headmaster patrolled the hedgerows with a torch in an attempt to catch people kissing.'

After leaving school, Dick and Terry went separate ways before reuniting for national service. While Terry worked in accountancy, Dick crossed the Atlantic on an exchange visit with an American school. He valued the twelve months spent in the States. 'It's one of the most important things that has happened to me,' he says. 'During my sixth form year, I became friends with an American who was on an exchange deal. I kept thinking how fantastic it must be to spend a year at school in a different country, learning about a completely new culture.'

After mulling over the opportunity, Dick applied for a place on the exchange scheme and was accepted. 'I'm proud I had the nous to go for it. Selection was based on an interview, and I'm reasonably good at talking, so I thought that if I couldn't get one of the 18 spaces available to 35 applicants, heaven help me.'

Sailing over on the *Queen Mary*, and returning on the *Queen Elizabeth*, Dick spent 1955–56 living in America, a rehearsal for where life would eventually lead him. 'It was a real love affair, I had a wonderful

Dick in his garden (*circa* 1964) with his eldest son, Andrew, and Fresco, the dog.

time,' he enthuses. 'We were like ambassadors in many ways, so we had to behave, but I found the work very easy and felt it was a fantastic experience.'

Dick feels the confidence gained from the exchange stood him in good stead for completing his national service upon returning. 'It helped me bull-shit my way into a commission, separating me from the herd,' he says. 'It was a very important experience for an 18-year-old.'

Upon joining the RAF, Dick was stationed in Norfolk. Based at the same training camp at Bircham Newton, was Michael Burridge, who played a key role in Dick's life after demob: not only did he play a part in introducing Dick to Ian La Frenais, but helped in his search for employment.

'After we'd finished national service, I saw a newspaper advert for the BBC, who were looking for studio managers. I sent it to Dick with a suggestion that he should apply.'

Michael's not surprised Dick has become one of the country's greatest comedy writers, having experienced his wit first-hand. 'He was always very funny; the humour of life never escaped him, whether it was the Air Force or something else. So the way his career has turned out is no surprise to me.'

Back on civvy street, Dick knew it was time to establish a career. After considering applying for RADA, he decided to respond to the BBC's advert for studio managers, and was successful in his application. 'I still wasn't entirely sure what I really wanted to do with my life, but joined the corporation because I felt in the vaguest possible way that it was the right direction for me.'

Dick started his media career as a studio manager, or what he terms a 'glorified sound man'. After training he joined Bush House, where broadcasts were transmitted all over the world. Even though his duties entailed working shifts, he enjoyed himself.

'It was very interesting at first, and although the work got boring after a while, the people were great. A lot of the time you were putting out new broadcasts, whether it be in Albanian or Polish, and you couldn't understand a word.'

His subsequent transfer to the African Service afforded him the chance to complete his first piece of professional writing. 'I wrote a script in English, which was translated into Somali: that's the first time I put words on paper in a specialist capacity.'

While working for the BBC, Dick started writing for pleasure, contributing sketches and ideas to the Corporation's own drama group, the Ariel Players. His involvement with the Players grew, as he began using the revues as a vehicle for developing his writing of comedy and satire.

His association with the group was memorable in other ways, because it was during the after-show party of the 1961 performance – which had included the 'Double Date' sketch – that Dick met his first wife. Jenny had played no part in the performance, but was invited along by Brenda Punshon (née Shepherd), who'd appeared in seven of the sketches and arranged the dance numbers for the Christmas show.

'I shared a flat with Jenny, while Dick shared a flat with Terry Taylor, who I went out with for a while,' she says. The party was held at Dick's flat in Earls Court, and Brenda recalls introducing the pair of them to each other.

'That was the end of Jenny for me!' laughs Brenda. 'We'd planned to go to America together the following year, but she pulled out and ended up marrying Dick instead. I was still in the States at the time, much to my annoyance, but I managed to phone them at the wedding from San Francisco.'

Jenny later returned the compliment by introducing Brenda to her husband, Richard.

Jenny remembers hitting it off with Dick immediately, partly because of their penchant for a little bear! 'We both adore Winnie-the-Pooh,' she explains, 'and were able to quote huge sections from stories, as well as reciting the poems to each other. I found Dick quite imposing when we first met, because he's very tall. But intellectually we hit it off from the start, and began dating straight away. We continued talking about Winnie-the-Pooh from that first meeting, and as you can imagine, our children were brought up on the bear as well.'

Back at the BBC, Dick's duties started encompassing magazine programmes, voice work and producing, but after about five years, he was ready for a change. 'I was desperate to get into mainstream broadcasting; I felt that I was in an incredible backwater,' he says.

To achieve his aim he applied to join the BBC directors' course, which led to the filming of the 'Double Date' sketch – previously performed by the Ariel Players – on the strength of which Dick and Ian were commissioned to write the first series of *The Likely Lads*.

When the series began its life, Dick was still employed by the Beeb, but as the show's success picked up momentum, he left to pursue a career as a freelance scriptwriter.

Nowadays Dick is based in the States, where he lives with his second wife, Nancy. When it comes to recreation, his main interest is playing tennis in the Californian sun. 'I play as often as I can, usually two or three games a week. It's good fun and ideal for keeping fit. It's also a great way to unwind, especially after a hard day's work.'

Dick (back row, 3rd from left) enjoyed a game of cricket. Here, in 1964, he guested for High Wych village team.

Ian La Frenais

Like so many teenagers verging on leaving school, Ian La Frenais didn't know what he wanted from life. His father was a corporate accountant, but Ian, an only child, knew that wasn't the career for him. 'I was interested in art, but also had a leaning towards writing, or wanting to write, but didn't know how to progress the idea,' he says. 'In addition to writing essays at school, I wrote for pleasure, so for a while I considered being a journalist.'

Mike Thompson has known Ian since junior school, and grew up in an adjoining street in Whitley Bay. 'At school he was good at English, and always keen to get into writing; but I think he probably saw himself as a novelist, rather than writing for television. One of his great talents is instant recall of situations and conversations he'd had, or overheard, stretching back to his childhood, which has made him a good raconteur.'

Fellow schoolmate, Horace Jeffcock, remembers Ian as a 'fun guy'. 'He was always imagining funny situations, trying to create an amusing scene out of something we were looking at, or talking about. That sense of humour was built in to him.'

Ian's ambivalence about a future career extended beyond his school days. After leaving the Dame Allan's School he had a year to kill before university. It was during this period that he decided against higher education, and joined the army instead, to complete his national service. 'Even then I'd tell people I was going to be a writer, but it was a lie because I didn't have any clear ideas about what I wanted to do; it just sounded a glamorous thing to say,' he observes.

Although he served his national service at Blenheim Barracks, Aldershot, Ian regularly returned home, as old friend Vin Welch recalls. 'He managed to get a job in the office where leave passes were issued, so ended up with an inordinate amount of weekend passes!'

Vin remembers a time when Ian went AWOL. 'After coming back for a weekend, a few friends went to the train station to see him off, before going on to a party. Ian was so annoyed about missing the do that he decided not to return.' He ended up going to the party with his friends and visiting the doctor the following day feigning some illness, which prevented trouble when he reached his army base.

Another friend who joined up the same day as Ian was David Hallwood. 'We thought it was best to get

Ian (front row, 2nd from right) spent his square-bashing days at Aldershot.

national service over and done with,' he says. 'We were put on the London train by our folks in September 1955. Although neither of us had ever spent any time away from home before, we laughed from dawn till dusk as Ian came to terms with the army. The "regular" NCOs couldn't get their brains round the name La Frenais and Ian was known as "Lee Francis" for the term of our square-bashing.

'Ian was constantly inventing characters in his imagination,' recalls David, who attended Bygate Infant School at Monkseaton, and Park Primary in Whitley Bay, with Ian. 'I remember one was a mild little creature who dribbled and kept looking up into the eyes of his corporal and did everything he was told to the letter! If he saw a railway hoarding advising people to go to Margate for their summer holidays, then Ian's make-believe character was organized into going off to Kent.

'Another of his ruses was to get the whole platoon, when marching from one place to another, to stamp on every seventh step, which caused drill corporals to have near seizures as they struggled to work out what was happening.

'Ian was liked by all our fellow rookie soldiers and we were a mixed bunch with university graduates, public school leavers, ordinary working-class lads and at least one or two thugs mixing in together and producing a winning "B" Company in the drill competition at the end of, I think, ten weeks. Ian was immaculate at all times.'

After returning to civvy street he moved between various temporary jobs. 'For a while it felt as if my life was in limbo, and it was quite nice,' admits Ian. But his father started pressing him to make something of his life, so he joined Gallahers, a tobacco company, as a sales trainee; he spent the next two years working throughout the British Isles. 'I spent a lot of my youth smoking free cigarettes!'

Ian's life reached a crucial juncture during 1961 when some of his friends ditched their jobs and moved to London. Brian Flint, who started off as a teacher before going into advertising, and Maurice Hardaker, a physicist, wanted to break into the world of entertainment themselves. While living in the North-East, they had secured a weekly slot on Tyne Tees – the regional independent television station – performing a satirical song, as Maurice explains. 'While Brian wrote the words, I composed the music. We appeared every week for a couple of years, back in the late Fifties. We enjoyed it so much,

Ian (far right) donning his top hat and tails with (left to right) Geoff and Anthony Hardaker, Brian Flint, Maurice Hardaker and Bob Joie.

we moved to London to see if we could make a career out of it. If we didn't make a lot of money, we'd already agreed to pack it in and return to something sensible.'

With another of his friends, Horace Jeffcock, already in London, Ian began getting itchy feet for the capital's bright lights. 'During that period when economically everything was going well, "going to London" had a certain significance,' Ian explains, 'and didn't beg the question: "What are you going to do when you get there?" It was simply a state of mind, I had no idea what I was going to do!'

Ian headed south, escorted by Mike Thompson. 'A friend and I took him down, as he went to start his career as the author of the century!' smiles Mike. 'He had ambitions of being interviewed by John Freeman on *Face to Face*, having written his first novel,' he adds.

Initially Ian lived in Earls Court with Maurice and Brian – whose budding careers making satirical comments to music didn't take off – before sharing a flat with Brian Flint in Pond Street, Knightsbridge.

To earn some money, Ian worked for a cleaning company and had other jobs before joining Marketing Advisory Service, a market research company. He was recruited by George Murray, who later set up his own company, Marketing Economics, and invited Ian to join. They became good friends.

'Ian was always an amusing character,' says George, who was aware of his employee's writing ambitions. 'Ian was working for me when *The Likely Lads* first started. He has a very creative and distinctive talent, so I wasn't surprised when he eventually went part-time, then gradually filtered out altogether to spend more time writing. And, of course, he was obviously making more money from his writing.'

George enjoyed working with Ian. 'I wouldn't say he was born to be a market researcher, but he had a good analytical mind, could do research and was able to write reports – I wouldn't have employed him if he hadn't been competent.'

One thing George remembers clearly about Ian was his eye for a fast car. 'When he was working for me, he demanded a company car. I thought he was going to choose a Ford Cortina, or something, but he wanted our red Sunbeam Alpine. Later, when he had a bit more money he bought himself an E-type Jag, then a Rolls Royce – he even had his own chauffeur for a while.'

Writer Patrick Tilley, who'd already written several episodes of the Rediffusion series, *Crane,* when he first met Ian, also recalls this passion for cars. 'When Ian and Dick's stardom was beginning to go into ascendancy, Ian came round to my house in Highgate and asked me to look out the window. There was this dark blue E-type Jag; it was a real "bird-puller". He was absolutely thrilled with it, and had bought it on the strength of the money he'd received for one of *The Likely Lads* series.' Patrick asked whether his family were delighted about his

Left: Ian (far right) dining out, while (right) shows Ian holidaying in Spain.

Right: Ian (left) and Maurice Hardaker chat with the owner of a Spanish bar.

success. 'He replied: "Yes, but my mother told me not to give up the day job!"'

Eventually Ian – who's married to Doris, and has one stepson, Michael – decided it was time to quit his market research job and concentrate on writing full-time. 'Throughout the period Dick and I wrote the first two series of *The Likely Lads*, as well as our first screenplay, *The Jokers*, I continued working in market research. But I began feeling I was missing out on all the fun of recording the episodes, and when the BBC ordered a third series, it seemed the ideal moment to do something about it by putting "professional writer" on the passport!' he concludes.

The Writing Partnership

There aren't many writing partnerships that have lasted as long as the one forged nearly four decades ago by Dick Clement and Ian La Frenais. When they started penning skits for amateur productions of the BBC's Ariel Players, little did they know their talents would take them to Hollywood. Without question, their partnership is one of the most respected and sought-after in the entertainment business, as their ever-increasing list of credits and awards proves.

Since the mid-1970s, Dick and Ian have lived in Beverly Hills. 'We sort of explored the idea of moving here in 1974,' explains Ian. 'But it wasn't until the end of '75 that we actually moved. Even though we were based in the States we constantly did work for the British market throughout the remainder of the Seventies and early Eighties, which meant commuting for some time. Even in 1979, when we formed a production company and had offices in America and England, nearly all the work was generated in London.'

Gradually the writers began to settle. 'As the years passed, and I married an American, established more and more American friends, I began realizing my life was in America.'

Initially, Dick and Ian moved to the States to be near the centre of the movie industry. After the success of *The Likely Lads*, they branched out into writing film scripts, starting with *The Jokers* in 1967, and followed a year later by *Otley*, which Dick also directed, and *Hannibal Brooks*, telling the story of a POW escaping over the Alps with an elephant.

But it was the writers' track record in sitcoms that agents seized upon when they touched down on American soil, and it wasn't long before they were involved in negotiations concerning an American version of *Porridge*.

In 1976, *On the Rocks* was screened, but it never progressed beyond the first series. 'The plots translated quite well,' explains Dick.

'We really felt it could work,' adds Ian, 'and saw it opening up all sorts of possibilities. But everyone was terrified it was going to be too gritty for the American market, and it ended up being a poor version of the original.'

Neither Dick or Ian would consider returning to England: they enjoy their lives in Beverly Hills too much for that. 'It's a hard-working town, very work oriented,' says Dick. 'We have a routine: Ian comes around at about 9.30 each morning, and we work till 4.30 most days. He's better at dialogue, while I'm better at structure, so together we work well.'

'I'm very happy here,' says Dick, 'but we'd never stop writing for Britain. Our recent movie, *Still Crazy*, is very much a British movie from beginning to end. We like showing we're flexible, and capable of more than one style, but it's enormously comfortable writing with a British voice.'

Although they've written for the American market, it's something they find difficult and not particularly gratifying. 'We haven't been very successful at it, apart from writing for *The Tracey Ullman Show*, which is great fun,' says Dick. 'But that's for cable, where you have a lot more freedom; in fact, it's the nearest we've come to the freedom we were given on British television,' he explains.

In the early days, Bob and Terry's adventures were often scripted at the kitchen table in Dick Clement's house.

Writing for network television in the States is a 'young man's game', claims Dick. 'You also need a lot of stamina because it's not really a writer's medium; it's a producer's medium. But that's not to say all American TV isn't funny; the best American comedy is fantastic, and, in many ways, they're better at writing comedy than the British.'

Much of the duo's success is due to their understanding of each other, something that has developed over the years. 'We have minor disagreements but never row,' says Ian, who lives two blocks from Dick and his wife, Nancy. 'We're all great friends.'

'It's been an enormously long and successful working marriage,' Dick says proudly. 'We respect each other and have done things on our own: Ian has written *Lovejoy* and *Spender*, while I've directed movies and a stage play on my own. The break has always been productive and refreshing, but we've never wanted to break up the partnership. It's more fun writing a script together: you can prop each other up as well as make each other laugh.'

Although they've enjoyed many successes during their careers, you'd be hard-pressed to find a series to beat *The Likely Lads* and its sequel when it comes to universal acceptance from journalists and viewers.

Clement and La Frenais appreciate the flow of compliments, but don't rate the show as their best. 'I wouldn't pick it out as my favourite,' says Dick. 'I have great respect for it because the original series got us started, but I wouldn't want to put it ahead of *Porridge* or *Auf Wiedersehen, Pet* – they're equally important. But obviously the fact it still connects with so many people is satisfying,' he affirms.

Ian agrees the show isn't necessarily the best thing they've written, but appreciates it's probably the most significant landmark in their careers. 'I still enjoy watching some of the episodes, even though a few seem very overwritten. But after *Whatever Happened to ...?* we were very assured and confident. It was a prolific period for our writing: it was a very important time because it changed everything for us, and you never forget that. *The Likely Lads* enabled us to become successful in television – and films, too. It changed our lives and for that we're grateful.'

Ian's not sure of his favourite piece of writing. 'You write shows at different periods, so it's difficult pinpointing one in particular. I enjoyed writing *Porridge*, and it was definitely the hardest to pull off. But you continue to learn; I feel we're better writers now than we were three or four years ago, which means it's not easy picking the best work we've done.'

Dr. Les Gofton – a lecturer at the University of Newcastle, and an avid fan of *The Likely Lads* – feels Clement and La Frenais are 'terrific writers' who 'have a grasp of the language, and the little nuances in the language which convey so much. They also have a nose for things people really do talk about, or think: they understand what people's priorities and values are, and that's not accidental; they research their subjects well. They always explore issues gently, but where their own sympathies lie is quite clear from the way they represent their characters.'

The strength of characterization is one of Clement and La Frenais' trademarks. Pick up any of their scripts and, instead of a barrowful of gags, you will see a depth of character an actor can really get his teeth into. 'We're not gag writers,' says Ian. 'We obtain our humour from the characters themselves.'

You don't need to look any further than *Porridge* and *The Likely Lads* for proof: the situation in both sitcoms is harsh, but the grimness is cleverly balanced by the vigour and colour of the characters.

Fellow writer Patrick Tilley, who co-wrote several sketches for the Ariel Players and later novelized several scripts for the BBC book *Whatever Happened to The Likely Lads?*, has known Dick and Ian years, and admires their work. 'They're on the same wavelength, and have a certain magic between them. It's a unique collaboration and fascinating to watch.'

It's something Patrick's been fortunate to experience. 'While Ian was walking around, Dick was sprawled out on a chaise longue, scribbling everything down. They work directly onto a computer these days, but when I saw them, Ian would spark off things, perhaps snatches of dialogue, and Dick would organize it and write it all down.'

Many writers would give anything to taste a little of the success Dick and Ian have experienced in the field of sitcoms. Despite the critical acclaim they've enjoyed – they won the Society of Film and Television Arts' award for both *Whatever Happened to The Likely Lads?* and *Porridge*, as well as picking up a Screen Writers Guild award for their prison-based series – Dick and Ian are in no rush to return to the genre. 'Situation comedy is not my favourite genre,' Dick admits. 'I like everything we do to contain comedy, but I don't really want to go back to situation comedy. I find the tyranny of having to be funny all the time exhausting. I like it when you can be both. When we previewed our recent film, *Still Crazy*, to an audience, it was still tremendously satisfying sitting in the dark, hearing people laugh at something you've written. But it's gratifying to occasionally write a scene where the audience go quiet and are touched by what they see. In a way, the juxtaposition of the two is the ideal.'

Despite the success we all associate with Clement and La Frenais, they have also endured the odd disappointment, their 1993 comedy drama for ITV, *Full Stretch*, being a prime example.

'I really felt that would work,' says Ian, 'but the programme wasn't really given the chance to settle, because there were changes taking place in ITV at the time. It was a shame because the casting was wonderful and we believed we could have created the new *Minder*.'

But whatever they write in the future, humour will always be an integral component. 'I would never want to write something without humour,' says Dick, 'because I think it's essential. Even in the darkest, most heavy movie it's important because life contains humour, often in the most inappropriate places, and I like that.'

Writing situation comedy is an enervating exercise, and not to be taken lightly. 'It's great when you finish it, but, boy, it's hard work,' says Dick. 'When you set out to be funny and people don't laugh, you've failed 100 per cent. And you know it because you can hear the silence, whereas if you write a thriller and people are fairly thrilled, it's not such a dramatic failure. It's only comedy where you have this absolute situation: do they laugh or not? And when they don't, it's very, very painful.'

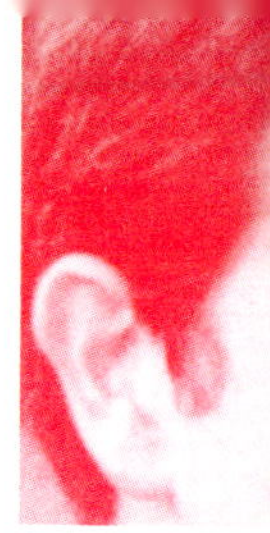

FILM CREDITS INCLUDE:
The Jokers
Otley
Hannibal Brooks
Villain
The Likely Lads
Porridge
The Prisoner of Zenda
The Commitments
Excess Baggage
Vice Versa
Still Crazy

THEATRE CREDITS INCLUDE:
Billy
Porridge sketch for *The Two Ronnies* stage show

TV CREDITS INCLUDE:
The Likely Lads
Mr. Aitch
Whatever Happened to The Likely Lads?
Thick As Thieves
Porridge
Going Straight
The Further Adventures of Lucky Jim
The New Adventures of Lucky Jim
Auf Wiedersehen, Pet
Mog
Freddie and Max
Ronnie Barker Playhouse ('Prisoner and Escort' and 'I'll Fly You for a Quid')
The Old Boy Network
Full Stretch
Over the Rainbow
Billy Liar (short series for US TV)
On the Rocks (US TV)
Dick also directed the second series of *Not Only... But Also* in 1966, as well as writing material for the show.

Bewes on Clement and La Frenais

'There have been many successful writing pairs in British television, and every one seems to have a straight one and a swinger, like Ian. When he bought his first Rolls Royce, there was a copy of *Melody Maker* on the back seat.

'You can tell a lot about a person from the car they drive: while Dick stuck with [illegible] Ian went from a red Sunbeam [illegible] later traded in for [illegible] Jag, to a Rolls.

'Whenever [illegible] we up to Whitley [illegible] next series, but rea[illegible]d got there we'd pick up his [illegible] and his daughters, Debra and Denise, [illegible] actress with a regular role in *Coronatio*[illegible]d take them for a spin along the sea fr[illegible]member Denise, aged five and a half, saying [illegible] got out after a posh car ride, "Aye, well, back [illegible]ity!"

'We were all very close, and to w[illegible]ith them was absolutely smashing. Ian's very [illegible] and boy-like, while Dick's jolly in a grown-up [illegible]t he was always very serious when it came t[illegible]cting the episodes.

'We rehearsed in the Addison Road [illegible]s' Club, a church hall, and I remember once being filmed for a documentary about the show. Jimmy Bolam and I had made a little pact beforehand, so when Dick – being the director and the grown-up – said: "On that line, Rodney, if you stand up and go to the door", I replied: "Oh, Dick, that's rubbish, Bob wouldn't do that!"

'Conscious of the TV cameras, Dick said quickly: "OK, fine, lovely, let's just get on." He then told Jimmy to get up and go to the door on his next line, but Jimmy refused as well.

'We did a few more lines at the sofa before he asked me again, but still I refused. Of course, Dick has a cutting point to the next scene to think of, and it doesn't work unless somebody gets to the door.

'Eventually he twigged what was going on: he realized we'd planned all this resistance bec[illegible] being filmed for this [illegible] pro[illegible] He shouted: "You bastards, how could y[illegible] screamed at the film crew: "Cut! You [illegible] that." But it was the best bit, of cours[illegible]

'Dick's got an amazing memory; he [illegible] [illegible]les and scenes. It must have been very ner[illegible] [illegible]ng for him, not just because *The Likely Lads* was his first series on television, but he came from Southend while everyone else was from the North, and we used to tease him about it.

'He's a very conscien[illegible] and I'm sure he was swea[illegible] He always paid particular [illegible] because cutting between [illegible]e in situation comedy is [illegible] laughs, or make them.

'A close-u[illegible] may kill the whole sequence, where[illegible] stayed out and caught the body language between the characters, it might have worked [illegible] these are all things a director has to be conscious of. Dick's gone on to direct movies, so it proves [illegible] good visual eye.

'Both are extremely [illegible] always the grown-up, the prefect of the [illegible], which is why he made such a good job of directing *The Likely Lads*. They have a tremendous sense of humour, but are completely different in so many ways. I suppose that's why their writing partnership works so well.'

RODNEY BEWES • BOB FERRIS

Bob – who used to be a boy scout – is a maudlin figure, and is always struggling to let go of the past. Influences and attitudes, which should simply be memories, plague Bob, preventing him, at times, looking forward to his future with Thelma. Thelma realizes Bob is incorrigible and stubborn, and any attempt at changing her partner will always be an uphill battle, try as she might.

Before settling down with Thelma, Bob lives with his mother, enjoying good home cooking, like his favourite breakfast of pease pudding and bacon. He savours his life as a bachelor, has a string of girl-friends and a penchant for girls in smocks, including florists and hairdressers. He is forever falling in love, and even announces his engagement to Helen in the episode, 'Talk of the Town'. But he is drunk at the time and quickly realizes his mistake once he has sobered up again.

He is easily led by his best mate Terry, whom he's known since infant school back in 1948. As Terry says: 'We've had the same friends, hobbies and girls.' Their long-standing friendship extends to secondary education – where Bob was secretary of the Lonnie Donegan Appreciation Society and president of the Deirdre Birchwood Fan Club – and out into the workplace.

Life consists of girls and beer until Thelma enters Bob's life. Although he never lets go of the past, and suffers serious bouts of melancholy, married life also offers security, something Bob needs in life. While Terry is in the army, Bob progresses and begins enjoying the little luxuries of a steady income, thanks to his management job in Mr Chambers' building and civil engineering firm. He starts appreciating the finer aspects of life, which for him includes wine, tennis and travelling abroad.

'The monster has begun' were the words that convinced Rodney Bewes that *The Likely Lads* would become a hit series. The late actor and director, Bill Fraser, best known for playing Claude Snudge in Granada's popular sitcom *Bootsie and Snudge*, watched the first episode being recorded.

'I admired Bill very much, and asked him to be in the audience,' says Rodney. 'In the Television Centre bar afterwards, I asked what he thought. "The monster has begun" was his reply; he knew it was going to be big.'

But the thought of such huge success initially caused Rodney unease. 'Jimmy Bolam and I met Dick and Ian at Television Centre, and we were given six scripts to take home and read. I hardly knew Jimmy: I'd seen him around the West End, and by then he was very successful at the Royal Court, while I was doing a lot of good plays on TV. We were both worried about situation comedy; if it became successful would we end up being typecast?

'But when I asked for his views on the scripts, he replied: "They're wonderful, aren't they?" I agreed. "Any actor would be a fool not to want to play those characters," I said. The quality of the scripts decided it for me; they were incredibly well-written, often with a brilliant twist at the end.'

Rodney enjoyed playing Bob. 'I liked him very much, but I'd never worked in front of a studio audience before, and that worried me: not only were you performing for the camera, but also the studio audience and people sat at home – it seemed strange.

'But I never had to think through Bob's character; the lines definitely told me everything I needed to know. A journalist once asked whether I minded playing the boring one. I couldn't believe his question because, as far as I was concerned, he wasn't boring at all – far from it.'

The first series was favourably received back in 1964, but its early repeat on BBC1 three months later exposed the sitcom to a much wider audience. People began stopping Rodney in the street to talk about the show. 'The reaction from the public was fantastic,' he says. 'My family were really pleased too, and lots of my relatives would come along to recordings. Being recognized and receiving fan mail was amazing. But the best reaction was when people said: "The Lads are just like we used to be." Fellas identified so much with Bob and Terry, just one reason it became such a success.'

The relationship between Bob Ferris and Terry Collier, forged during their schooldays together, is the linchpin of the show's success, and Rodney is keen to point out that, contrary to what some journalists think, his professional relationship with James Bolam was fine. 'We had a mutual respect for each other that was kind of immediate,' he explains. 'When we were doing *Whatever Happened to…?*, for example, we had thirteen scripts to learn each series. That's six and a half hours, with each of us having a big chunk of the dialogue. It worked out to be bigger than *Hamlet*, so to learn and record all of that we had to get on.

'We also needed to help each other if we made mistakes, so we set up a code consisting of the words: "Oh, well" and "Still". If Terry said: "In half an hour we're going to the pub," and I had no idea what line came next, I had a habit of stalling for time by saying: "Still…"

'All the journalists who said we didn't get on were wrong: we got on terribly well professionally and socially we had a great time. When the show began, a group of us would go out to dinner after the final rehearsal and once we'd recorded the episode. I remember lots of times arriving at the studio the following day and having to ask the BBC nurse for Alka Seltzers because we'd had such an evening!

'When it came to *Whatever Happened to…?* we were that much older, and the evening before a recording would entail going to bed early to read the script; but I'll never forget those early days, being out nearly every night having fun, and enjoying every minute.'

But reports over the years about Bolam's absence from Rodney's wedding, non-appearance on his *This Is Your Life*, and his refusal to talk anymore about his time playing Terry, have fuelled rumours that these days, at any rate, the actors do not see eye-to-eye. 'I won't talk about that,' says Rodney, 'because I don't think it's right – I can't think about someone else's point of view.'

The erstwhile Likely Lad has nothing but fond memories of playing Bob Ferris, and feels the scripts more than anything else made it such a pleasure. 'Each episode was so well-constructed; in fact, the whole recording process was fun. When we were making *The Likely Lads* we had no executive producers, no one telling us what we could or couldn't do. We owed a debt to Tom Sloan, Bill Cotton and David Attenborough because they let us get on with it. Everything worked and it was considered a good show, earning sparkling reviews in all the papers, including the *Financial Times*.'

When the transmission of the episode 'Goodbye To All That', on 23 July 1966, marked the passing of *The Likely Lads*, one could have forgiven Rodney feeling sad: after all, it had established his name in the world of television. Fortunately, as one door closed, another opened. 'I was on such a high that I didn't feel too sad about giving up Bob,' Rodney explains. 'I wrote a television series called *Dear Mother…Love Albert*, which ran for three years. It did well, averaging number seven in the ratings. I produced it, wrote it, edited it, appeared in it, and even sang the signature tune – it was a fabulous time.'

But if it hadn't been for a bout of flu, Rodney may never have dreamt up the idea. He'd spent 10 days in bed, pole-axed and unable to get up, so decided that he would write a letter to his mother.

'I've always been a tremendous letter writer, and I wrote saying: "I'm having such a great time here in London: I went out with Ian [La Frenais] last night; he collected me in his Rolls Royce, and we went down the King's Road to an Italian restaurant and Princess Margaret was there."

'You never write home with bad news, else your mother would be on the next train. Suddenly it gave me an idea for a series, where each episode began with a weekly letter home to mum, saying how well I was doing and showing the opposite!'

As soon as Rodney had recuperated he met Philip Jones, who was Director of Light Entertainment at Thames TV, for lunch to discuss the idea. 'I told Philip the basic outline: a man lives in London and tells his mum he's got an incredible flat, while the camera reveals a depressing basement apartment. The character says he's doing well at work and will soon receive promotion, before cutting to a scene where he's fired.'

Jones loved the idea and commissioned a series, with Rodney playing the lead role, Albert Courtnay. 'I don't think you could ever get a series off the ground today at lunch!'

The opening series was well received, but Thames were unable to commission any more, as Rodney explains. 'Philip Jones asked to see me. He got out plans of Thames' future programming, showing his three studios were fully booked; it would be a year and a half before another series could be filmed. He was very sorry, but told me not to drop the idea. I loved the fact he took time to sit me down and explain his decision, I'll always admire him for that. I don't think a television executive would be bothered today.'

But Rodney didn't give up and a chance meeting with Donald Baverstock – then programme director at Yorkshire Television – at a Christmas party led to a further three series being commissioned between 1970–72. 'Donald told me how much he loved my programme, and when asked whether he wanted it, he jumped at the chance.'

By the end of the fourth series, Rodney had to confront one of the toughest decisions of his career. Dick Clement and Ian La Frenais had already mentioned their idea of bringing the Lads back to the small screen, but if Rodney agreed to return as Bob, it would mean the end for *Dear Mother...Love Albert.* 'I was writing, producing and doing very well; it was also incredibly lucrative. But I knew in my heart of hearts I longed to do *Whatever Happened to The Likely Lads?* I couldn't wait to see the first script, I just wanted to devour it.' After much ruminating, Rodney opted for Bob Ferris instead of Albert Courtnay. 'I gave up a great deal to play Bob again, but feel I made the right decision.'

Born in the Yorkshire town of Bingley in 1937, Rodney's early years were spent ill in bed. 'I had chronic bronchitis and asthma, so missed a lot of school.' He occupied his time reading stories and making theatres out of shoe boxes, nurturing his dreams of becoming an actor.

Rodney has always believed in the power of letter writing, and it paid dividends when, at the age of 12, he noticed an article in his father's newspaper saying that the BBC were looking for children for a new television production.

'I wrote the producer, Joy Harington, a letter, and she invited me to meet her, which I did. She ended up giving me a part in a thriller for children's television.' But Rodney's luck didn't stop there. 'She then introduced me to another producer down the corridor, who was casting for *The Pickwick Papers*, and I ended up playing Joe, the fat boy – probably because I had a very round face.'

Years later, when Rodney's career was at a low ebb, another letter proved valuable. 'I was in Cornwall going through a dull time, so decided to write to Bill Kenwright, now one of the West End's biggest producers. Before long, I was working for him in the West End, which led to another job. A letter can change your whole life.'

After his childhood appearances for the BBC, Rodney took the advice of one of the corporation's producers and applied for RADA's preparatory school. Upon being accepted he moved to London. 'Looking back, I suppose it was a brave move for someone so young,' says Rodney, who was fourteen at the time. 'But it was the best thing I could have done because, as soon as I started acting, the asthma and bronchitis disappeared.

'The pupils in my class were very sophisticated, and I remember being invited to this party at a girl's posh home in Hampstead. They were all different from me: I lived in a basement flat in Belsize Avenue, and earned some much-needed money washing-up at the Grosvenor House. I didn't have a clue what to wear, and ended up buying a blazer. But when I got to the party everyone was dressed in jeans and T-shirts – I felt completely out of place. I drank gin all night and ended up feeling sick; it's a night that will always stick in my mind.'

After finishing preparatory school, Rodney spent the summer working at the Royalty Theatre, Morecambe, before moving on to RADA, where he enjoyed his first year. 'I was there until I was seventeen and a half, and loved every minute of it.'

His time at the Academy was interrupted by national service, but when he was able to resume his studies, it wasn't long before he was thrown out! 'It was a mistake to go back,' he admits. 'I returned to RADA the day after finishing in the RAF, and I couldn't get my head together. I went to parties, had fun, and ended up being expelled after the first term, which I deserved. What I should have done was spend a year back in theatres and rep.'

Although Rodney wasn't upset about his expulsion, his mother was; she thought her son was destined to become the next Olivier or Gielgud. 'She was terribly upset,' says Rodney, 'especially when she read the letter from the principal saying: "I think Rodney's talents should be channelled in a different direction." In other words, give it up.'

The experience didn't dent his confidence, and, in hindsight, Rodney feels being kicked out of RADA was a blessing in disguise. 'It was probably good for me because I went off to lots of different theatres in the North and had a ball.' It also gave him time to ponder where his future lay. 'I loved appearing in weekly rep, but after three years decided I didn't want to do it forever: I wanted to get into TV, so moved back to London to try and achieve it.'

While he began the arduous task of breaking into the world of television, Rodney earned a living selling antiques from a stall in Portobello Road. After writing hundreds of letters to people in the industry

he was eventually offered work in TV plays, including his first leading part in the ATV's series, *Love Story*, attracting some positive reviews. 'Television fascinated me,' he says, 'and at that point in my career I wanted to do it more than theatre.'

In the early 1960s Rodney struck up a friendship with actor Tom Courtenay, which led to an appearance in the 1963 film *Billy Liar*. 'I saw Tom in the stage version several times; I'd also seen Albert Finney in it as well. I was totally obsessed by *Billy Liar* as a play; it blew my mind; I thought plays in London were all about butlers and tennis! After one performance I went around to see if I could meet Tom, and luckily he agreed. We got talking, went to a pub and quickly became friends, and went on to share various houses and flats. When he was offered the role in the film I happened to read the script,

(Left) Earlier this year, Rodney completed a successful tour of his one-man show, *Three Men in a Boat.*

(Right) Rodney has nothing but fond memories of playing Bob Ferris.

quickly realizing that I would love to play Billy's friend, Arthur. I couldn't ask Tom to put in a good word for me because that would have been using him, so I wrote to the director, John Schlesinger.' Shortly after, Rodney met Schlesinger and was offered the role. Among the film's admirers were Clement and La Frenais, who were decidedly impressed with Rodney's portrayal.

In recent years Rodney has spent his time in the theatre, most recently touring in his successful one-man show, *Three Men in a Boat.* But he hasn't been seen on TV for some time, not that this causes him undue concern. 'Financially I'm very settled: I have houses in Putney and Cornwall without mortgages, and I've done well, so I'm not disappointed because I have a lovely life.

'I made a huge killing with my one-man show at the Edinburgh Festival in 1998; the year before that I was in a Ray Cooney farce called *Funny Money*, then appeared with Jack Klugman and Tony Randall in *The Odd Couple*, both in London. I also enjoy playing dame in panto each year: it's incredibly hard work, but great fun. So overall I'm very happy,' says Rodney, who shares his life with wife, Daphne, whom he met in a London restaurant, and his daughter and three sons.

'Daphne worked as a waitress at a restaurant in Victoria I used to visit with Tom Courtenay, Mike Hugg, Dick and Ian. The waitresses all wore miniskirts and were like Pan's People: having a date with one of them was unimaginable, but I was lucky.' For their first date Rodney took Daphne to watch a football match! 'I asked whether she wanted to see Chelsea play, and she agreed,' he smiles.

'Daphne told me subsequently that she tried phoning to get out of the date, but couldn't because my number was ex-directory.'

Today, 35 years since stepping into Bob's shoes, Rodney never tires of being linked to *The Likely Lads*. He's proud to have been associated with something so good, a piece of classic television. 'Journalists often ask whether I mind talking about the show; if I minded I would deserve a swift kick because it was a good programme, and to be famous for something that good makes me feel lucky. It's also been nice to get some wonderful repeat cheques.'

As a consequence of *The Likely Lads*' never-ending appeal, Rodney is frequently asked whether there's any chance the Lads will be revived again, a mouth-watering prospect as far as he's concerned. If it were feasible, Rodney would have no hesitation accepting. 'It would be a laugh,' he enthuses. 'Over lunch a couple of years ago, Ian said it would be interesting if Bob had become a member of the new middle-class poor and was struggling, while Terry owned a Rolls Royce and had really made it in life. It would be very funny, but I don't think for one moment it would be possible.'

Even if the Lads aren't reunited, at least repeats will continue opening up the series to new generations of fans, just as recent reruns on BBC and UK Gold have done. 'I've had a mega response from new fans,' says Rodney. 'When you think how gentle and laid back it is compared to many shows today, it's amazing it still gets a response. But it's down to the writing, which is so accessible; and the issues being explored are just as relevant today, so people can relate to it.'

However, Rodney, who can't choose a favourite episode, finds it difficult watching repeats. 'I did actually watch one, "Guess Who's Coming to Dinner?", recently and thought it was brilliant, particularly how it focused on snobbery. But I couldn't sit on a sofa and just watch it. I pace around commenting on how good someone was. I wish I could just sit down and enjoy it for its entertainment.'

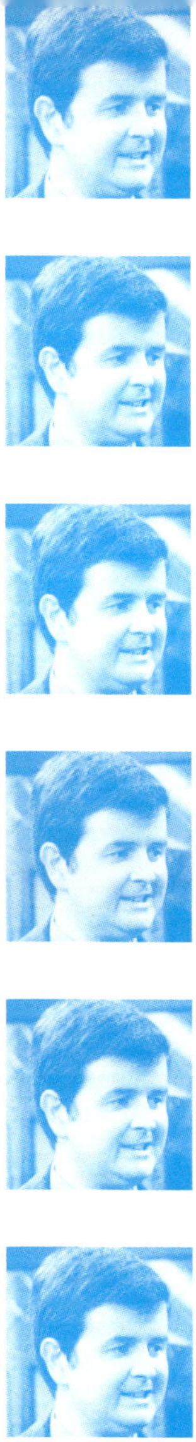

TV CREDITS INCLUDE:

Dear Mother...Love Albert (29 episodes as Albert Courtnay)
The Plane Makers
Emergency – Ward 10
Z Cars
The Basil Brush Show
East Lynne (Earl of Mountsevern)
Love Story
Doctor Who
The Max Bygraves Show
Camera Club
'Tis Pity She's a Whore
Just Liz (one series as Reg Last)
Spender (Norman Ellerson)
She Stoops to Conquer
Jonah and the Whale
My Friend Dennis

THEATRE CREDITS INCLUDE:

A Night Out
Little Malcolm
Middle Age Spread
And Then There Were None
Little Malcolm and his Struggle against the Eunuchs
Big in Brazil
Midsummer Night's Dream (played Flute while touring South America and Europe)
Three Men in a Boat (one-man show)
Funny Money
The Odd Couple
Various pantomimes, including *Cinderella*, *Aladdin* and *Jack and the Beanstalk*

FILM CREDITS INCLUDE:

Billy Liar
Spring and Port Wine
The Spaceman and King Arthur
The Wildcats of St. Trinian's
The Gothic Chimney
Saint Jack
Alice in Wonderland
We Joined the Navy
The Three Musketeers
Decline and Fall
Dance to Your Daddy

La Frenais on Bewes

'My first meeting with Rodney and Jimmy was rather strange. I wasn't around for casting; I still had the day job in market research, and although Di[illegible] consulted with me and I knew of the two a[illegible]om their work, it was his final decision. So I [illegible] personally met either of them until a fe[illegible] after they'd landed the roles.

'I was in Soho, where I work[illegible], get[illegible]wich one lunchtime. I passed [illegible] Bolam and Bewes at the bar! [illegible] on a wardrobe trip to do with the [illegible]ember thinking, if I say, "Are you Jam[illegible] will Bewes be miffed at second billing, [illegible] Bolam feel the same if I recognize Rodn[illegible] In the end I marched up to them and a[illegible] "Hi, I'm Ian La Frenais." Even in my professio[illegible]ancy I was obviously attaching more weight to [illegible]er's credit!

'We all became close friends although I spent more time with Rodney, especially at soccer grounds and in restaurants and clubs. The restaurants, or bistros, were staffed then, as now, by deadly, skinny girls in black stockings who always seemed to be looking somewhere else when they took your order. Meanwhile we only had eyes for them and made desperate efforts to "pull" them. Rodney eventually did! The lovely Daphne, with whom he continues to share marital bliss in Putney.

'We managed to get in most of the coolest clubs in spite of our haircuts and shoes. Rodney was convinced he was a brilliant dancer. He would tell me, in all seriousness: "If all else fails, I'll still have my dancing." The truth is I was a better dancer than Rodney, and still am today.

'Rodney was always great with aunts and uncles, he had legions of them himself, so he was terrific value when he visited the North-East and met my relatives. He loved the area and over the years was a frequent visitor. In turn, Rodney introduced me to Cornwall, as far away from Newcastle as you could possibly get, and I loved that; the people, the pubs, the lo[illegible]ttas, the fishermen crowded into the local, sing[illegible] the night fortified by some frightening conco[illegible]d rum 'n shrubs.

'Rodney had a [illegible]hich could be embarrassing. When he'd drunk too [illegible] red wine, which we all frequently did, he liked to [illegible] Music Hall monologues. His favourite was som[illegible]g about Albert and his horse's head handle, performed in an uncompromising Lancashire accent. It went down a [illegible] all the aunts but was less well received [illegible] Rodney recited it at a party in Beverly Hills, which I took him to on his first visit to California.

'The party was given by the famous writer and producer Larry Gelbart and his wife Pat. The guest list was star-studded and a few of them put on a cabaret. The few included Mel Brooks, Tim Conway, Anne Bancroft and Carl Reiner – seriously talented and funny people. Perhaps if Rodney had given his "Albert" first it might have been excused or excusable. As it was, he announced himself after the cabaret and proceeded. At least he elicited a definite response from comic icon Mel Brooks who asked everyone within earshot "Who the f— is that guy!?"

'Rodney always loved being Bob, as either an actor playing the part or as a television personality. He enjoyed the attention the role brought him and was always grateful for that. Jimmy was never comfortable. Not so much with success or the part itself – he loved Terry Collier – but with the problems a recurring role can bring to an actor. Over the years his talent and versatility have proved those fears groundless, but I'm not sure he looks back on The Lads with the same nostalgia and affection as the rest of us.

'For myself I look back with both affection and gratitude. It was our first taste of success. It was the f[illegible] my life I could put my occupation as w[illegible]n I filled in a form. It was exciting and it w[illegible] And we were young.

W[illegible]ver happened to that?'

JAMES BOLAM • TERRY COLLIER

The feckless Terry Collier – a qualified electrician – inadvertently played a key role in bringing Thelma and Terry together. After yet another disturbance at school, the class teacher decided to split up Terry and Bob, by moving Thelma's desk next to her future husband's.

With a liking for girls in uniform, especially bus conductresses and garage pump attendants, Terry's life changes dramatically when he joins the army. During five years spent in the REME, he reaches the rank of lance corporal while serving in Germany and Cyprus. When he returns to civvy street, it isn't long before he announces he's married a German masseuse, but has split a year later in 1970, the day England lost to West Germany in the World Cup. It is news that shocks everyone, particularly Bob.

Terry finds his return to the North-East difficult to cope with at first, especially when he discovers all his old haunts are long gone, demolished in the face of so-called progress. Even Ellison's, the factory where he served his apprenticeship, no longer exists. With most of his friends married, including Bob, life isn't as carefree and easy anymore, a fact Terry has great difficulty accepting.

Terry Collier's return from the Army had a lasting effect on everyone, while he struggled to adjust to a new chapter in his life.

When James Bolam and Rodney Bewes were offered the chance to play Terry and Bob, back in the early Sixties, they were concerned about being typecast if the sitcom took off. Many thespians, particularly those involved in soaps, leave successful jobs only to find the public and casting directors unable to accept them in any other role.

Although James no longer gives interviews about his days in *The Likely Lads* and its 1970s sequel, he only needs to glance at his extensive curriculum vitae to realize his career, which spans all strands of the profession, hasn't been hampered by playing Terry. Michael Glynn, who produced and directed *The Beiderbecke Tapes* and *The Beiderbecke Connection*, in which Bolam played Trevor Chaplin, welcomed the actor's varied acting experience when casting both series. 'I was thrilled to have James in the show because of his track record,' he says. 'Naturally I admired his work in *The Likely Lads*, which I enjoyed, because he gave such superb performances throughout the series.'

As Tim Rostron pointed out in the *Daily Telegraph*: 'Any well-travelled theatre-goer for the past 30 years will have an even better idea of Bolam's range.' It's the actor's ability to feel equally at home playing comedy or drama that has helped his career prosper. But he's been fortunate enough to work alongside some of the industry's 'greats'. Shortly after leaving drama school he joined the Royal Court, acting with the likes of Laurence Olivier, John Gielgud and Alastair Sim – which anyone would agree was a priceless opportunity for any novice actor.

James Bolam – who lives in Sussex with his partner, actress Susan Jameson – was born in the Sunderland Maternity Home in 1938. By the time he finished his education at Bede Grammar School, he'd decided he wanted to be an actor. He trained at the Central School of Speech and Drama, thanks to a London County Council grant, graduating in 1961. He quickly found employment at a repertory company in Dundee, where one of his fellow actors was Ralph Richardson. After a spell north of the border, he moved back to London and into the West End production of *Semi-Detached*, before becoming involved with the Royal Court.

His first real success on TV came with Terry Collier. In an interview with the *Sunday Times*, James expressed his views about the role. 'In those days I'd never done any comedy, and then Ian La Frenais and Dick Clement recommended me for *The Likely Lads*. I don't know why they decided on me – it was luck. Like with all these things, you need to have a lot of luck on your side.'

But he also pointed out the immediate effect it had on his career, adding: 'Or maybe I got unlucky with that, because it's taken years to get rid of the image. After *The Likely Lads* I didn't work for eighteen months.' Offers of work came his way, but there was a dearth of well-written scripts. That changed when Clement and La Frenais decided to reunite

Bob and Terry for a sequel. James agreed to return to the role, once he had had time to realize just how good the scripts were.

Although he may have been offered his fair share of duff examples, James is first to admit that he's been lucky enough to have recorded some real gems. Shortly after finishing *Whatever Happened to…?* he appeared as Jack Ford in over 50 episodes of James Mitchell's highly successful saga, *When The Boat Comes In*, depicting Northern life during the Depression. Mitchell was pleased Bolam accepted the part. 'In my view, he was the only actor of real stature who could do a good Geordie accent, and that was because he was one, like me. When I first spoke to him it took about ten minutes to realize we were onto a winner with him in the part. Once we'd gone a little further down the road, I couldn't think of anyone else playing the part, nor did I want to contemplate it – he was great.'

When James Mitchell first floated Bolam's name for the lead role, everyone else in the decision-making process agreed he fitted the bill. 'He brought an enormous acting skill,' says Mitchell. 'He was also totally aware of the kind of person Jack Ford was: a deviousness that was sometimes appalling, but who was sometimes extremely likeable. Each week we had 50 minutes to portray a highly complicated man and he did it every time. James was a very powerful driving force, but in some ways he's all wrong: he's too short and certainly not beautiful,' smiles Mitchell, 'but he's a born actor, and given ten minutes to play himself in, he's there for the duration.'

He continued to be in demand in the theatre, and went on to appear in two Shakespearean productions, *As You Like It* and *Macbeth* for the BBC, before taking to his sick bed as Roy Figgis in Yorkshire TV's amusing sitcom, *Only When I Laugh*. Between 1979 and 1982, four series and a Christmas Special were made, all written by Eric Chappell.

Appearing as the matron – a role she frequently played in those days – was veteran actress, Brenda Cowling, who has very fond memories of her time on the show, even though it was just one episode. 'Everybody made me feel welcome from the start,' she says. 'It was a very witty sitcom, and I enjoyed working on it. All the actors worked very fast and extremely hard during rehearsals, and I thought James was extremely good, very inventive. I have a lot of admiration for him, and would like to work with him again, but haven't had the opportunity.'

One of Bolam's biggest roles on TV has been Trevor Chaplin, an amateur detective, in *The Beiderbecke Affair* for Yorkshire Television in 1985. Six hour-long episodes were followed by two further series, *The Beiderbecke Tapes* (1987) and *The Beiderbecke Connection* (1988), both produced by Michael Glynn, who enjoyed working with Bolam. 'James is a true professional. He had an excellent quality, which you sometimes find in an actor, and that is the ability to stretch the writer, director and producer to the limit, which I admired him for. The reason for this, I believe, is his desire to have everything exact and correct, to deliver a performance, which, nine times out of ten, is terrific. But what it does is instil discipline into every aspect of work, meaning you can achieve that little bit more.'

Michael feels James Bolam was ideal for the part of Trevor Chaplin. 'His approach to the character was always excellent, and even in real life he seemed to fit the character like a glove. Alan Plater, who wrote the series, brought out the underdog quality, which James was able to project onto the screen.'

Looking back, Michael enjoyed his time working with James. 'He's a kind individual, particularly when other thespians working with him are having problems with a particular line or move – he's always willing to help and make it easier. He was always cooperative towards fellow artists, but a very private man. I would describe him as very similar to the sabra, an Israeli fruit: prickly on the outside, but soft and tender inside!'

Writer Alan Plater had only Bolam in mind when he created the character Trevor Chaplin, the dry-witted woodwork teacher. *The Beiderbecke* trilogy was conceived after Plater had been commissioned to write a further series of *Get Lost!* for Yorkshire Television in 1981, a 'tongue-in-cheek thriller about a couple of teachers in Leeds.' Alun Armstrong and Bridget Turner played the main characters, and after the success of the first series, a sequel was planned. By the time the project was ready to move into production, Armstrong was on Broadway with *Nicholas Nickleby*, and unable to carry on the role.

After discussions with his bosses at Yorkshire, Alan suggested Bolam for the part and everyone agreed he was an ideal replacement. The characters were redrawn and *The Beiderbecke Affair* was created. The names of the characters were changed, and production started with Barbara Flynn and James Bolam playing the leads.

'They turned out to be a dream team as far as I was concerned,' enthuses Alan. 'I'd first worked with Jimmy on a radio play in Leeds during the late Sixties, and we've always got on extremely well. What he brings to every part he plays is absolute truth and simplicity. He doesn't do anything that's superfluous; he doesn't thrill it out. There are lots of ways of dividing actors and one way is into those who do visible acting, and those who do invisible, and Jim is an invisible actor: you almost don't notice what he's doing; he's incredibly natural.'

(Top) Bob and Terry chat about the old days.
(Below) Terry enjoyed chatting up the girls.

Alan has enjoyed watching recent reruns of *Whatever Happened to The Likely Lads?* 'So much of the time Jim is throwing up the ball for Rodney Bewes to hit it. When the show first began I wondered whether there was mileage in the idea, but then I remembered one or two of my early plays were not dissimilar; they were about a couple of lads, one who's the leader, the other the follower; and there's a constant battle between the two. I thought the idea was good for a play, but not for a series – Dick and Ian proved me wrong, however.

'But Jimmy is good in whatever he does. I remember Barbara Flynn, in *The Beiderbecke Affair*, thinking he was wonderful because he gave so much support; he made everyone's job easier. If you get the right actors in a show, the game is won, and that's how I felt with *Beiderbecke*. I'm Jimmy's number one fan!'

During his career, James has been involved in several other popular shows, including *Second Thoughts*, playing Bill MacGregor on both radio and TV, with Lynda Bellingham as Faith Grayshot, two divorcees who strike up a fiery relationship. After 31 radio episodes, the programme was adapted for TV, with five series being recorded between 1991 and 1994. Three years earlier, he'd finished the second series of Yorkshire's sitcom, *Room at the Bottom*, playing the

leading role, Nesbitt Gunn, who works for Megla Television, run by the dislikeable Kevin Hughes, played by Keith Barron.

On stage, he's appeared in many productions, including *A Midsummer Night's Dream*, *The Knack*, the record-breaking national tours of *Butley* and *Time and Time Again* and the title role in *Macbeth*, at the Young Vic and on American TV. Meanwhile his film credits include films such as *Half a Sixpence*, *A Kind of Loving* and *The Loneliness of the Long-Distance Runner*, in which he played alongside Tom Courtenay.

Away from work, James leads a private life, shunning the spotlight associated with the acting business, preferring to spend his time with family, or indulging in his hobbies, including golf and horse racing.

TV CREDITS INCLUDE:

Take Three Girls
Rivals of Sherlock Holmes
Somerset Maugham (series)
Protectors
Macbeth
The Philanthropist
When the Boat Comes In (four series as Jack Ford)
The Limbo Connection
As You Like It
Only When I Laugh (four series as Roy Figgis)
The Beiderbecke Affair (Trevor Chaplin in all the Beiderbecke series)
The Beiderbecke Tapes
The Beiderbecke Connection
Room at the Bottom (two series as Nesbitt Gunn)
Andy Capp (one series in title role)
Love on the Dole
The Maze
Shades of Darkness
Father Matthew's Daughter (one series as Father Matthew)
Executive Stress
Sticky Wickets
Second Thoughts (five series as Bill MacGregor)
First Take
Eleven Men against Eleven (Ted Whitehead)
Jackanory (read *Tales From Moomin Valley*)
Budgie

THEATRE CREDITS INCLUDE:

The Kitchen
The Knack
A Midsummer Night's Dream
The Happy Haven
The Veterans
Treats
The White Liars
Who Killed Agatha Christie?
Arms and the Man
Run for Your Wife
Jeffrey Barnard is Unwell
How's the World Treating You?
Wild Oats (Sir George Thunder)
Sophocles
Semi-Detached
King Lear
Glengarry Glen Ross
Enjoy
Butley
Time and Time Again
The Seagull
Platanov
The Alchemist
The Bourgeois Gentilhomme
Endgame

FILM CREDITS INCLUDE:

Straight on Till Morning
Crucible of Terror
Otley
Murder Most Foul
In Celebration
The Great Question
A Kind of Loving
The Loneliness of the Long Distance Runner
Half a Sixpence
O Lucky Man!
Clockwork Mice
Stella Does Tricks
The End of the Affair

Clement on Bolam

'I remember a lot of laughs with Jimmy Bolam in the early days of the series. I also remember him staggering in to rehearsal at the Addison Road Boys' Club, a visual definition of the word "hangover"! Don't infer from this that he had a 'problem', we all drank a lot in those days, but it was still a memorable sight.

'Jimmy treated this work with great professionalism. He had a great respect for the text – a word I'd previously only heard applied to Shakespeare – which was flattering to writers as new as we were. He was fiercely self-critical, especially of anything obvious, which he dismissed derisively as "face-acting". 'And he hated any of the ancillary stuff, which goes with success, like being recognized in the street. He loathed being thought of as a "Likely Lad". Early on, when a passer-by recognized him and called out: "Hullo, Terry, where's your mate?" he turned round and snapped: "He's dead!"

'I understood this at the time. He was, and remains, a serious actor, terrified by the idea of being over-associated with one role. I understood it then, but I do not understand it now, so many years later, with a wide-ranging body of work behind him. And frankly, I am hurt and mystified by his attitude. Others involved with the series look back on it with great affection, especially since it represented for most of us a huge leap forward in our careers. He still seems to regard it as a threat to his integrity.

'Mind, the show is not the only recipient of his waspishness. His home town of Sunderland has suffered too. We held the premiere of *The Likely Lads* movie in Newcastle and he was asked by a local journalist how he felt about returning to his roots. His terse reply was something like: "I came up on the last available train and I shall be returning on the first available one in the morning."

'Rodney was on the receiving end, too. In fairness, there was a time when he went through a silly period himself and deserved quite a lot of it, but that's another story. When we decided to revisit our characters, we knew that the main stumbling block would be Jimmy. We took him to lunch at a fashionable King's Road restaurant. After the preamble we put our agenda on the table. His mouth tightened and he said firmly: "Not with Rodney Bewes, no." Less than encouraging. Fortunately, when we outlined what had happened to Bob and Terry in the intervening years, he started to laugh. That, and at least two bottles of Montepulciano, brought him around.

'Ian and I last saw him in Chichester, after an excellent performance as Napoleon. Not one member of the audience shouted out: "Hello, Terry, where's your mate?" We had a very good dinner afterwards, warm and friendly. There was no hint of personal animosity, nor did I ever feel he bore me any, but clearly he has not a trace of nostalgia for the work we did together all those years ago.'

SHEILA FEARN • AUDREY COLLIER

Audrey, just like her brother Terry is never afraid to speak her mind. This trait extends to views about her family: although she loves her brother, she realizes there were flaws in his make-up and isn't afraid to highlight them. She marries Ernie, a hairdresser – who she feels drinks too much – in the late 1960s, and she has two children: Emma Fleur and Wayne.

Sheila Fearn wanted the part of Audrey so much, she turned down two other jobs and a holiday to accept it. 'I knew it was going to be a good part,' she says. 'You only had to read the script to see that – the character leapt off the page. I liked her very much, and thought I could bring something to the part. Audrey was brilliantly written – all the characters were. In my view, Dick and Ian are unique in their ability to write comedy dialogue.'

From the beginning, Sheila felt confident the show would be a success. 'The dialogue was wordy and there was very little action, but I had a strong feeling episodes. Knowing Dick and Ian's writing so well at the time, I always felt confident I could spot who'd written which piece of dialogue.'

When 'Goodbye To All That', the last episode of *The Likely Lads*, had been transmitted on 23 July 1966, Sheila said goodbye to Audrey – or so she

thought. 'I was sad, but was already committed to other things, so it became part of history as far as my working life was concerned. But I always look back with tremendous joy, because I'd been part of a show that has become a classic. I think it's probably one of the best things that has been on television.'

Little did she know that six years later she'd be resurrecting the character in the sequel, *Whatever Happened to The Likely Lads?* But for a while it didn't look as if she'd be free to resume the role. 'I was working on a series for Anglia Television, and was committed to thirteen episodes, so the producer wouldn't release me. And as the BBC didn't have me on a retainer, I missed some of the episodes. It was irritating for Dick and Ian because they'd already written the scripts to include me and had to do lots of rewrites.'

Although she enjoyed appearing in the sequel, Sheila still holds a soft spot for the early black and white episodes. The sequel inevitably held a different focus in terms of story-lines, being based much more on Bob's environment, particularly with regard to his

that all the essential ingredients for success were definitely in the pot.'

The memory of her audition is firmly embedded in Sheila's mind. 'I'd finished working on a TV series in Manchester and had just returned when I was asked to go along and see Dick Clement. I did one reading and that was it,' she recalls. 'I remember we laughed a lot. We also talked about the Beatles because I'd just filmed a part as a make-up girl in *A Hard Day's Night*.'

When it came to deciding how to play Audrey, Sheila observed James Bolam very closely, gearing her own performance to his. 'I tempered my performance to be as sparky as Terry – after all, they were from the same pod.'

Sheila describes Audrey as 'very nosy and bossy – a typical sister', and it was undoubtedly one of the highlights of her career. 'I loved appearing in the show, but then one was always grateful to be offered work. It wasn't the biggest role, but it was definitely one of the best.'

With writer Dick Clement producing the three series of *The Likely Lads*, it meant that he was always around. Ian La Frenais, meanwhile, took as much time off as possible from his job in market research to be on the set, something Sheila appreciated. 'It was terrific, tremendous for confidence. Dick and Ian always hooted with laughter at their own dialogue, especially at the read-through. They seemed to enjoy the whole process enormously. In fact, that was the overriding feeling amongst everyone: after all, here was something new, in a sense a breakthrough from what had gone before, heralding a whole new batch of comedics.'

One of the qualities associated with the sitcom is its sense of reality, something Sheila recognised. 'It was "life", especially the early black and white

married life with Thelma. This obviously meant Audrey's profile as a character was somewhat diminished, but it didn't prevent Sheila enjoying her return to the role.

Born in Leicestershire, Sheila always wanted to be an actress, and after leaving grammar school went straight to RADA. Afterwards she worked for a year on the popular TV show *Emergency – Ward 10*, playing Nurse Elizabeth. 'It was very good experience, and enabled me to get my Equity card.'

Sheila appeared in rep for a while, and toured with several plays, including a production of D. H. Lawrence's *The Daughter-in-Law*, but it was the medium of television that dominated her career, with early appearances in shows like *Z Cars* and *The Expert* for BBC, *Public Eye* and *Special Branch* for Thames TV and *Hadleigh* for Yorkshire. 'I began my career playing a lot of working-class lasses, and then Northern girls, which was strange because in the early days – even before appearing in *Emergency – Ward 10* – I was turned down for a part in *Z Cars* because my Northern accent wasn't strong enough! I was told I should work on it, and from then on I seemed to do nothing but Northern girls – it was extraordinary.'

During this period, work was plentiful in the acting profession, and Sheila moved from one job to the next, never out of work. Although her earlier appearances were mainly in dramas, she's best-known for comedy. In addition to playing Audrey, she appeared in numerous hit shows, such as when she portrayed Ann Fourmile in five series of Thames' *George and Mildred,* and Ronnie Corbett's girlfriend, Freddie, in the BBC sitcom, *Sorry!*

One of her last TV appearances was in ITV's children's sitcom, *News at Twelve,* in 1988, playing Iris Swindley. Shortly after, she decided to spend more time with her son. 'When he was young he became very badly diabetic; I found I couldn't work six days a week and be with him as much as I wanted. Like most actors, I have high professional standards for myself and didn't think I could concentrate 100 per cent while my mind was so much on my son.'

Her son is now grown-up, but Sheila – who admits she was never particularly ambitious – has reached the point where being with her family and travelling with her husband are paramount in her life. 'Travelling has taken up a lot of my time over the last few years. I travel with my husband, who's a businessman, and his work has taken us to places we wouldn't normally see. He's American so we've travelled extensively in the States. It's a wonderful place to live, and we may decide to move there permanently one day.'

In recent years, newspapers have often speculated on the possibility of catching up, once more, with Bob and Terry, even though Dick Clement and Ian La Frenais have no plans for such a venture. 'There isn't much that would tempt me back to work, but playing Audrey again would.'

TV CREDITS INCLUDE:

New Scotland Yard
Sorry!
George and Mildred (five series as Ann Fourmile)
Z Cars
The Avengers
The Beverly Hillbillies (series for American TV)
Paul Temple
Menace
Thirty Minute Theatre
Crown Court
Your Move
The Flockton Flyer
Rainbow Story
Night People
Emergency – Ward 10
East of Ipswich
News at Twelve (one series as Iris Swindley)
Wear a Very Big Hat (lead in BBC play)
Walter (lead in BBC play)
Public Eye
The Expert
Special Branch
Hadleigh
Fly pn the Wall
Trial
Spy Trap
Masters and Servants
Rough with the Smooth

THEATRE CREDITS INCLUDE:

A tour of D. H. Lawrence's *The Daughter in Law* and *A Taste of Honey* at the Richmond Theatre.

FILM CREDITS INCLUDE:

A Hard Day's Night
A Kind of Loving
Time Bandits
George and Mildred
The Likely Lads

La[illegible]

[illegible] al[illegible] s sexy and funny and [illegible] L[illegible] in *A Hard D[illegible]y's Night* a[illegible] d [illegible]. She didn't [illegible] him as [illegible] Len[illegible] She [illegible] him Jo[illegible] ges[illegible] u[illegible] able to [illegible] est of us.

'She [illegible] ew lots of cool people. One night, in a club, s[illegible] duced me to Sandie Shaw and the wife of one [illegible] Hollies! Imagine.

'She [illegible] wonderful Audrey, with that under-stated [illegible] stoicism and matter-of-factness that a work[illegible] sister [illegible] Terry Collier and a young, marri[illegible] her [illegible] equired. Sure, life isn't a bowl [illegible] ries [illegible] with it, that's the way it is. Fa[illegible] line that d[illegible] the character? Audr[illegible] cussing married life with the hapless Bob. "[illegible] ten thought of leaving Ernie," she sighs, "but [illegible] ver fou[illegible] time."

'Sh[illegible] time for everyone and I think [illegible] her, and Audrey, with great affection. Audre[illegible] grandmother now. But she loves k[illegible] bars, [illegible] s salsa lessons [illegible] holidays, al[illegible] e, in Greec[illegible]

PRODUCTION TEAM

(Unless otherwise stated, the people mentioned performed the job throughout the three series.)

SCRIPTS: All episodes written by Dick Clement and Ian La Frenais.
PRODUCER: Dick Clement
PRODUCTION ASSISTANT: Sydney Lotterby
ASSISTANT FLOOR MANAGER: Keith Darby (series 1); Marilyn Gold (series 2 & 3)
COSTUMES: Sandra Reid (series 1 & episode 9); Ursula Reid (series 2, except episode 9); Rita Reekie (series 3)
MAKE-UP: Cecile Fox (series 1, except episode 5); Heather Stewart (episode 5); Monica Ludkin (series 2); Marie Brown (series 3, except episode 14); Janet Nethercot (episode 14)
TECHNICAL MANAGERS: Geoff Shaw (all episodes, except episode 19); John Green (all episodes, except episodes 3, 11, 12 & series 3); Derek Hobday (episode 3); Bill Miller (episodes 11 & 12); Clive Leighton (series 3, except episodes 14 & 19); Frank Rose (episode 14); Peter Catlett and Eric Furze (episode 19)
SOUND: Dick Chamberlain (series 1 & 2, except episodes 2 and 3); Chris Holcombe (episode 2); Norman Greaves (episode 3); Alan Fogg (series 3)
DESIGN: Geoff Kirkland (episodes 2, 4, 6, 8, 10 & 12); Richard Hunt (episodes 1, 3 & 5); Martin Johnson (episodes 7, 9 & 11); Alan Hunter-Craig (series 3, except episodes 16 & 19); Paul Allen (episodes 16 & 19)
VISION MIXER: Clive Doig (all episodes, except 4); Alan Russell (episode 4)
MUSIC: Ronnie Hazlehurst
FILM CAMERAMAN: Elmer Cossey (episode 15); Ian Stone (episode 20)
FILM EDITOR: Geoffrey Botterill (episode 15); Pamela Bosworth (episode 20)

SERIES ONE

(Rodney Bewes and James Bolam were ever-present throughout the series)

I. ENTENTE CORDIALE

Original transmission: Wed. 16/12/64, BBC2, 9.55p.m. (25 mins.)
Repeated on BBC1: Fri. 5/3/65, 8p.m.
(Viewing figures: BBC2 = not available, BBC1 = 8 million)

CAST:

Cloughy . . . . Bartlett Mullins
Jack. . . . . Donald McKillop
Audrey. . . . . Sheila Fearn
Mrs Collier . . . . Olive Milbourne
Louise and Colette . . . Christine Collins
. . . . and Bettine Le Beau
Café Assistant . . . . Joan Pickering

The Lads return from holidaying in Spain – their first trip abroad – and while Terry admits having not seen 'so much talent in all his life', Bob's fighting post-holiday blues and wonders what Louise – his holiday romance – is doing, even though he didn't even speak to her!

Bob is furious when Terry confesses to having given his, not Bob's, address to Louise, and when a postcard arrives, saying she's visiting the area and wants to meet, Terry can't believe his luck.

While Terry brushes up on his French and spruces himself up for the impending visit, Bob reluctantly agrees to tag along when he hears she's bringing a friend. But he has the last laugh when Louise doesn't live up to expectations, while her mate, Colette, is an attractive French au pair.

2. DOUBLE DATE

Original transmission: Wed. 23/12/64, BBC2, 9.55p.m. (25 mins.)
Repeated on BBC1: Fri., 12/3/65, 8p.m.
(Viewing figures: BBC2 = not available, BBC1 = 8.4 million)

CAST:
Deirdre . . . . Coral Atkins
Pat . . . . Susan Jameson
Audrey. . . . . Sheila Fearn

Bob's melancholic again, thanks to a broken romance. Sitting in a scruffy café with Terry, he tries justifying his deep despondency by the fact that he was unofficially engaged to Felicity. But Terry's seen it all before: his mate falling head over heels in love after the first kiss is par for the course.

When two girls – Deirdre and Pat – enter the café, Terry is keen to ask them out, while Bob agrees reluctantly to making up the numbers. They take the girls on the town, splashing out on drinks and food at a new Chinese restaurant, burning a hole in their pockets at the same time!

Reflecting on a successful evening, Bob admits to Terry that he's fallen in love again, so much so that he's given Pat all his luncheon vouchers.

3. OLDER WOMEN ARE MORE EXPERIENCED

Original transmission: Wed. 30/2/64, BBC2, 9.55p.m. (25 mins.)
Repeated on BBC1: Fri. 19/3/65, 8p.m.
(Viewing figures: BBC2 = not available, BBC1 = 8.6 million)

CAST:
Cloughy . . . . Bartlett Mullins
Jack. . . . . Donald McKillop
Sheila Mills. . . . . Sandra Payne
Waitress. . . . . Patricia Shakesby
Freda Winsor . . . . Yvette Rees

A new canteen manageress causes a stir among the male workforce at Ellison's, with everyone fancying their chances with Freda, an attractive divorcee. Terry bets Bob that he'll be going out with her by the end of the day, and is all smiles when he's invited round to her place to carry out a 'little job'!

Bob, meanwhile, has a date with Sheila Mills, but both Lads have a shock in store when Terry finds himself grappling with an immersion heater, and Bob's date isn't all she seems: not only is she just fourteen, she also happens to be the manageress's daughter.

4. THE OTHER SIDE OF THE FENCE

Original transmission: Wed. 6/1/65, BBC2, 10.15p.m. (25 mins.)
Repeated on BBC1: Fri. 26/3/65, 8p.m.
(Viewing figures: BBC2 = not available, BBC1 = 8.5 million)

CAST:

Judith Francis . . . . Anneke Wills
Sally Anne . . . . Didi Sullivan
Jack. . . . . Donald McKillop
Cloughy . . . . Bartlett Mullins
Blakey . . . . Richard Moore
Holgate . . . . Eric Dodson
Nesbit . . . . Michael Sheard
Roger . . . . Martin Redpath

Bob samples life as a white-collar worker when he's seconded to the drawing office. As Terry waits for him after work, Bob strolls up accompanied by two girls: Sally Anne, from Personnel, and Judith, a secretary he fancies. He invites Terry along to the office social, an ideal chance for him to meet his new workmates.

Bob's new status sees him working diligently on homework, discarding his bike because cycle clips crease his trousers and refusing after-work drinks with Terry. Bob reveals, for the first time, a desire to better himself.

At the social, the Lads find Sally Anne and Judith accompanied by Roger and Nesbit, and a row ensues. When it's discovered Terry is only factory staff, he's thrown out, but not before Bob tells his boss where to stick his drawing board. The evening is not a complete disaster because the girls head for the Black Horse with the boys.

5. CHANCE OF A LIFETIME

Original transmission: Wed. 13/1/65, BBC2, 9.55p.m. (25 mins.)
Repeated on BBC1: Fri. 2/4/65, 8p.m.
(Viewing figures: BBC2 = not available, BBC1 = 8.3 million)

CAST:

Audrey. . . . . Sheila Fearn
Cecile . . . . Veronica Lang
Cloughy . . . . Bartlett Mullins
Wally Ralph. . . . . Barry Linehan
Blakey . . . . Richard Moore
Jeffcock . . . . Garfield Morgan
Barman . . . . Eric Smith

The Lads have been stood up, and to make matters worse it's pouring with rain. They drown their sorrows at the Station Hotel's buffet bar and get chatting to Ralph, who's staying at the hotel with his daughter while visiting from Adelaide. He spends the entire evening extolling the virtues of life down under, encouraging the Lads to emigrate.

A £10 state-assisted passage is all that stands between them and a chance of a lifetime. Ralph – who boasts about owning his own factory – is willing to book their tickets, so long as they raise the money pronto. But any plans of a new life are short-lived when it transpires that Ralph is a fraud.

6. THE SUITOR

Original transmission: Wed. 20/1/65, BBC2, 9.55p.m. (25 mins.)
Repeated on BBC1: Fri. 9/4/65, 8p.m.
(Viewing figures: BBC2 = not available, BBC1 = 10 million)

CAST:

Audrey. . . . . Sheila Fearn
Mario . . . . George Layton
Mrs Collier . . . . Olive Milbourne
Barman . . . . Tony Bates

Audrey's been dating Mario – alias Ernie from Hull – far too long, as far as Terry's concerned. She's even dropped her mates, thanks to the charms of the smooth-talking hairdresser. Knowing his sister's pet hate is men who drink and stand her up, Terry devises a plan to get Mario down the pub.

When her boyfriend is late returning, she knows Terry's up to something. As part of the plan, Bob arrives and asks an agitated Audrey out to a party, where she'll bump into her old mates; but she sees through the ruse and decides to get her own back on Terry, who sees Mario in a different light upon discovering he plays rugger and darts and also drinks.

SERIES TWO

(Rodney Bewes and James Bolam appeared in all episodes)

7. BABY, IT'S COLD OUTSIDE

Original transmission: Wed. 16/6/65, BBC2, 9.40p.m. (25 mins.)
Repeated on BBC1: Mon. 23/8/65, 8p.m.
(Viewing figures: BBC2 = not available, BBC1 = 6.9 million)

CAST:

Audrey	Sheila Fearn
Jack	Donald McKillop
Margaret	Dorothy White
Rose	Kate Storey
June	Janet Kelly
Barman	John Scott-Martin

Terry and Bob have a date with a couple of nurses – Rose and June – from the local hospital's radiography department. As they're leaving the area in a few days, the Lads feel they don't have to worry what they get up to – trouble is, they need somewhere to take the girls. With Audrey entertaining Mario at home, their chances look bleak until they meet Jack in the pub, and end up babysitting while he takes his wife to a supper dance.

They tell the girls it's their flat, but when the baby starts crying, Bob's attempts at blaming it on the cat next door are completely unconvincing and fail dismally, and the girls spend the entire evening cooing over the kiddie.

8. A STAR IS BORN

Original transmission: Wed. 23/6/65, BBC2, 9.40p.m. (25 mins.)
Repeated on BBC1: Mon. 30/8/65, 8p.m.
(Viewing figures: BBC2 = not available, BBC1 = 9.4 million)

CAST:

Jack	Donald McKillop
Blakey	Richard Moore
Cloughy	Bartlett Mullins
Rhona	Dilys Watling
Freddy Fyfe	Bernard Spear
Mrs Collier	Olive Milbourne
Mr Collier	Alex McDonald
Singer	Jessie Robins
Ronnie (pianist)	George McCallum
Drummer	Wally Thompson
Pop Group	The Cordinates
Miss Water Board	Gillian Moore
Glass Clearer	Frank Cowley

It's Jack's 42nd birthday, and he's out celebrating with Cloughy, Blakey and the Lads at a scruffy pub in town. Jack, who's had a few, is persuaded to get up and sing, but when Terry and Bob take the mickey out of him, Rhona – the pub's waitress and resident singer – tells them to enter Saturday's talent night if they can do better.

With £25 prize money at stake, Terry and Bob are tempted – even though they can't sing! However, for Terry, the real prize is not the cash, it's Rhona. But it's not long before stage fright sets in.

9. THE TALK OF THE TOWN

Original transmission: Wed. 30/6/65, BBC2, 9.10p.m. (25 mins.)
Repeated on BBC1: Mon. 6/9/65, 8p.m
(Viewing figures: BBC2 = not available, BBC1 = 7.2 million)

CAST:

Audrey	Sheila Fearn
Blakey	Richard Moore
Jack	Donald McKillop
Cloughy	Bartlett Mullins
Mrs Ferris	Irene Richmond
Helen	Helen Fraser
Big Duggie	Michael Coles
Elsie	Patricia Shakesby
Factory Hand	Douglas Harris
Barman	John Scott-Martin
Man in Pub	Martin King
Commissionaire	Roy Denton

Bob wakes up with a hangover, remembering nothing about the previous night's party after which he walked home a girl called Helen. When he reaches work he can't understand why everyone's offering him their congratulations and claiming he has good reason for being late.

It's not long before Bob's reminded of the night's events: in the middle of someone else's engagement party he stood on the sideboard and announced his engagement before putting a ring on Helen's finger. To make matters worse, there are now rumours running around that she's pregnant!

Bob has to summon up the courage to tell Helen he's made a mistake, but he's saved humiliation when she apologizes first: an old flame has returned and her heart lies elsewhere.

10. THE LAST OF THE BIG SPENDERS

Original transmission: Wed. 7/7/65, BBC2, 9.10p.m. (25 mins.)
Repeated on BBC1: Mon. 13/9/65, 8p.m.
(Viewing figures: BBC2 = not available, BBC1 = 9.2 million)

CAST:
Audrey . . . . Sheila Fearn
Angela . . . . Wanda Ventham
Lynn . . . . Wendy Richard
Nesbit . . . . Michael Sheard
Julian . . . . Roger Brierley
Miss Moppet . . . . Pamela Greer
Bouncer . . . . Alister Williamson
Barman . . . . Paul Lindley
Croupier . . . . Elsa Fell

The Lads visit a local department store and notice two pretty girls – Lynn and Angela – conducting an in-store demonstration of the 'Miracle Mop' and 'Wonder Foam' floor cleaner. As a ploy to gain their undivided attention, the Lads buy a plethora of products, only to find themselves short of cash when they achieve their goal of fixing a date with the girls.

Because of the extravagance shown at the demonstration, Lynn and Angela – who only agree to go out to ease the boredom of hotelling it in Newcastle – assume the Lads are loaded, so suggest eating and drinking at a new, palatial roadhouse, outside town.

After a meal, they move on to a gambling club. By now, Bob and Terry are fretting so much about the evening's soaring costs that they are relieved to lose the two spendthrifts when they're chatted up at the club.

11. FARAWAY PLACES

Original transmission: Wed. 14/7/65, BBC2, 8.50p.m. (25 mins.)
Repeated on BBC1: Mon. 20/9/65, 8p.m.
(Viewing figures: BBC2 = not available, BBC1 = 8.7 million)

CAST:
Audrey . . . . Sheila Fearn
Mrs Collier . . . . Olive Milbourne
Archie . . . . Norman Chappell
Labour Exchange Clerk . . . . Roger Avon
Eva . . . . Gay Hamilton
Mr Clipboard . . . . Jay Denyer

At the local billiard hall, Bob and Terry discuss their forthcoming holiday. But money is short after squandering a small fortune entertaining Lynn and Angela, the store demonstrators. Terry floats the idea of a break in a holiday camp, but Bob's thinking further afield, to more sunny climes.

To help ease their financial shortcomings, Archie – who owns the billiard hall – suggests the Lads find part-time jobs to earn some extra cash, so a visit to the labour exchange is now called for.

12. WHERE HAVE ALL THE FLOWERS GONE?

Original transmission: Wed. 21/7/65, BBC2, 9.15p.m. (25 mins.)
Repeated on BBC1: Mon. 27/9/65, 8p.m.
(Viewing figures: BBC2 = not available, BBC1 = 10 million)

CAST:
Audrey . . . . Sheila Fearn
Mrs Collier . . . . Olive Milbourne
Mario . . . . George Layton
Beryl and Elaine,
the Bridesmaids . . . . Janina Faye
. . . . and Tracy Rogers
Aunt Peggy . . . . Ruth Kettlewell
Uncle Walter . . . . John Henderson
Cyril . . . . Peter Hempson
Aunt Hannah . . . . Lucy Griffiths
Colin . . . . Ian Norris
Miriam . . . . Cathy Ash
Vicar . . . . James Cossins

One of Terry's relatives is getting married and the Lads attend the event. It seems everyone they know has opted for married life. While their old friend John Webb has got another kid, Cyril, Terry's cousin, got engaged shortly after leaving school and it's only a matter of time before he announces the wedding date. Even Aunt Peggy thinks it's about time Terry and Bob settled down. The Lads are fed up with everyone wondering when they'll get hitched, and are more interested in the young bridesmaids, Beryl and Elaine.

Before leaving for the evening do at the Hand and Flower, a new pub, Bob and Terry agree that weddings depress them. Terry says: 'It wasn't so bad when the girls you were at school with got married, but now it's the blokes.' Just to add to their depression, they take a quick look at an old school photo and count off friends who have got married, including Mike Thompson and Mike Williams.

With the likes of youngsters such as Cyril about, the Lads start feeling old, especially when they're told they wouldn't like a particular nightclub because it's full of young people.

SERIES THREE

(Rodney Bewes and James Bolam appeared throughout)

13. OUTWARD BOUND

Original transmission: Sat. 4/6/66, BBC2, 9.40p.m. (30 mins.)
Repeated on BBC1: Tues. 4/10/66, 7.30p.m.
(Viewing figures: BBC2 = 0.6 million, BBC1 = 11.3 million)

CAST:

Jack	Donald McKillop
Cloughy	Bartlett Mullins
Café Proprietor	Keith Roberts
Scoutmaster	James Cossins
Postmistress	Amy Dalby
Valerie	Nerys Hughes
Susan	Sandra Blaine
Boy Scouts	John Shelley and Gary Neilson
Large Lady	Parnell McGarry

Terry's suddenly interested in Bob's idea of a break when he hears about a place on the coast where beatniks go. Believing they're advocates of 'free love', Terry is keen to experience the delights of this coastal resort!

They plan hitchhiking all the way, but their adventure gets off to a bad start when Terry is not only late arriving at Bob's, but is carrying a suitcase. As the journey progresses, matters worsen when Terry gets blisters and moans all the way.

Finally, they arrive at their overnight stop, the Old Manor, only to find it has been demolished to make way for a new housing estate. With the railway station closed and the last bus into town departed, the Lads are in a fix, until they spot Valerie and Susan, who are camping in a nearby spot.

14. FRIENDS AND NEIGHBOURS

Original transmission: Sat. 11/6/66, BBC2, 9.40p.m. (30 mins.)
Repeated on BBC1: Tues. 11/10/66, 7.30p.m.
(Viewing figures: BBC2 = 0.4 million, BBC1 = 11.2 million)

CAST:

Grandad	Wilfred Lawson
Mr. Perrin	Glenn Melvyn
Mrs Perrin	Noel Dyson
Lorna Perrin	Angela Lovell
Barmaid	Rita Ramano
Customers in pub	Ray Golman and Steve Pokol

While Terry's auntie is visiting Canada, his grandad stays in her house, but it's not long before he's upsetting Mr. and Mrs Perrin, the snooty neighbours, by hanging out his washing. Meanwhile Bob is dating seventeen-year-old Lorna, the Perrins' daughter, and finds himself in an awkward position when they tell him about the horrible old man living next door, who wears braces and spits.

The Lads are on opposing sides in the class war: Terry is backing his grandad, while Bob, who'd normally be right behind him, has a vested interest in seeing the middle-class family's point of view on this occasion.

15. ROCKER

Original transmission: Sat. 18/6/66, BBC2, 9.30p.m. (30 mins.)
Repeated on BBC1: Tues. 18/10/66, 7.30p.m.
(Viewing figures: BBC2 = 0.5 million, BBC1 = 12.1 million)

CAST:

Nurse	Carole Mowlam
Mr. Sydney	Derek Sydney
Carol	Patti Dalton
Scooterist	Tex Fuller
Mechanic	Derek Seaton

Bob's acquired his first set of wheels, even though it's a second-hand scooter. With an outlook stretching beyond the immediate horizon, he dreams of taking a 'bird' out into the country on Sunday mornings, enjoying the freedom his own transport could bring.

After a few scrapes, he gets the hang of his scooter and Terry helps him prepare for his test by quizzing him on the Highway Code. But when it comes to practising the all-important emergency stop, Terry ends up in hospital!

16. BRIEF ENCOUNTER

Original transmission: Sat. 25/6/66, BBC2, 9.35p.m. (30 mins.)
Repeated on BBC1: Tues. 25/10/66, 7.30p.m.
(Viewing figures: BBC2 = 0.5 million, BBC1 = 11.2 million)

CAST:

Jack	Donald McKillop
Cloughy	Bartlett Mullins
Ursula	Isobel Black
Cloakroom Attendant	Derek Benfield
Girl	Joan Pickering
Barman	Lewis Teasdale
Drunk	Donald Oliver
Waitress	Maggie Riley

At the local dance hall the Lads are on the prowl for dancing partners, and split up to help their cause. Eventually Bob strikes lucky with Ursula, who's from Blackpool and visiting her sick aunt. They get on well and agree to meet the following day, but Ursula refuses Bob's offer to walk her home because someone else has that pleasure. What Bob doesn't know is that Terry's the chosen one.

17. THE RAZOR'S EDGE

Original transmission: Sat. 2/7/66, BBC2, 9.40p.m. (30 mins.)
Repeated on BBC1: Tues. 1/11/66, 7.30p.m.
(Viewing figures: BBC2 = 0.6 million, BBC1 = 12.8 million)

CAST:

Mrs Collier	Olive Milbourne
Jack	Donald McKillop
Cloughy	Bartlett Mullins
Mrs Ferris	Irene Richmond
Darby	Antony Baird
Godfrey	Donald Gee
Monica	Vickery Turner
Podge	Geoffrey Hughes
Barmaid	Penelope Goddard
Barman	John Scott-Martin

With Bob suffering from chicken pox, Terry has made sure he doesn't catch anything by staying away throughout the entire three-week incubation period. Finally he musters up the courage to visit Bob, only to find the patient has changed in more ways than one – he's grown a beard, the result of lying in bed so long.

When he returns to work Mr. Darby is unhappy with Bob's new look and orders him to shave it off. Bob's annoyed because he's not the only bearded person at work, but Terry takes the matter more seriously, claiming victimization; he's prepared to stand up for his pal's rights, even if it means he has to go on strike.

18. ANCHORS AWEIGH

Original transmission: Sat. 9/7/66, BBC2, 9.35p.m. (30 mins.)
Repeated on BBC1: Tues. 8/11/66, 7.30p.m.
(Viewing figures: BBC2 = 0.5 million, BBC1 = 13.1 million)

CAST:

Mrs Collier . . . . Olive Milbourne
Sam. . . . . Hamish Roughead
Sally West . . . . Rosemary Nicols
Barman. . . . . Patrick Carter
Marion . . . . Glenda Ramsay

When friends pull out of a boating holiday on the Norfolk Broads, Bob suggests to Terry that they take up the opportunity, even though they know nothing about boats. Terry's nervous about the idea, but soon perks up when Bob tells him it'll be a great way of finding some girls – especially when he sees Sally West, who runs the boatyard.

Before they even leave the shore, Terry's fixed up a date with Sally, but to his disgust Bob launches the boat before he has chance to meet her. At the next stop, Terry phones Sally and she agrees to drive over, but Bob scuppers his plans again by sailing on to Yarmouth.

When Bob meets Marion, who's on a boat moored nearby, it's Terry's turn to play spoilsport. But things get worse yet again for Terry when Bob ends up dating Sally West!

19. LOVE AND MARRIAGE

Original transmission: Sat. 16/7/66, BBC2, 8.50p.m. (30 mins.)
Repeated on BBC1: Tues. 15/11/66, 7.30p.m.
(Viewing figures: BBC2 = 0.4 million, BBC1 = 13.5 million)

CAST:

Jack. . . . . Donald McKillop
Cloughy . . . . Bartlett Mullins
Helen . . . . Helen Fraser
Duggie . . . . Derek Newark
Archie . . . . Norman Chappell
Mrs Foster . . . . Elizabeth Begley
Podge . . . . Geoffrey Hughes
Old Dan . . . . Frank Cowley

The Lads drink at the social club while waiting for Norman Elliott's stag night to begin. When Duggie, an old friend who's married with a new baby, pops in on his way home from shopping, he's persuaded to stay for a quick half.

It will soon be the social club's annual outing to Morecambe and Terry asks Duggie whether he's going, but he can't because of his child. When Duggie confesses he hasn't been out with mates for years, Bob and Terry persuade him that he should stay, and he ends up drunk.

When the groom-to-be fails to turn up, Terry and Bob realize they've got the wrong night and help their inebriated friend home, before considering how every example of married life seems far from special.

20. GOODBYE TO ALL THAT

Original transmission: Sat. 23/7/66, BBC2, 8.40p.m. (30 mins.)
Repeated on BBC1: Tues. 22/11/66, 7.30p.m.
(Viewing figures: BBC2 = 0.6 million, BBC1 = 13.7 million)

CAST:

Audrey . . . . Sheila Fearn
Jack . . . . Donald McKillop
Cloughy . . . . Bartlett Mullins
Mrs Collier . . . . Olive Milbourne
Mr. Collier . . . . Alex McDonald
George . . . . Barry Stanton
Army Sergeant . . . . Tony Caunter
Mrs Ferris . . . . Irene Richmond
Youth . . . . Andrew Robertson
Recruit . . . . Hugh Walters

Over a pint in the pub, the Lads debate what the town has to offer. While Terry champions its plus points, Bob classes it as 'the muckiest town' he's ever seen, and considers getting himself out of a rut by joining up and seeing the world.

Terry doesn't think he's serious, and believes he's trying to run away after getting the push from Thelma Chambers. But when Bob hands in his notice and a collection is organized, he knows it's for real.

Terry struggles adjusting to his pal's departure, and in an attempt to reunite their friendship, joins the army, too – only to find that Bob's discharged due to his flat feet!

CHRISTMAS SPECIAL

CHRISTMAS NIGHT WITH THE STARS

The Lads appeared in a five-minute sketch, directed by Dick Clement, during the broadcast.

Original transmission: 25/12/64, BBC1, between 7.15p.m. and 8.45p.m.
(Audience = 18.6 million)
An edited repeat was shown on BBC2 on Sat. 21/12/91, 6 – 7p.m. as part of *A Perfect Christmas*

CAST:

Terry . . . . James Bolam
Bob . . . . Rodney Bewes
Audrey . . . . Sheila Fearn

FAMILIAR FACES

The Likely Lads

SUSAN JAMESON
(b. Barnt Green)
Role: Pat Welsh
(episode 2)

When the episode 'Double Date' was last repeated – Susan played one of the girls the Lads date – it caused much amusement amongst local children. 'Several I know were very tickled, and kept imitating my character describing how she'd been kissed! Once I'd recovered from the shock of how I looked, I enjoyed watching it. The episodes are just as relevant and funny today – even our daughter, Lucy, thinks so.'

Susan was certain the series would be a hit. 'I remember reading the scripts and thinking how funny they all were. In Terry and Bob, Dick Clement and Ian La Frenais created the perfect pair of characters: they were real and a wonderful contrast. Conflict existed all the time, which is where the humour sprang from.' Deciding how to play the character was easy. 'It was self-explanatory how I should play her because the two girls were written so clearly; they were just like girls we all knew. Coral Atkins, who played the other girl, was quite different to me, so it worked well.'

Susan knew from the age of ten that she wanted to be an actress. Due to her father's job – he was an artist and teacher – she moved around the country, an experience she believes gave her 'a good ear for accents'.

Susan joined the Birmingham School of Speech and Drama straight from school, but left before completing the course to spend eight months as an ASM/juvenile lead at Weston-super-Mare, starting with an appearance as Anne Frank. After returning to complete her drama course, she went on to appear at various reps, including Birmingham, Canterbury and Cheltenham.

She made her TV debut in *Z Cars*, but her first significant role was the year (1963–64) spent playing Myra Booth in *Coronation Street*. 'While appearing in a play at Coventry, I was called for an audition and got lucky.' Her TV career blossomed with a semi-regular role as P.C. Nelson in *Softly, Softly*, Kate in *Take Three*

MEMORABLE SCENES

EPISODE

Double Date

(Terry is in a café with Bob when two girls – Deirdre and Pat – arrive; a date is on the cards, but first the girls assess Bob.)

DEIRDRE: Well he's a miserable-looking devil.

PAT: *(looking under cover of seam straightening)* Oh, I don't know – I like that. Serious. Looks a bit like Roy Orbison.

DEIRDRE: Huh!

PAT: Well, he does.

DEIRDRE: Stop whisperin'. They'll think we're talking about 'em.

PAT: What would you like to do tonight, Deirdre? I mean, I'd like you to have a good time while you're here. We could go to a dance if you like, or pictures...

DEIRDRE: Eh, I wouldn't make too many plans if I were you, I've got a feeling our evening's all being arranged for us.

Girls, Jessie Seaton in four series of *When the Boat Comes In*, *To Serve Them All My Days*, Kathleen Ferguson in *Band of Gold* and many more. And she has played in theatre, Lady Macbeth in *Macbeth*, Constance in *The Constant Wife* and national tours of *Getting On* and *Pride and Prejudice*.

She also appeared in films, such as *International Velvet* and the lead in *Catherine – Brief Lives*, exploring anorexia. 'It was based on a true story and lots of people who had problems themselves sent mail; it was reassuring to think we'd made a film that had helped people.'

Susan met her partner, actor James Bolam, on the set of *The Likely Lads*, but it was some time before they became friends, and she still holds happy memories of her single appearance in the show. 'It was such a pleasure to do.'

GEORGE LAYTON
(b. Bradford)
Role: Mario
(episodes 6 & 12)

If George Layton had had his way, he would have been playing Terry. 'I auditioned for the part but, being a young actor with hardly any television credits to my name, I didn't have enough experience,' recalls George, who's 56. But Dick and Ian liked him enough to offer him the role of Mario, Audrey's boyfriend, a hairdresser.

Fresh out of drama school, George – who's also a writer and director – was excited to be involved in such an innovative show. 'When you watch *The Likely Lads* today you don't realize it was the cutting edge of its time, and it was great working with two new writers like Dick and Ian.'

Mario was George's second TV part, and he went on to appear in *United!* and numerous other TV shows. 'Television began dominating my career, and during the 1970s I was never off the screen. I was in the lucky position of picking and choosing jobs.'

Recently he spent time in Cyprus filming the BBC drama series *Sunburn*, but his favourite role was Paul Collier in the long-running *Doctor* series. 'It started off as a poor part but developed well as the series progressed. I also enjoyed appearing in *Minder*, and playing Bombardier Solomons in *It Ain't Half Hot, Mum* before leaving after two series due to other work commitments.'

Other TV roles include Vernon Potter in two series of *Robin's Nest*, Brian Booth in *My Brother's Keeper* and a presenter on the first series of *That's Life*!

During the 1980s, George's writing career took up much of his time, and he became an infrequent visitor to the small screen. He hit a rich vein when he began writing *Don't Wait Up*, which ran for six series between 1983 and 1990. This success story was followed by three series of *Executive Stress* with Penelope Keith and Geoffrey Palmer/Peter Bowles. 'That took care of the 1980s very nicely,' says George, 'but it meant I had to turn down acting work which was a shame – not that I'm complaining.'

A RADA graduate, where he won the Emile Littler Award, George Layton wanted to be an actor from the age of seven, but upon leaving school worked in a hospital for a few months until joining drama school. Afterwards he went straight to Coventry and joined one of the leading reps of the day; he stayed 18 months before appearing on Broadway in *Chips With Everything*.

Nowadays, George, who has also written several novels, is making a concerted effort to return to acting. 'Writing was starting to take over, so I'm really trying to get back to acting.'

DONALD McKILLOP
(b. Carlisle)
Role: Jack
(episodes 1, 3, 4, 5, 7, 8, 9, 13, 16, 17, 19 & 20)

Donald played the bluff foreman of the little workshop where Bob and Terry worked, a character he enjoyed bringing to life. 'He was a very nice foreman, really, always mucking in with the lads and getting on well with them. He was ex-army and I could see him as a sergeant. It was a lovely job, a super cast and a good production team to work with.'

Having Dick as the director, as well as one of the writers, was an immense advantage, as far as 70-year-old Donald is concerned. 'Anything that didn't work in rehearsals, he'd simply rewrite it – it worked out very well.'

Donald trained as a draughtsman, but when he moved to Ashton-under-Lyne he joined the local rep and stayed five years. After a spell in various companies, he joined RADA in 1959 as a mature student.

MEMORABLE SCENES

EPISODE

Love and Marriage

(Bob and Terry discuss how their friends, especially Duggie, have changed since they got married.)

BOB: Take the blokes in the Club. They're always saying things like 'Oh I've got the night off from the wife' or 'the wife's away for a couple of days, thank God'. Well what's it all about? I mean, if I'm gonna be so pleased to be out of the wife's sight for a couple of hours, why am I married to her in the first place?

TERRY: Well, of course, you know why most of the blokes we know get married.

BOB: Yes but – not all of them. Doesn't seem to be all that much difference, though, does it? They all end up the same. Like Duggie.

TERRY: Ee, it's incredible. You wouldn't have known it was the same bloke, would you? D'you remember how he used to be?

BOB: Aye. There was always some action when Duggie was around.

TERRY: There was that. He was a real good lad was Duggie. Never a dull moment. Last time we went out with him he knocked your teeth in.

BOB: *(nostalgically)* I know.

Upon graduating two years later, he joined the BBC's own repertory company on the radio, where he first met Dick Clement.

'I worked for the BBC's rep company for two years, before leaving in 1961 and doing three plays at the Royal Court, including *The Changing Room*.' Don appeared in a few small parts on TV, including *Coronation Street*, but *The Likely Lads* was his biggest role at that point in his career.

When he finished the series he worked for three years in Scotland, playing Sergeant McKechnie in *Sutherland's Law*. He also continued working on the stage. He was last seen on the screen in BBC's *South of the Border*, back in 1988, while his last theatre job was with the RSC. His only film appearance was in *An American Werewolf in London*.

For the last ten years Donald has lived in Spain. 'When a planned house purchase in Stratford fell through, we decided to move to Spain. Initially we only intended living here for a year or two, but the weather is wonderful in Southern Spain, and we're only minutes from the sea, so we've stayed. While I was still in England I got very bad arthritis in both knees, and although I was able to have an operation, I just felt it was important to have a change – and I've never regretted it.'

OLIVE MILBOURNE
(b. London)
Role: Mrs Collier
(episodes 1, 6, 8, 11, 12, 17, 18 & 20.
Whatever Happened To. . .? *episodes 6, 8, 19 & 26)*

Olive – who played Terry's hard-working mother – was constantly rushing between rehearsals when she started appearing in *The Likely Lads*, as her widower, Ellison Bayles, explains: 'When the show began she was already appearing in *Clough*, a series with Leslie Sands. She was hardly ever out of work at that time.' Although her character appeared less in the sequel, Olive – whose father was in the leather trade – still enjoyed recording the occasional episode.

Her acting talents were spotted at school. When one of her teachers suggested she took up acting, Olive, a regular in school productions, joined PRADA before moving on to RADA. She graduated in 1927 and quickly made her West End debut, appearing in *Mr. Prohack* at the Royal Court, with Charles Laughton. After a couple of tours, she spent three years in weekly rep at Northampton.

Olive remained busy in the theatre, establishing herself as a small-part character actress until war broke out, during which she joined ENSA and met her future husband. 'We were both working at Malvern in 1940,' says Ellison Bayles. 'Then we both toured abroad with ENSA, following the British army from Paris to Berlin.'

After the war ended she returned to the stage, initially at Worthing, but it wasn't long before she was making her film debut in the 1947 picture, *Veterans' Rendezvous*. During her career she was seen in a few other movies, including *Edward My Son* (1949), *The Woman with No Name* (1950), *One Way Out* (1955) and *Happy Is the Bride* (1955).

Her TV career began just before the war, and she was soon back on the small screen in shows like *Billy Bunter of Greyfriars School* in 1952. She was also seen as Aunt Mabel, the butcher's wife in Rediffusion's *Six Penny Corner*, a probation officer and traveller in *Shadow Squad* and appearances in *Emergency – Ward 10*.

Olive died of cancer in 1984; she was 85.

RICHARD MOORE
(b. Burnley)
Role: Blakey
(episodes 4, 5, 8 & 9)

'Like many of the names given to Dick and Ian's characters, Blakey was probably an old friend, because when we recorded one of the episodes, we were getting some big laughs that I wasn't expecting. I found out a lot of Dick and Ian's friends were in the audience, and they must have recognized the name,' says Richard, who regrets not appearing in the sequel.

'Dick and Ian asked whether I wanted to be in *Whatever Happened to…?*, which left me with an interesting dilemma: I'd been offered a part in a world tour of *Midsummer Night's Dream*, so had to make a choice. I probably made the wrong one because I chose the world tour. It's just that *The Likely Lads* had been so good, I didn't think they could revive it successfully, but I was wrong.'

Richard felt confident *The Likely Lads* would be successful. 'It was the Sixties, the time of the Beatles, and it seemed that anything from up North was fashionable. I played a Northerner in a series around that time called *Diary of a Young Man*, directed by Ken Loach, which was a success, too. Playing Blakey was just good fun: I liked it so much, I named my cat after the character. It's extraordinary how people still remember the part, after all these years.'

Upon leaving school, Richard worked for four years as a photographer at the *Burnley Express*, before joining a Bristol drama school at 19. Rep work followed, but by the start of the 1960s he was also appearing on TV, his debut in *Z Cars* earning him £90.

He continued working in the theatre and was engaged by the RSC for some years. More recent small screen credits include *Band of Gold*, and a regular role in *McCallum*, playing Professor Paddy Penfold, head of the pathology department.

Richard has appeared in five movies, including Twentieth Century Fox's *Robin Hood* in 1991. 'Latterly, I've become more a drama actor, and haven't done any comedy for a long time.'

BARTLETT MULLINS
(b. Crosby)
Role: Cloughy
(episodes 1, 3, 4, 5, 8, 9, 13, 16, 17, 19 & 20)

Bartlett Mullins developed interests in amateur dramatics and carpentry whilst in the merchant navy, and both of these skills stood him in good stead later in life.

Upon leaving school he worked in an office, but soon packed it in to join the navy. Ill health forced his retirement and he decided to concentrate on a career in the entertainment business. When a repertory company arrived in his home town, and they lost the services of their carpenter, Bartlett joined and toured the country as the company chippie. 'But he wasn't content with just doing carpentry, and was soon playing small parts, which made him realize he wanted to pursue an acting career,' explains Bartlett's widow, Dorothy Mullins.

Bartlett – whose father was in the removal business – particularly enjoyed working in the theatre, and in 1927 he moved to London and started appearing in touring shows like Dorothy L. Sayer's *The Six Men of Dorset.* He was seen in the West End either side of the Second World War, in shows including *Goodnight Mr. Peeps* and *Tobias and the Angel.*

During the war he worked for the rescue service, meeting his wife in the process. 'We were both stationed at Kensington,' says Dorothy, who was working for the ambulance service. 'We met in 1941 and were married the following year.'

After the war, Bartlett worked as assistant to the borough engineer of Kensington. But from 1946 onwards he appeared on Broadway, and regularly in the West End. Then, when TV came along, he knew it was time to broaden his horizons.

He made his screen debut in the early Sixties, and regularly appeared in small parts in shows like *Emergency – Ward 10*, *Steptoe and Son* and *Hancock's Half-Hour.* One of his last jobs was Granada's thirteen-part series, *The House of Caracus*, but he's best remembered as Cloughy. 'Bartlett enjoyed playing the character,' says Dorothy. 'He always had a mischievous sense of humour, so Cloughy suited him down to the ground.'

Busy throughout his career, the diminutive character actor appeared in several films, including *Conflict of Wings*, as the eel catcher, *Daughter of Darkness, Gone to Earth, Innocent Sinners, Sapphire, No Room at the Inn, Stolen Face, The Quatermass Experiment, Half a Sixpence* and *Peeping Tom.*

In 1972 Bartlett and Dorothy moved to Exmouth, Devon, but he continued appearing in the occasional commercial or TV show. He suffered a stroke in 1982, and remained unwell until his death 10 years later, aged 88.

SANDRA PAYNE
(b. Cambridge)
Role: Sheila Mills (episode 3)

When she played the new canteen manageress' daughter who Bob dates, only to discover she's 14, Sandra Payne was, in fact, 20. 'Because of my age and the fact I could play very young characters, I never stopped working. I'd only been in television a year when I appeared in *The Likely Lads*; I was still learning the trade and remember just wandering on and trying to look like Brigitte Bardot, which every girl wanted to do in those days.

'I had no real understanding of what you did in front of the camera, so it was just as well Sheila was only a tiny role. I'll always remember watching the regulars during rehearsal, which was a good way to learn.' Sandra later appeared with Rodney Bewes in Thames' 1980 sitcom, *Just Liz,* playing Liz Parker, the lead role.

After finishing her education, Sandra spent a few months at the Italia Conti Stage School before accepting her first professional job in panto at Weymouth during the Christmas of 1960. Rep work followed, beginning at Cromer, where her stage manager was Gareth Gwenlan, who's now one of the BBC's top producers. He's since employed Sandra several times, including an appearance in *Only Fools And Horses.* She also worked at Northampton and Croydon rep before TV really started to dominate her career.

Sandra, whose mother was an actress and father a solicitor, made her TV debut in a 1963 episode of *Compact.* Her other TV credits include *The*

Troubleshooters, *Riviera Police* for Rediffusion, Pam in the pilot of *Roger, Roger*, Marion in five series of *Waiting For God*, Christine Harris in two series of BBC's *Triangle*, *The Professionals*, Belinda Leydon in *Never The Twain*, Mrs Micawber in *David Copperfield*, Caroline Ackland in the TV film of *Jack the Ripper* with Michael Caine and four years as Janet Langley in BBC's early soap, *The Newcomers*, one of Sandra's favourite roles.

In the mid-1970s, she lived in New York, before returning to England and resuming her career, which in recent years has included a lot of Shakespeare, including Queen of France in *Henry V* and Katherine of Aragon in *Henry VIII*, directed by Robert Hardy in 1998.

JOAN PICKERING
(b. Sheffield)
Role: Café Assistant
(episode 1);
Girl (episode 16)

Joan Pickering was the first person seen in *The Likely Lads*, thanks to her role as the tea-spilling café assistant at the railway station where Bob and Terry wait for their train. She popped up again in a later episode 'Brief Encounter'.

Upon completing her education Joan joined a drama school, after which she began her professional career in rep. Although she mainly worked on the stage – including one foray into the West End – she made a living playing small parts on TV, like an appearance in *Z Cars*.

Joan married in 1965, and moved to Jersey a year later. While her husband produced shows at St. Helier's opera house, Joan acted in them. But when her husband died in 1975 she retired from professional acting and worked behind the scenes, helping shows coming over to the island.

Towards the end of her life Joan got involved in several local amateur productions. After a long series of illnesses, she died in 1991, aged 59.

IRENE RICHMOND
(b. Gresford)
Role: Mrs Ferris
(episodes 9, 17 & 20)

Welsh-born Irene Richmond enjoyed playing Bob's mother, Mrs Ferris, who doted over her son, in three episodes of *The Likely Lads*. 'It was tremendous fun; I loved the boys, they had such a wonderful sense of humour,' she says enthusiastically. 'I'm a very good North country speaker, very authentic, so I felt happy playing the part.'

Sadly, when it came to casting for *Whatever Happened to…?*, Irene, now 87, was in the middle of an extensive tour and couldn't be released from her contract, so actress Barbara Ogilvie replaced her.

Irene was only six months old when her family left Wales for Pontefract – her father worked as a colliery cashier. After leaving school she had a few jobs, including shop work, until she joined a drama school in Oxford. Her first professional job was at the Henley Playhouse, where she played an assortment of characters during a six-month period. Once she had earned her Equity card she joined ENSA for three years until the end of the Second World War.

Her early career was very much dominated by theatrical work – including many plays at London's Q Theatre, such as *Point of Departure* and *Sailor Beware* with Peggy Mount. However, as the years passed she was seen more and more on TV, including in *Z Cars*, *Crossroads*, ATV's *24 Hour Call*, *Probation Officer*, *No Hiding Place*, *The Dickie Henderson Show*, *Harry Worth* and *My Husband and I*.

Irene, who now lives in Bournemouth, retired from the business 15 years ago through ill health. 'I'd just finished working at the Royal Court, and I fell down some steps and broke my hip, which led to arthritis. I couldn't go on working, and didn't really want to, so I decided to move to Dorset, where I'm living very happily.'

The Return

You tread carefully when contemplating reviving a television show, especially if the original has been a success. If it's solely nostalgia that drives writers or producers to consider such an exercise, they do so at their peril. Fond memories don't always stand the test of time, and any revival has to achieve more than secure the allegiance of diehard fans: it must win over an entirely new, critical audience, many of whom may be too young to have any recollection of its predecessor.

If a revival does get off the ground, it very often fails to reach the heights scaled by its forerunner. But there is always an exception to the rule, and when Bob and Terry resurfaced, six years after the Lads waved goodbye in the final episode of *The Likely Lads*, critics and fans alike regarded it as even better than the original three series.

Journalist and TV presenter Clive James, classed *Whatever Happened To…?* as his favourite sitcom. He wrote: 'Dick Clement and Ian La Frenais continue to write with unfailing comic invention. Sequels are rarely as strong as the originals, but *Whatever Happened To…?* is currently breaking the rule. The lines are acted out with engaging clumsiness.'

A journalist in the *Sun*, meanwhile, answered the question of what happened to the Lads, stating: 'They got funnier, that's what. It was funny enough years ago…But the present series is even better.'

Such accolades are gratefully acknowledged by Dick and Ian, who were holidaying in Cornwall when they considered answering what did happen to Bob and Terry? 'Quite independently Ian and I had been thinking about what the characters would have been up to,' says Dick. 'Neither of us could believe it when we discovered we'd been thinking the same.'

'Dick and I were working on something else at the

time,' says Ian, 'but we talked about the possibilities of revisiting Bob and Terry. But it was unusual, especially then, to bring a show back.

'About six years had passed since the last series, and we realized that the Lads would have reached a crucial period in their lives,' Dick explains. 'It was, perhaps, the greatest change they would ever face: settling down and getting married.' Exploring such shifts in circumstance and responsibilities formed the foundations on which the sequel was built.

Another helpful factor was the manner in which the final episode of *The Likely Lads*, 'Goodbye To All That', had finished, as Dick explains. 'We knew Terry had ended up in the army, so his eventual return would be an ideal launching pad. Nothing had happened which would make it difficult to revive the series.'

As to whether the sequel eclipsed the originals from the Sixties, Ian La Frenais appreciates why critics might have adopted that viewpoint: '*The Likely Lads* was very raw, whereas *Whatever Happened to…?* was probably better because our writing had improved. We were more experienced and had learnt something about our craft.'

Dick agrees. 'The writing for *Whatever Happened to…?* is more mature. We'd travelled a little further down the road and had learnt a lot by then. I think the sequel was better than the originals, partly because the Lads were that much older which meant we could dig a little deeper in terms of all their various issues and attitudes.'

Penning the new episodes was a job the writers enjoyed. 'It was enormous fun,' says Dick. 'The first three just poured onto the paper; one episode was way too long, but we just couldn't stop writing.' The writing flowed so well they held back on the news that Terry had got married. 'We originally put it in episode two, but it was moved to the third episode

because there was too much story to tell – it was all such great fun.'

Even though writing the scripts went smoothly, getting the show commissioned wasn't so easy. The original three series were transmitted by the BBC, but when Dick and Ian's agent approached the corporation to discuss financial terms for the sequel, money became a stumbling block. 'The BBC would not pay us what we thought the scripts were worth,' explains Dick. 'The difference between what we wanted and what they were prepared to pay was about £100 an episode. We were sticking out on principle, and if the BBC didn't want it, we'd take it to somebody else.'

That's exactly what they did, and if it hadn't been for a last minute change of heart from the BBC, *Whatever Happened to The Likely Lads?* would have been shown by Thames.

Philip Jones, then Head of Light Entertainment at Thames Television has Rodney Bewes to thank for telling him the show was up for grabs. 'I'd made a series, *Dear Mother...Love Albert*, with Rodney, which was successful. In the course of that, Rodney mentioned Dick and Ian wanted to revive *The Likely Lads*, but the BBC was dragging its feet. Like most people, I'd been a fan of the original series, so naturally I pricked up my ears and went off to investigate; sure enough, the series appeared to be available.'

Philip – who welcomed the idea warmly – moved quickly to sort out contracts and had agreed terms with Bewes and Bolam, as well as finalizing matters with Clement and La Frenais, when one of his colleagues threw a spanner in the works. 'Someone from the contracts department pointed out that we'd be taking a risk if we went ahead. He felt that as Dick Clement was a BBC employee when the original series was commissioned, the BBC would have a legitimate claim on the new package. We could have found ourselves in the unfortunate position of recording several relatively expensive programmes, but not being able to show them because of a possible injunction from the BBC.'

Philip Jones admits to being 'green' in those days, and regrets not chancing his luck. 'The lesson I learnt from this exercise was not to be so intimidated. The BBC probably wouldn't have done anything, but I didn't want to take the risk. For a long time after losing the opportunity, I kept three of the scripts in my bottom drawer, labelled: "Why didn't you go ahead, you fool?"'

By the time the Beeb had agreed to Clement and La Frenais' price, the entire 13 scripts of the first series had been written. Although he feels a tinge of regret every time he watches an episode of *Whatever Happened to…?*, Philip Jones enjoyed the sequel. 'In all the years I worked in TV, it was rare a memorable sitcom arrived on our screens. Jimmy and Rodney made a great couple, and the whole casting was brilliant. The sequel gave the writers the chance to reflect the changing times facing the Lads. In the hands of such smashing writers and performers, it couldn't fail.'

Throughout the three series of *The Likely Lads* Dick Clement had been at the helm, producing all twenty episodes. By the time *Whatever Happened to…?* was finally commissioned, he was busy with other projects, as well as planning a move to the States. The job of producing the new series was given to Jimmy Gilbert, who was taken off another show to work on the sequel. 'I'd been directing a movie in Australia and expected to produce a chat show-cum-comedy series upon my return, which I wasn't looking forward to,' he recalls. 'Instead I was put in charge of *Whatever Happened to The Likely Lads*.'

Rodney Bewes was disappointed Dick wasn't available. 'I was giving up such a lot with Yorkshire Television, and when I heard Dick was too busy to direct, I was concerned. Jimmy Gilbert was an imponderable, but it went very well, as it did with Bernard Thompson, when he took charge of the

THE DIRECTORS OF
WHATEVER HAPPENED TO THE LIKELY LADS?

JAMES GILBERT

After studying at Edinburgh University and spending four years as a pilot in the RAF, James joined RADA and trained as an actor, but he made his name in the field of television directing.

During his extensive career he has directed shows such as *Frost Over England, The Frost Report, Not Only But Also, It's a Square World, The Two Ronnies, Pickwick, Kiss Me Kate* and *Last of the Summer Wine*. He also directed the film *Sunstruck*, starring Harry Secombe, in Australia. Over this period, he received three BAFTA awards.

In 1973 he was promoted to Head of Comedy at the BBC, a position he then held at Thames TV between 1982 and 1991. Later he worked as a freelance producer for the BBC, before retiring in 1997.

BERNARD THOMPSON

Bernard's career in the entertainment world began with acting, a period which saw him touring America and Canada for two years. On his return he began working behind the scenes, initially with Granada Television, and then the BBC as a floor manager. But he's best remembered for his credits as a director, working on shows like *Potter, Rosie, Only Fools and Horses* and *Last of the Summer Wine*.

When he left the BBC he joined Granada, directing, amongst other shows, *Brothers McGregor*. Bernard died in 1998.

second series. I'm not decrying Jimmy or Bernard, it was just that I missed the foursome of me, Jimmy, Dick and Ian.'

When Jimmy Gilbert returned to his office from Australia he had a pleasant surprise. 'I got back to find 13 completed, beautifully bound scripts sitting

on my desk – the entire series waiting for me, an almost unprecedented event in my experience.'

People kept telling him to avoid revivals, but he relished the challenge. 'The idea didn't fill me with any foreboding. The new series was so different, and superbly written. I'd also read the scripts and anybody who didn't like them was out of their skull.'

Jimmy was not altogether surprised at the standard of writing. 'Dick and Ian are skilled writers. Dick is also an excellent director, and a good producer. Our paths first crossed when he was doing a series of *Not Only…But Also* with Peter Cook and Dudley Moore. I produced the third series while Dick had been responsible for the second. It was obvious that he wasn't going to stay with the BBC just directing; he was destined – along with Ian – for greater things.'

Restrictive budgets had meant most location work for *The Likely Lads* had taken place within a stone's throw of Television Centre, but Jimmy Gilbert was always keen on location filming, something he wanted to do with *Whatever Happened to The Likely Lads?*

'Going out filming is expensive, and for some time I felt the BBC didn't think it necessary,' he says. 'Initially filming was all about establishing a scene: going in and out of buildings, cars coming up to doors, that sort of thing. There weren't any great two or three week shoots.'

Jimmy experienced no resistance when he broached the subject with his bosses, so arrangements for filming in the North-East were put in place. Mixing location shooting with studio work added an extra dimension to the show, a fact that was acknowledged by Kenneth Tossell, writing in the *Daily Mirror* in 1974. He maintained that: 'One of the strengths of this series is its authentic North-East flavour. This is a situation comedy that is helped by geographical situation.'

The Concept

The success of *The Likely Lads* was partly due to the light-hearted examination of everyday life, seen through the eyes, actions and attitudes of Terry and Bob. Its study of everything ranging from sex to the laddish ritual of getting thoroughly tanked up at the local boozer every Friday night, was beautifully exploited by Clement and La Frenais. But time moves on and it was clear to the writers that the sequel would have to confront new issues and take on board quite a number of fresh attitudes.

'Whereas *The Likely Lads* had been about girls and booze, *Whatever Happened to…?* concentrated on class issues,' remarks Dick. 'The Lads have become more introspective. While Bob sees himself climbing the social ladder, Terry – the lazy sod that he is – feels this is working-class betrayal.

'There's a great deal of hypocrisy about Terry because Bob is progressing in life and he isn't. Because he's stuck in a time warp, he falls back on the cosy clichés of class betrayal and not seeing the need for improving oneself. But all Bob is trying to do, in a very modest way, is better himself.'

While the curtain fell on *The Likely Lads* with Terry heading off in the back of an army truck for a spell in the Forces, the sequel kicks off with the two Lads reuniting, unexpectedly, on a Newcastle-bound train. Although it is only five years since they last met, their contrasting fortunes couldn't be further apart. While Terry feels an unjust victim of circumstance, almost as if he's been barred from the outside world, Bob has moved into adulthood. Not only is he holding down a job with prospects, but he owns a car, smokes cigars and is marrying Thelma Chambers.

Throughout the 20 episodes of *The Likely Lads*, Bob and Terry's relationship is rock solid. Although at times they resemble sparring partners, arguing over everything from girls to football, their friendship remains unscathed by anything life throws at it. They are just lads, not yet experiencing the trappings of adulthood, such as mortgages, steady relationships and marriage.

But when Terry leaves the North-East in the back of an army truck their lives are irreversibly affected. When Terry meets Bob in 'Strangers on a Train' he is returning home, expecting time to have stood still; he yearns for a warmth and congeniality rooted in the past. But a lot of people have moved on to a different platform in life, including Bob, who's adjusted

to life pretty well without his best mate to hamper him – he's enjoyed his passage into adult life.

Through the course of two series, Terry's return to the North-East creates its fair share of headaches for Bob and Thelma as he adjusts to his life back on civvy street.

Ian La Frenais agrees that Terry cuts a sad figure in *Whatever Happened to…?*, drifting along without a job or a future. 'He's sad because all his talk about the working class and people fighting against the odds is really an alibi. Seeing Bob's advancement as a kind of betrayal is a ridiculous attitude to have; but his identity and roots are all he's really got left, so his attitude is understandable in a way.'

Terry's spell in the army has done little to enhance his social or professional prospects: he is demobbed without a trade or any real skills that are apposite to life outside the military. Life has left him behind and it is going to be an uphill struggle to catch up.

'Terry takes a stance of bitterness in the belief that he deserves a break, or a spell of recuperation,' comments Ian, on this unhappy situation.

'There's one scene where Terry makes a speech about Bob's new house, his new friends and the badminton club. He speaks in a voice that sounds like one of envy, but at the end he says: "And I despise all that!" Terry always manages to stop himself going too far,' says Ian.

Clement and La Frenais' preference for displaying comedy through situation and character was ideally suited to tackling the social elements of *Whatever Happened to The Likely Lads?* Class struggles, snobbery, losing grip on one's roots as well as the past are handled in the series with acute observations and a degree of pathos that makes for enjoyable viewing.

This element of realism was crucial, as far as Ian is concerned. 'We never felt pressured to supply the sheer volume of laughs expected of writers today, so having pathos and complexity in there, something a little deeper, was essential.' It has become one of their trademarks in situation comedy.

Although Bob and Terry are both used as vehicles for exploring such social issues, Terry's dilemma lent itself much more readily. 'When we started writing the series we decided Terry needed to recover the past,' explains Ian, 'and the main component of that was Bob, who's just about to put it all behind him by getting married to Thelma.'

The forlorn figure of Terry was symptomatic of the earnestness of the subject matter. 'It wasn't something to run away from, and we never thought it conflicted with the comedy. In fact, we felt it made everything richer.'

Terry's reluctance to secure a job led the benefits office to threaten withholding his money unless he bucked up his ideas.

The serious moments in the series were written with great aplomb, juxtaposing the more lighthearted scenes brilliantly. In 'Countdown' class differences and the idea of forgetting one's past are tackled. With the wedding day approaching, Bob and Terry argue while trying on their top hats and tails. Terry believes Bob's wish to bring a touch of Belgravia to Station Road is a gesture of discarding his working-class values. As far as Terry is concerned, Bob has become very materialistic: possessions and status are worth more to him than anything else, obscuring his judgement, in Terry's eyes, of the true values in life. Bob vehemently disagrees; to him everything he believes in is about working hard to earn a slice of life's luxuries, rather than scraping along and under-achieving.

Meanwhile, Bob continues with his liaisons with depression, producing a poignant piece of dialogue. Realizing just how fast life is slipping away, he says to Terry, over a bag of chips: 'Suddenly the past seems so much larger, and the future is shrinking. And I haven't got time for the present.'

Such moments of realism and *gravitas* added a quality fans and, in most cases, the Press enjoyed. Leonard Buckley wrote in *The Times* : 'These writers can take such unsubtle stuff and root it in reality. Their script has its serious moments that add conviction to all the rest. In short, their characters and their situations are equally true to life.'

It's rare to find a sitcom that can tackle social issues so cleverly, but its success is down to the writers expressing thoughts and feelings we all share. After all, Ian La Frenais was once quoted as saying he was a sentimentalist, and resented the passing of every week of his life.

Casting

One of the dangers that befall television revivals is being unable to reunite the original cast. For secondary characters, this isn't such a problem but when it comes to the main characters, major changes can cause irreparable damage, so it was essential Bewes and Bolam agreed to return.

Believing James Bolam would be the most likely to hold doubts about resuming the role, Dick and Ian

MEMORABLE SCENES

EPISODE

Cold Feet

(Bob's wedding is approaching, and he tells Terry that he's fancied Thelma since childhood. But he feels socially inferior to her.)

BOB: That's when I lost contact with her, when she went to the grammar school, when you and I were banished to the blackboard jungle. I became her social inferior.

TERRY: In that school we were everyone's social inferior.

BOB: I used to watch her through the railings, skipping, her blouse tucked into her thick navy blue knickers. As Paul Anka put it at the time: 'So near, and yet so far away.'

TERRY: Billy Fury!

spoke to him first. 'We took him out to lunch and asked what he thought about having another look at *The Likely Lads*.' Dick volunteered an overview of what they had in mind. 'We made him laugh so much that by the end of lunch we had him hooked. Again he was seduced by the writing, and it was a very productive meal!'

Rodney Bewes, meanwhile, first heard about the idea for a sequel while travelling back from Cornwall with Dick and Ian. Rodney had been relaxing at his cottage in the Cornish village of Cadgwith, and Dick and Ian had rented a house nearby in which they had begun their musical, *Billy*, as well as grabbing the opportunity to take a few days' break. Deciding whether to play Bob Ferris again was no easy task for Rodney.

'I had a tremendous thing going with Yorkshire Television, so when they told me they were thinking of doing *Whatever Happened to The Likely Lads?*, I realized I faced a huge decision. At that point, I didn't know anything about the journey they had in mind for the marriage – I certainly hadn't envisaged a wife coming into the story-lines. But the whole thing worked out well because the casting of Thelma was brilliant – Brigit Forsyth was incredibly good.'

Choosing the right actress to play Thelma Chambers, who marries Bob in the final episode of series one, 'End Of An Era', was the biggest piece of casting in *Whatever Happened to The Likely Lads?* In many ways, Thelma was deemed the catalyst for the changes occurring in Bob's life, which ultimately affect his relationship with Terry.

Without a doubt, Thelma – who is first mentioned back in the 1966 episode, 'Rocker' – was one of the highlights of *Whatever Happened to The Likely Lads?* Beautifully crafted by Clement and La Frenais, and adroitly played by Brigit Forsyth, the no-nonsense librarian injects order and meaning into Bob's pedestrian lifestyle. Dr. Les Gofton, a lecturer at the University of Newcastle, feels that Thelma is not the sort of female character traditionally seen in shows of the era. 'She was more the emerging, respectable, out-in-public, on-the-way-up kind of woman – much more an equal partner in marriage than we were used to seeing.'

Dick Clement knew the vital importance of finding exactly the right person to play Thelma. 'It was a crucial piece of casting because it was such a big part,' he says, 'Brigit was a wonderful actress, and I'm glad she accepted the part. I know she's miffed

about her character being termed the "dreaded Thelma", and assure her we never set out to turn Thelma into an ogre; it was the Press that gave her that tag. There were moments when Bob would have driven anyone mad!'

Ian La Frenais appreciates just how difficult the role of Thelma must have been to play. 'We all loved Brigit and thought she was ideal for the part. We could have written the character as one-dimensional, but tried our hardest not to. She could easily have been disliked and seen as the obvious, archetypal threat to the boys, but Brigit managed to change that and create a character of her own. Thelma may be bossy, but she's not a snob: she's just a likeable, good person, with an understandable point of view as regards Terry.'

The man credited with bringing Brigit Forsyth into the fold is Jimmy Gilbert, who produced the first series. 'I only saw one person playing the part, and that was Brigit,' he admits. 'I didn't really know her, but had seen her in a production of *The Sinners*, an Irish drama series written by Hugh Leonard and recorded by Granada.

'I thought Brigit was Irish, and as I'd recently worked with Hugh in Ireland, and he seemed to

MEMORABLE SCENES

EPISODE

Storm in a Tea Chest

(Terry helps Bob move his belongings into his new house, but Thelma doesn't want the 'useless remnants of his past', in their new home. Terry persuades him to take a stand, so he phones Thelma from the pub to tell her.)

BOB: *(returning to the pub table)* I didn't need these. (*gives Terry some coins*)

TERRY: Oh aye, short call was it?

BOB: To the point.

TERRY: What did you say?

BOB: I said that I was not prepared to give up my heritage, that it's my home as well as her home and where those things go, I go.

TERRY: Well put. What did she say?

BOB: She gave me one of her ominous silences.

TERRY: So what did you do?

BOB: I gave her one of my ominous silences.

TERRY: Pretty pointless phone call really then, wasn't it?

BOB: It made its point, then the pips went.

know everything about Irish actors and actresses, I rang him up and asked about Brigit. He said: "She's not Irish, she's Scottish." I replied: "I want her to play North Country; what do you think?" Without hesitating, Hugh said: "She's so good, she could do anything." That confirmed what I felt.'

Hugh Leonard has always admired Brigit Forsyth as an actress. 'She's got what a writer likes: precision. She's very sharp and doesn't have to go round saying: "I can't say this!" She makes any difficult lines bend for her.'

Hugh was able to catch her playing Thelma, and was suitably impressed by her. 'She did a super job. You know Thelma is a caring person, but at the same time takes no nonsense; she's the kind of wife you'd be afraid to come home to if you weren't quite upright!'

Brigit's audition was arranged to take place in Jimmy Gilbert's office at Television Centre. 'It must have been daunting for her because so many people were present: Dick and Ian, Rodney and Jimmy Bolam as well as me, but we all liked her. She had this wonderful, serious style of comedy. She never acted funny for one moment; she just had the character in one,' recalls Jimmy.

When Brigit made her entrance, Rodney Bewes knew that she was right for the role. 'I had such a strong feeling I begged Dick to give her the part, and when she began playing Thelma it was obvious she was the right choice.'

Introducing a new character, to play an integral part in a show that had been dominated by two well-defined characters like Bob and Terry, was a major task. 'When Brigit started playing Thelma,' explains Rodney, 'she was very conscious of the fact that Jimmy and I had worked together for so long, and that her character was crucial to the plot; it was a hell of a position to be in, but she was marvellous. Even now people tell me how much they liked Thelma; the public certainly took the character to their hearts.'

The same feeling of warmth was felt by the Press. In April 1975, a journalist in the *Sun* wrote: 'One of the unexpected bonuses, when Bob and Terry returned to television in *Whatever Happened to The*

Likely Lads?...was Thelma.' He added: 'Far from being just a figure in the background, Thelma emerged as a vital comedy ingredient in the series. And this was largely due to the acting of the girl who plays her, Brigit Forsyth.'

Leonard Buckley in *The Times* was also impressed with Brigit's contribution. While reviewing an episode, his favourable comments ran: 'Not for the first time, Brigit Forsyth's Thelma nearly stole the show...We have long since taken Messrs. Bewes and Bolam to our hearts as *The Likely Lads*. And here indeed is a likely lass.'

As far as Jimmy Gilbert is concerned, Brigit portrayed Thelma beautifully. 'She played it just as I would have wished. In some ways, Thelma was grim, almost lacking a sense of humour. But Dick and Ian rounded the character off so well, it meant you were allowed to see her soft, attractive side. Thelma was a very caring person, and although the Press called her the "dreaded Thelma", she wasn't like that at all.'

Several other characters were seen for the first time, including Thelma's parents, played by Bill

Owen and Joan Hickson (later replaced by Noel Dyson). 'I was very keen on casting,' says Jimmy Gilbert. 'I went to the theatre a lot, watched plenty of TV and was always making lists of people who interested me. Unlike ITV, there were no casting directors at the BBC; bookers contacted the artists, but the actual casting was the producer's responsibility. Everyone helped each other, suggesting people for particular parts, if asked. I'd always talk to other producers and directors, which was helpful, too.'

As far as Bill Owen was concerned, Jimmy had worked with him a lot and thought he was 'very funny'. 'I first saw him at the Lyric, Hammersmith, where he was playing a scruffy manservant with Spike Milligan berating him all the time. I cast him as Compo in *Last of the Summer Wine*, and used him as a gangster in a production of *Kiss Me Kate*. I've always thought Bill has great versatility, and that's why I cast him as Mr. Chambers. Joan Hickson was

Thelma was shocked to discover her father entertaining his secretary, Beryl (Anne Hamilton) in 'Affairs and Relations'.

MEMORIES...

'I loved the scripts and couldn't wait to get started, but I realized I was the newcomer in an old-established team. Dick, Ian, Rodney and Jimmy had worked very well together, and were understandably concerned about me taking over from Dick.

'Would we get on? We met for lunch at a small hotel, just off Leicester Square, to try and find out. They arrived, half an hour late, having had a meeting to discuss what they should say. In the event, we all got on very well and lunch broke up at around four o'clock. I think the clincher was when Dick started to tell me about the locations he had used in Willesden that were very similar to a town up North, and I told him I had the budget to do the real thing, and wanted to film all the locations in and around Newcastle.

'They were very pleased by this and when we all agreed to meet in my office, to cast Thelma, I knew I was accepted. It wouldn't be the same, but I would do; and when, later, I brought Brigit Forsyth along to the meeting, they thought I might even do quite well.'

JIMMY GILBERT

wonderful, I was an enormous admirer of her work, but eventually she wasn't well enough to continue, so Noel Dyson came in.'

Two semi-regulars were Jack and Gloria, who ran the Black Horse pub, one of Bob and Terry's regular watering holes. Played by Norman Mitchell and Lorna Wilde, they'd both worked for Jimmy before. 'Norman is a very good actor who never stops work,' says Jimmy. 'I'd worked with him – in fact, we all had, he's a well-known actor. I cast Lorna in *Sunstruck,* the film I made in Australia with Harry Secombe, about a timid school teacher who goes off to teach in Australia after he's spurned by a beautiful PE instructor in Wales. Lorna played the instructor and was very good.

'Anita Carey, who appeared as Thelma's sister, was very good, too. I'd seen her in plenty of shows, but she auditioned with several other actresses. I went on to use her again in *I Didn't Know You Cared.*'

Bob Ferris' progression up the middle management ladder demanded a secretary. Elizabeth Lax played Wendy in one of her first TV appearances. 'I felt Elizabeth had a fresh, original quality, probably because she hadn't done much TV,' explains Jimmy.

Other semi-regulars were Donald Gee – who'd already appeared in *The Likely Lads* – and Christopher Biggins. They played a vicar and Podge, a friend of Bob and Terry, respectively. 'I'd seen Donald in other shows and just thought he had a very humorous, lively face. Christopher Biggins also

Tony entertains Thelma's sister, Susan (Anita Carey), while Bob's dutiful secretary was played by Elizabeth Lax (right).

had a humorous face and personality, so he was brought in, too.'

It was important having some consistent faces dropping into the series every now and then, as the late Bernard Thompson, Gilbert's production assistant on the first series and producer of the second in his own right, explained. 'If you go to your local, it's jolly nice seeing a familiar face behind the bar.' Thompson believed that characters who were seen quite frequently, as semi-regulars, provided a degree of solidity to the series. 'I tried to feature these people as often as I could.'

The Theme Tune

A catchy theme tune always helps a TV programme, and the song used for *Whatever Happened to The Likely Lads?* appealed to fans – so much so that it was released as a single, reaching number 35 in the charts in April 1973.

Mike Hugg, who played drums for Manfred Mann, became friends with Ian La Frenais, who

MEMORABLE SCENES

EPISODE

Countdown

(It's nearly the day of the wedding. At the suit fitting, Terry gets annoyed when Bob says top hat and tails will bring a bit of Belgravia to Station Road, where he's getting married.)

TERRY: Station Road doesn't need a bit of Belgravia. Station Road, mate, is perfectly happy with honest-to-goodness, no-nonsense, salt of the earth. All this is just another concession to your middle-class mother-in-law.

BOB: No it isn't, it was my suggestion.

TERRY: Never in the world, it was hers. And it wasn't a suggestion, either, it was a royal command. They're all the same, that lot – middle classes, especially those who have just been promoted from the lower divisions.

BOB: You know what you are, don't you? Shall I tell you what you are? You're an inverted snob, that's what you are. We're just hiring a suit of clothes, clothes that are suitable for an occasion. We'll only have them on for five hours. You see that as a betrayal of your entire class.

decided to ask him to write the music that would accompany the opening and closing credits. While Ian wrote the lyrics one afternoon, Mike – who also wrote the music for Clement and La Frenais' 1974 sitcom, *Thick as Thieves* – enjoyed himself when he was putting them to music. 'It was a straightforward job: Ian gave me the lyrics and I went in the studio with the musicians. We made it as a record, which was always an intention, and just used the chorus for the programme. I was very pleased with the result, and it's been a good little earner over the years, thanks to the repeats on television.'

Mike, who has written the music for countless commercials, has fond memories of all the times he spent socializing with Ian, Dick, Rodney and other friends. 'We'd often eat and drink at lunchtimes, finishing up with quite a big bill. To decide who should pay we'd place a serviette, with a penny in the middle, over the top of a bowl; a cigarette was then passed around and everyone took turns to burn a hole on the edge of the serviette. Whoever burnt the hole that caused the penny to drop, paid the bill. Luckily, I never forked out a penny!'

The Credits

Tasked with the job of creating the opening and closing credits was graphic designer Mic Rolph, who joined the BBC straight from art school in 1966. Each episode finished with scenes of boys playing amongst ruins and high-rise flats, denoting the passing of time, one of the themes explored in the series.

Dr. Les Gofton is one of the first to appreciate the significance of such scenes. 'There is a kind of mourning for neighbourhoods that are being pulled down. In terms of symbolism, it means more if you're actually from the North-East, like me, because many of the streets in the title sequences don't exist anymore. The 1960s and 1970s was the time neighbourhoods were being demolished because the local environment was being remade.'

The opening sequence, meanwhile, featured photos of the Lads, mixed with snatches of film. One of the photographs showed Bob and Terry holding a crying baby. The baby girl was none other than Sian, Dick and Jenny Clement's daughter, who now runs her own publicity company in New

Zealand. 'It was funny because Sian was crying, and Jimmy and Rodney were trying desperately to stop her but didn't have a clue how to deal with it, which shows in Jimmy's face!' says Jenny.

Sian was chuffed to have her photo, which had been taken in her bedroom at home, appear in the show; but it wasn't the first time she'd appeared: for *The Likely Lads* episode, 'Baby, It's Cold Outside', a baby was required and Sian was chosen. Publicity shots were taken, one of which was splashed across the front cover of *Radio Times*.

Costumes

It's easy underestimating the importance of the costume department in a show like *The Likely Lads* or *Whatever Happened to…?* Despite the fact that it wasn't a period production, the department's role is far from inessential. A great deal of attention to detail and research is required if the show is to look accurate and credible.

Roger Reece, one of the costume designers who worked on the sequel, was keen to make sure the style of clothing reflected the trends seen in the North East. 'You had to bear in mind where the series was set, so as far as dressing was concerned, especially for Jimmy, it was important to know what Northern working-class lads were wearing.' Roger travelled to the region to further his research. 'I wanted to get a flavour for where the sitcom was set,' he says. 'I'd spend time just looking at people, seeing what they wore and how they wore their clothes – little things like that are important.'

Another vital role is continuity. When a break in filming occurs, the eagle-eyed continuity assistants must ensure the scene restarts as it finished: a different colour handbag or a missing scarf will be instantly noticeable to the viewers.

Sally Adams, production assistant on the first series, was in charge of continuity whilst on location. She admits it could be a difficult job at times. 'Because we filmed the whole series in one go, we'd find ourselves working on episodes one, three and six, one day, and two, four and five the next – it could get confusing. It was quite difficult keeping aware of everything, but I'd make sure I wrote things down or, perhaps, used my Instamatic camera. Luckily, the Lads didn't have huge wardrobes and the majority of shots were in the studio, which made my job easier.'

On one occasion, Sally remembers she donated her own jumper to the wardrobe! 'We were filming outside what was supposed to be Audrey's house. Sheila Fearn didn't like the jumper she was going to wear, and said to me: "I like the one you've got on, can I use it?"

'I agreed and we did a swap. But that meant it had to go into wardrobe until the actual episode was recorded because she'd be seen inside the house and needed the same jumper. As a result, I lost it for about six weeks!'

Sally worked closely with the costume supervisor to make sure there were no mistakes. 'Between us we'd record what was required if there was a break in filming. By the time you get back to the studio, the job is made a little easier because by then the edited film is available to look at.'

Roger Reece – who worked on shows such as

MEMORABLE SCENES

EPISODE

The Old Magic

(Out for his last bachelor meal, Bob discusses their long friendship with Terry – who's just been told that Frank Clarke will be the best man.)

BOB: It's amazing how character shows at such an early age. Even at five you were trouble, a hazard to other children. 'Don't talk to Terry Collier', that was like our school motto.

TERRY: I was your first friend. I was the first person who stole your tricycle pump, the first person who split your head open with a brick. Frank Clarke can't claim things like that in his wedding speech. He can't recall colourful anecdotes from the past.

BOB: I don't think many colourful anecdotes from our past are fit to go into a wedding speech.

Robinson Crusoe and *David Copperfield* – believes that being a costume designer in TV is all about collaboration. 'The producer has his views, the actors theirs, and the designer has some, too. It's a case of discussing all the possibilities and coming up with something that, hopefully, everyone is happy with.'

For *Whatever Happened to The Likely Lads?* it was important the costume designs were played down, as Roger makes plain.

'The last thing you want is for someone to remember the programme because of the costumes. Rodney was the more suave of the characters, so for him wearing a suit and tie was the right thing to do, partly because Thelma would have expected him to dress that way. With Terry, it was a case of dressing in a style that was slightly more with it, but not quite making it. It was a fun show to work on.'

Set Design

Five designers were employed during the life of *Whatever Happened To The Likely Lads?* Tim Gleeson and Allan Anson split the work for the first series, and enjoyed being involved. 'It was one of the best sitcoms,' says Allan, who'd worked on numerous shows, including the original series of *The Liver Birds*. 'A lot were pretty indifferent stuff, but Clement and La Frenais' show was real quality.'

Allan noticed the scripts contained a sometimes hard-to-find ingredient: humour! '"Shitcoms" was the term we used in the design department because lots of shows were so diabolically awful. But working on *Whatever Happened to…?* made me feel I was doing something worthwhile.'

Although the sitcom presented few difficulties – Tim and Allan class it as 'bread and butter stuff' – Tim views getting everything ready for recording as a 'triumph of organization'. Assembling the set in the studio overnight following another television production was a major feat. 'Getting everything stood up, dressed, doors working, furniture fitted and curtains hung ready for rehearsal at half past ten was very hard work.'

To make matters more complicated, half the studio was taken up with audience seating, which meant the sets were cramped. This caused Allan a headache when Jimmy Gilbert requested as many camera traps as possible. 'If you have a set, which would normally be four walls, you put the cameras where the fourth wall would go. But Jimmy wanted cameras right up inside the set, which is impossible because rugs and pieces of furniture get in the way. The only option was to take the camera round the outside and take a

wall away, or a section of it. I remember designing a set where there were so many walls to be removed Jimmy thought I was sending him up!'

Budgets were tight, so designers had to be frugal. 'You didn't waste money. Some people think designers are arty-farty types who are on ego trips, but that

MEMORABLE SCENES

EPISODE

Birthday Boy

(Terry's feeling depressed and unwanted, so Bob points out the facts.)

BOB: Well you're here aren't you? Living proof.

TERRY: Proof! Proof of what? That my dad had a couple of jars too many one night on a 48-hour pass. I was probably conceived in an Anderson shelter. He probably only did it to keep my mother's mind off a doodlebug.

isn't the case at all. You did what you had to; you didn't use unnecessary stuff because there was no space in the studio,' says Allan, who remembers designing plenty of pubs as well as the church used in the popular episode, 'No Hiding Place'. 'It would have been built by one of the workshops, or possibly a contractor, and was shot through a wide-angle lens to make it look bigger.'

Some sets were inherited, but one of the most important had to be built: Bob and Thelma's new home. 'I was struck by the architecture of the housing estate chosen for the filming,' says Tim. 'It was such that the picture windows in the lounge were in line with all the other picture windows in the streets parallel to the one in which we filmed. You could stand in one house and, by looking through the windows, wave to someone several streets away.

'When we designed the house in the studio, we had a photo enlarged, or a painting, to show the houses across the street. But there's never enough room to light the backing the way you'd like, even though it was used weekly,' says Tim, who remembers Dick and Ian more than the characters in the show. 'They looked like a mismatched couple: Dick was tall, elegant, and very urbane, vaguely an Oxbridge type. Ian was short, dark and slightly dour. I got the impression the series was a reflection of the writers' own relationship.'

As with the costumes, it was absolutely necessary for the designers to record how their sets were dressed. Photographs were taken so that every prop, even something innocuous like a child's spade, reappeared in the studio in the same position. 'Someone might see something as rubbish and throw it away,' says Tim. 'The number of times you'd lose an essential prop because someone had tidied up, and not realized the importance of a particular object. It's important you have an eye for detail – and a trusty camera, because you'll probably need several copies of reference photos.'

Another task designers have to tackle when making a set more realistic is 'dirtying down'. 'If you're doing a scene in a pub, everyday wear and tear will mean there'll be a certain amount of grime around the place. When it came to building the set at Television Centre, you'd have the extraordinary situation where something newly painted had to be dirtied down by the scenic painters to make an accurate copy of what existed on location,' says Tim. 'The painters were so good at their job, you wouldn't want to eat off a table that had been dirtied down; it was that convincing.'

The house used for the location filming was loaned by a family called the Whalans, who enjoyed the experience, though Tim Gleeson readily admits giving up your home for filming usually causes plenty of disruption.

'It's the production manager's job to keep everyone happy, else we might not be allowed back again. But I've left standing instructions with my wife never to allow anyone to film in our house, because money will never recompense you enough for the aggravation involved.'

One of the main things Tim remembers about working on the show was how pleasant it was filming in and around Newcastle.

'The people were great, very relaxed about everything. When you are filming around London the public become so cheesed off and world-weary because they've seen it all before. They only look at the disruptive effect we have on their lives, whereas the Newcastle people seemed genuinely interested. It was a pleasure working there.'

Sounding Right

In charge of sound for most of the first series was Trevor Webster, who always felt the success of his department was unfairly judged on how much people laughed! 'There was a feeling at the time that a studio audience helped people at home enjoy the show so the pressure was on to create a comedy where the audience laughed, and to some degree the success of the sound operation was judged by how much laughter was generated.'

Trevor remembers discussing the problem with Jimmy Gilbert. 'I said: "The trouble with this show is that it's a million smiles. It's very funny but people sit there happily smiling at everything; it's not filled with great belly laughs," Jimmy agreed and thought "million smiles" was a nice quote.'

One thing that helped Trevor, who now works freelance, to do his job was the quality of the scripts. 'I used to read them at home as preparation, and found them so funny. But the actual job was no more difficult than it is today. The equipment may have been different, but the operation and requirements were the same. You had to paint a picture in sound that complemented the picture in vision. The eye is very dominant and we think that pictures are tremendously important. They are, of course, but in terms of getting your message across, 90 odd per cent of information is in the sound; at a pinch you can carry on in sound only, whereas pictures don't make sense on their own.'

The most challenging part of the job, as far as Trevor is concerned, was working on the show when post-production was in its infancy. The early 1970s was a time when production techniques were in transition. 'It was a changeover period from having to do everything live, to finding oneself with a tremendous freedom in editing. Vision editing had developed quite well, but sound editing was still breaking through. We did as much as possible live, with planned breaks for the actors to change costumes, or have a rest. After reminding the audience of where we'd got to, recording would restart.

'In earlier days, things were always done live, or were recorded as if they were live, because editing was so expensive. I've heard directors tell actors: "If you get into trouble, you get yourselves out because I'm not stopping, whatever happens."'

Trevor enjoyed his days on *Whatever Happened to…?* and loves watching repeats. 'I think they stand up very well as far as the production side is concerned. Obviously you have to bear in mind fashions change, and things that were the norm back then are no longer done the same way.

'The audience has become more educated, too: there was a time when you had to be careful how you handled flashbacks. You really had to point them up with music and wavy lines across the screen. Nowadays you can jump backwards and forwards and people work it out. I'll always remember the period I spent working on the show as happy.'

MEMORABLE SCENES

EPISODE

The Ant and The Grasshopper

(Terry thinks Bob's working too hard, and that all Thelma's got to look forward to is when his life assurance pays out.)

BOB: And what kind of future…what are you going to leave your wife? A few old IOUs, torn betting slips and stubs from the Odeon.

TERRY: Well, I'll tell you one thing, mate, I shall outlive you because I have dropped out of the rat race.

BOB: You what? You what? You were never in it, you. You've been on the dole since you came out of the army. No attempt to look for a job.

TERRY: Well I'm happy enough, there's nothing wrong with my existence. I bet you'd rather be going to the pictures this afternoon than going 30 miles up the A1 to some barren, freezing moor to stick up your theodolite?

Out and About

Unlike its black and white precursor, where tight budgets meant location work was carried out within a short distance of Television Centre, except for the occasional episode like 'Anchors Aweigh', which took the crew and cast off to the far corners of Norfolk, *Whatever Happened to …?* travelled further afield. Relaunching a successful sitcom from the Sixties attracted lots of hype, and the budget was a little more generous. Bernard Thompson believed the locations played a significant role in the sequel's success. In an interview shortly before his death, he said: 'It's a strange thing, but for most actors it's best if you can take them to the real locations in which the production is based. I'm not suggesting we couldn't find buildings in London that were similar to the ones used in Newcastle, but the actual fact we were there, hearing the accent and chatting with the people, was incredibly helpful.'

As far as Bernard was concerned, finding locations was one of the most difficult jobs when planning a television show, but also one of the most pleasurable. 'It's time-consuming, but once you find a location you've been looking for, it provides a solid background on which to build the rest of the series.'

Unless a specialist company is employed to identify suitable locations, there's no alternative but for the producer and/or production assistant to pick up a copy of the local Ordnance Survey map and tour the countryside, which is what Bernard did. 'I always took my production manager, Evan King, along,' he said. 'We'd just drive around and, when we spotted somewhere we liked, I'd send Evan in to agree everything with the owners, while I double-checked the script to make sure it was exactly what I wanted. The owners would be paid and asked to sign a document of consent, because you wouldn't want them changing their minds halfway through recording.'

Throughout the life of the sequel, Bernard and the rest of the production team found the people of the North-East always willing to help. Mrs Dobson, who managed the Imperial Hotel in Newcastle, is one such example, as Evan King explains. 'We all stayed at the hotel, and when it came to arranging payment, Mrs Dobson told me that as long as Jimmy and Rodney were there, we could all come in for nothing. I had to tell her that the BBC didn't work like that; we all had to pay, but it shows just how welcome we were made to feel.'

MEMORABLE SCENES

EPISODE

Boys' Night In

(Bob – who, much to Terry's amazement, has decided against a stag night – is having trouble sleeping, as Terry finds out when he stays with him; it's 4 a.m.)

TERRY: What are you doing now?

BOB: *(walking over to his writing desk)* Keep your voice down, you don't want to disturb my mother.

TERRY: Charming. *(speaking quietly)* What are you doing?

BOB: I'm rewriting my wedding speech.

TERRY: Well, can't you do that downstairs?

BOB: I don't want to disturb the cat.

TERRY: What? You what?

BOB: Well, he's been out all night.

TERRY: Lucky bloody cat!

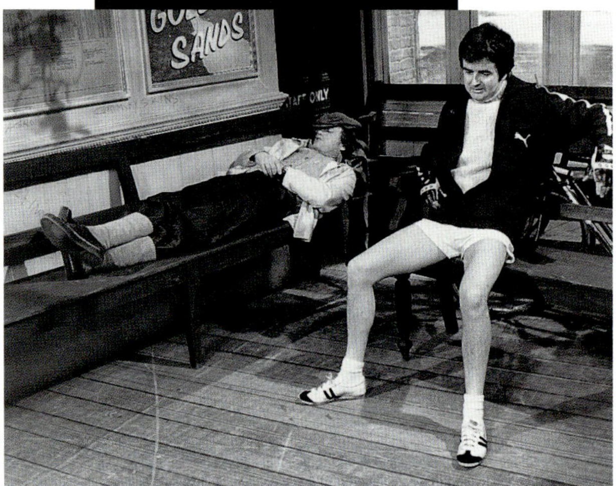

Evan always tried returning such kindness. One particular moment of amiability served him well later when he experienced unforeseen difficulties. 'We were filming outside Newcastle one horrible, freezing night, and it was discovered that an essential handbag had been forgotten, so Peter Grant, my wonderful assistant, and the costume lady dashed back to Newcastle to get it.

'While we were waiting, this guy, wearing a camouflage jacket, and his little boy, came up to me and asked whether I minded them watching. Of course I didn't mind, and got chatting to them, explaining what was going on. Next morning, the man called me. He said he'd enjoyed the previous evening, and that he was the Chief Inspector of Police, in charge of film liaison in the area. He also left his phone number, just in case I needed his help at any point.'

It wasn't too long before Evan was reaching for the Chief Inspector's phone number. 'When we recorded the Christmas episode, we couldn't get a fire engine. The cleaning lady had to be rescued from the bedroom window by a fireman, but we failed to find an engine.' After exhausting every possible avenue, he turned to the Chief Inspector. 'I told him my problem, and he replied: "As it happens, I'm going to a dinner tonight with the fire people – leave it to me." And he fixed it for me, so the answer is to be nice to anyone who approaches you – who knows when you might need their help?'

On another occasion Evan and Bernard were bombarded with offers of help. While touring the region looking for somewhere to film sequences for the episode, 'The Great Race', they stopped off at a pub for a bite to eat. Casually they mentioned to people what they were looking for, unaware of the deluge of suggestions that would come their way. 'I had to find a country road that went downhill; at the bottom there had to be a border where some people could be picnicking, before the road veered right,' Bernard explained. 'It's not always easy finding all these things together. When we asked if anyone knew of a location like this, everyone leapt to their feet and suggested all sorts of places – someone even insisted on taking us to a place they had in mind. But it didn't turn out to be right; it's amazing how we all see things differently.'

Evan King describes the negotiating involved in location work as 'fun'. 'Usually as soon as you mentioned *The Likely Lads*, you were away, but occasionally people were difficult.'

One of his beliefs regarding securing locations, is if there's the slightest doubt over any part of the negotiation, pull out. However, that wasn't possible for one location, as he explains. 'Jimmy Gilbert told me we needed a particular location for a fishing scene, but we were really dropped in it by the owner, who insisted the only time we could film there was in the afternoon. I knew the sun was going to be too low by then, but the owner was adamant. It was an added complication we could have done without.'

Every producer has their own method for finding locations, and Jimmy Gilbert preferred doing it for himself. 'Some people would get their PA out finding locations, but I'd usually go off for a week on my own, armed with the scripts. By the end of that time, I'd return with a rough idea of where all the shots were going to be. That way, when it came to organizing the shooting script, I had particular places in mind – I didn't want to just go somewhere and try and fit the script around it.

'Before we went off on location, I'd usually go back with my PA and show him the places; it was then his responsibility to arrange all the permissions.'

One of the primary locations required for *Whatever Happened to…?* was Bob and Thelma's new house. After scouring the region for something suitable, a property was discovered in what Jimmy Gilbert describes as a 'new estate for newly-married

young executives, a few miles north of Newcastle'. In the series, the estate is known as Elm Lodge Housing Estate, named after a house of Dick Clement's, as his first wife, Jenny, explains. 'We had owned a house in Petersham, called Elm Lodge, and when Dick was looking for a name, he decided to use it.' Terry always refers to the estate with a slight sneer, because it represents the orderly path of social progression along which Bob is travelling. 'I think Dick also used it to send us up a bit,' suggests Jenny. 'Elm Lodge was a mansion, ridiculously big but lovely. It was a very grand house.'

In reality, Elm Lodge Housing Estate was Highfields, a newly-built estate in Killingworth, Newcastle-upon-Tyne. Bob and Thelma's house was No.8, Agincourt, one of the streets on the estate. Graham Whalan owned the property when the BBC recorded the second series and the Christmas Special, and with the story-lines focusing heavily on Bob's new lifestyle, the house became an integral part of the series. Graham was 'thrilled' when the BBC asked to use his house. 'We watched the first series avidly, and hoped that they would make a further series, and when they did we had a great time.'

The Whalans were aware the BBC had used the house when they bought it. 'The original owner told us that the BBC suddenly turned up on the doorstep one day. As the estate had just been built it was exactly what they were looking for.' The state of the garden was another important factor in the house being chosen. 'It hadn't been touched, unlike others around, so the house looked newer than the rest,' says Graham, who remembers clearly the arrival of the BBC entourage on the first day of filming.

'When all their catering vans and equipment arrived, we just couldn't believe how much they brought with them. We were sorry we couldn't hang around a little bit more, but my wife and I were both working, so we left them to it. On the days we could stay we were banned to the back of the house and had to keep quiet whilst they were doing their shots, so we couldn't really see very much of what was going on.'

While the Whalans occupied themselves in the back of the house, their lounge was pressed into service as a busy waiting-cum-changing room. 'Everyone would have refreshments and eat their meals there. We were allowed food from the catering wagon, so it saved us having to cook,' Graham

Bob and Thelma's new house on the Elm Lodge Housing Estate was actually filmed on a newly built estate in Killingworth, Newcastle-upon-Tyne.

recalls. 'But it was never a hassle and we were excited to be involved.

'All the actors were very nice, particularly Brigit Forsyth, who was lovely. My wife, Helen, was pregnant at the time, so they were all very interested in her progress.'

In particular, Graham remembers Tony Haygarth, who played Les, the milkman. 'He knew some stunning card tricks, and kept everyone entertained between takes. The crew was very friendly, too, and appreciative of the opportunity to use the house. They were always worried about causing us too much disruption, particularly for one episode when they devastated the garden with a forklift truck.'

The Whalans received £150 for having their garden dug up. 'It was enough for a colour TV,' says Graham, 'which must have been a good buy because it only packed up a couple of years ago.'

Reports over the years have suggested that loaning property to a television company for location purposes can be a lucrative pursuit, and Graham was pleased with the disturbance fees received from the BBC. 'We got about £20 a day, which was quite a lot in 1973.'

Bernard Thompson appreciated the Whalans' help. 'They let Jimmy and Rodney be made up in one room, while another was being used for costumes. They were amazingly hospitable, especially as filming occasionally went on right into the early hours of the morning!'

Although it was the Whalans who experienced most disruption to their lives, filming in a residential area inevitably affects others, but everything ran smoothly in Agincourt, as Graham explains. 'None of the neighbours had any problems with it: I think they were just excited that the street was being involved in a successful TV programme. A couple of them had the exterior of their houses used in a scene, which they were pleased about.'

Local youngsters, who frequently congregated around the house in Agincourt, also felt the excitement. 'Some of them were a bit of a menace,' says Graham. 'They wanted to cheer and make a noise, and there were difficulties, at times, getting them under control. Occasionally they'd throw little stones at the window, while the film crew was using the house, just to grab their attention. But it was nothing unpleasant, just the usual things kids get up to.'

Graeme Ford, who was nine at the time, moved to the estate shortly after the second series was completed, but he regularly visited a friend living at Bannockburn, situated at the bottom of Agincourt. Although he's keen to point out he wasn't one of the kids who caused a nuisance, he was eager to be involved in the filming, if possible. 'As a young lad growing up in the Seventies, watching this series was a must,' says Graham, who's now 34. 'Not only did it give us the chance to see many local landmarks, but the characters were just like my Dad's friends. Obviously the constant references by both Terry and Bob to Newcastle United were important, too.'

Together with his mate, Graeme succeeded in sneaking in to the final moments of filming one day. 'I remember they were shooting a scene outside the house, and we kept trying to get in the picture, but were moved on by the director.' When the light began to fade, Graeme and his pal grabbed their opportunity. 'As the cameras began rolling we rode down the street, one of us giving the other a "backer" on a red Chopper bicycle – we were so pleased with ourselves!'

The Whalan's house was used chiefly for exterior shots, everything else being recorded in the studio. But they did film one interior shot at No.8, Agincourt. 'They used our bedroom for one shot,' says Graham. 'It was a scene where Bob arrived home late and was lifted up to the window in the forklift truck, while Thelma was in bed.

'They used our bed, but fixed on their own headboard, and propped up a board behind, which was covered in a wallpaper they could match when they got back to the studio.'

Although only one scene was actually shot inside, the studio set was closely based on the interior of the house. 'It was pretty accurate,' Graham says. 'The only real difference was that the entrance door and serving hatch were in slightly different places, but that was all.'

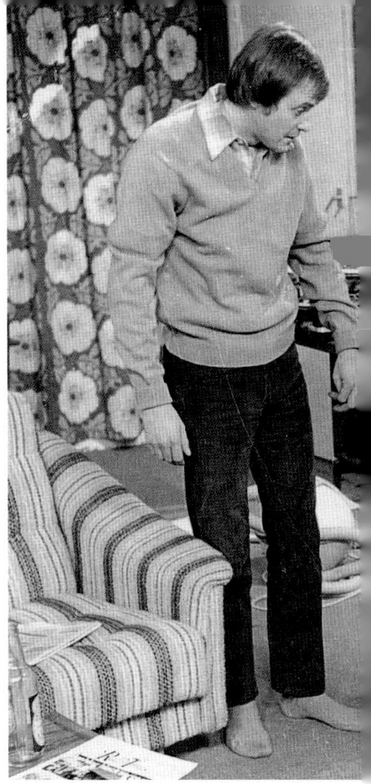

Just one scene was shot inside the Whalan's home, but the studio was based on the house's interior.

The house was going to be used for the movie, but EMI decided against it for cost reasons. It was utilized for the Christmas Special, at the end of the second series, even though Graham and Helen Whalan were away at the time. By then, they had got to know the production crew so well that they trusted them completely. So they were happy to give them the keys and let them get on with it. 'We were over with my family in Barrow,' recalls Graham. 'The BBC had left arrangements quite late and we got telegrams and phone calls, because they were anxious to start filming at the start of the New Year, but we weren't back until January 3. They wanted to begin earlier than that, so Evan King and his assistant came over to Barrow to pick up the keys.'

Bernard Thompson remembered the filming well, because the street was deserted. 'It was New Year's Day and we started filming at eight in the morning. Everyone in the neighbourhood must have been celebrating New Year's Eve very heartily because there wasn't a sound, not even a bird singing. We filmed for about three hours before we saw or heard any sign of life.' The street was so quiet Bernard had to dub in sound effects when he got back to Television Centre. 'It sounded like we were filming in a place that was unpopulated – it was very strange.'

Overall, Graham and Helen Whalan enjoyed their involvement with the series. 'It was interesting watching the street and remembering some of the sequences they filmed while we were there,' says Graham. 'My wife and some of the neighbours were pulled in to be extras in one episode. They didn't get paid for it, but it was a nice thing to be involved in.'

The entire production team was grateful to the people of the North-East who helped make the show such a success.

'The show was appreciated very much by the Geordies,' said Bernard. 'Whenever we were filming in and around Newcastle people were always very enthusiastic and helpful – they were so friendly and we were always made welcome.'

On Air

Producer Jimmy Gilbert had been a fan of *The Likely Lads,* and thought it was his birthday when he read the scripts for the sequel. Such was the quality, no reworking was necessary, except for the closing scene of 'End of an Era', the last episode in series one. He says: 'When Bob and Thelma are at the airport leaving for their honeymoon, the original version saw Terry's German wife arrive. That was Dick and Ian's

'It's difficult picking a favourite episode, but "Conduct Unbecoming" and "The Go-Between" are very special. But I'm particularly fond of "No Hiding Place", which was a one-off potboiler about not wanting to know the result of a football match. It struck a chord with so many people, who'd all been there. It was completely inconsequential but just happened to be liked by everyone.'

DICK CLEMENT

'It has to be "The Great Race" where Bob challenges Terry to a bike race. But it would only be by a whisper because I don't think there was a bad episode in the whole of the series. They were of such a high standard, it wasn't surprising the show worked so well.'

The late BERNARD THOMPSON

'It's hard to choose. I like "Strangers On A Train" very much, as well as the dinner party scenes in "Guess Who's Coming To Dinner?". But "No Hiding Place", where Bob and Terry are trying to avoid hearing the score of a football match, is another wonderful episode. It's used as Polyfilla: every time there's a cup final, or a big international, and there's half an hour to spare, they transmit this one.'

JIMMY GILBERT

"teaser", the springboard for another series with Terry having to cope with his wife back again. But I thought it best to finish the final episode with just Bob and Thelma's departure, and Terry's wry smile – a very touching ending.'

Producing a sequel obviously means inheriting an established set-up, leaving little room for one's own ideas. Although he didn't want to make drastic changes to the sitcom's format, Jimmy Gilbert felt he was able to stamp a little of his own style on the show, without losing any of the original qualities.

Getting out on location was one example. He also set out to heighten the realism. 'That was something I was particularly interested in achieving,' he says. 'At that time, music was being used in many sitcoms which, I felt, took away a lot of the realism. Some shows used music at the end of scenes, which had become something of a trend in situation comedies. I wanted straight cuts. Because we shot it more like a drama, we didn't want something reminding the audience that the scene was ending and was supposed to be funny.'

Jimmy also favoured the use of a studio audience, largely because he felt it was a real help to the performers. 'It's difficult for actors to react in comedy without an audience. There was a lot of reaction comedy in the show, particularly scenes between Rodney and James. You'd start a scene with somebody, then you'd take their reaction and play it off the other character, and I felt the actors needed the audience to help them.'

Anyone watching the first instalment knew instantly the show was going to be a hit. Over 13 million people tuned in to 'Strangers on a Train', a response that pleased Jimmy Gilbert, who won the BAFTA's 1973 award for best producer. 'We got a terrific reaction from the viewers.'

Respectable audiences were maintained throughout the whole 13-episode run, resulting in a new series being commissioned, with a new producer, Bernard Thompson, in charge. Between the two series, Jimmy Gilbert had a job promotion, to Head of Comedy at the BBC, and had to relinquish responsibilities for *Whatever Happened to The Likely Lads?* 'I was very disappointed when I had to pass it onto someone else. It was one of the best shows I'd ever worked on.'

Bernard Thompson was initially assigned to produce alternate episodes, sharing the series with someone else. 'I went on holiday delighted at the prospect,' he said. He returned to a letter from Duncan Wood, the departing Head of Comedy, explaining changes that meant Bernard would produce the entire series, accentuating his joy.

Even though he marvelled at the earlier shows, Bernard felt the second series was even better. 'I couldn't change much – not that there was much need,' he said. 'But the show became more and more like a comedy drama, with situations closer to a natural performance than ever before.' He also tried to ensure that all the new characters coming in were genuine Geordies, if possible, adding even more authenticity.

The first thing that impressed Bernard about the show was the quality of the scripts. 'They were beautifully written and had such strong situations and characters; we hardly ever changed anything. And when the episodes came to life at rehearsals, I realized they were even better than what I'd imagined from reading the script.'

He was pleased with how the sitcom evolved. 'It developed much more than most sitcoms. If you take some of the classics, like *Steptoe and Son*, there is virtually no change in the scenario throughout the whole series. Because of its style of comedy, once they stepped out into the real world it, somehow, didn't seem quite as funny.

'With *Whatever Happened to....?*, you had a developing story, and weren't confined to one location. It's not absolutely essential to have a story; comedy can be done anecdotally, providing you have the right characters and dialogue. But in *Whatever Happened to...?* we had tremendous variety.'

The first episode Bernard was in charge of was 'Absent Friends', which received a warm welcome from the public. The BBC's Audience Research Department carried out a survey, which revealed people felt 'the relationship between the "lads" was skilfully developed...and the episode was written with the sure, light touch that characterized the series'. The style of humour that had become one of the trademarks of the series was acknowledged. The author of the report relayed the views of the sample audience, saying: 'There were no "belly laughs" but the humour was pleasant, down-to-earth and consistent, and it was "nice to have them back".' Although some viewers felt there was a 'certain predictability' about the show, approximately 12 million viewers watched the Lads every week, thus maintaining the show's audience share.

Quite often, Bernard would be driving home from work at the time *Whatever Happened to...?* was being screened, and he saw for himself the impact it was having on the public.

'I'd be driving through streets that were virtually empty, and the realization that millions of people were sitting in front of their television watching the show was a wonderful feeling. It was a very happy period for me.'

One of the things Bernard noticed was how quickly the actors slipped into the shoes of their small-screen alter egos.

'It didn't take them long at all,' he commented. 'It was quite remarkable; as soon as they started playing the roles, they wore their characters like a glove.'

None more so than Bolam and Bewes. 'I can't think of two other actors I've been associated with who worked better together. It was like a Morecambe and Wise situation with each one knowing how the other would behave.

'Rehearsals were sheer delight. Jimmy, Rodney and Brigit are all inventive actors, and it was great working with them. Dick and Ian came along to the read-through, then we'd rehearse for four or five days before the technical run-through. Dick and Ian were always pleased with the job we did. As far as they were concerned, the level of performance balanced the standard of writing.'

T12/1,478/1

Bernard Thompson 7021 TC

(Week 1)

WHATEVER HAPPENED TO THE LIKELY LADS?

by Dick Clement and Ian la Frenais

Producer: Bernard Thompson

Tuesday, 1st January 1974. 8.30-9.00 pm. BBC-1

1. Size of audience (based on results of the Survey of Listening and Viewing).

It is estimated that the audience for this broadcast was 23.5% of the United Kingdom population. Programmes on BBC-2 and ITV at the time were seen by 1.2% and 31.4%.

2. Reaction of audience (based on 332 questionnaires completed by 21% of the Viewing Panel).

The reactions of this sample of the audience were distributed as follows:-

A+	A	B	C	C-
%	%	%	%	%
8	42	42	7	1

which gives a Reaction Index of 62.

3. There was a generally warm welcome for the return of the Likely Lads and most of those reporting appear to have enjoyed this opening episode, which saw Bob and Thelma honeymooning in Norway while worrying about the havoc that Terry might be wreaking in their new house. As always, the relationship between the 'lads' was skilfully developed, it was agreed, and the episode was written with the sure, light touch that characterised the series - there were no 'belly laughs' but the humour was pleasant, down-to-earth and consistent, and it was 'nice to have them back'.

4. While finding the episode entertaining enough, however, quite a few viewers in the sample evidently felt that there was now a certain sameness and predictability about The Likely Lads: this new series looked like being scarcely different from the old ('it has almost reached the stage when you can anticipate the next remark') and there seemed to be little room for development - 'it's a very narrow story line - wife hates husband's bachelor friends ....' A small group thought the episode rather crude at times, or 'just not one of their funniest'.

5. As has been said, however, the overall response was cordial and, even if they were not all that impressed with the script, viewers thought the performance excellent. As always, James Bolam and Rodney Bewes played their parts to perfection, it was said, and the supporting roles - the long-suffering Thelma (Brigit Forsyth) and Bob's father-in-law (Bill Owen) in particular - were well taken. Camera work, costumes and settings were also approved, although a handful felt that some snow scenes might have been included to give the atmosphere of a ski-ing holiday.

6. 95% of the sample watched the whole programme, 2% came in in the middle, 1% tried a bit and 2% switched off before the end.

Copyright of the BBC
RG/MH

Audience Research Department
22nd January 1974

As the BBC's audience survey reveals (left), the sequel was warmly welcomed, with many viewers commenting that: 'As always, the relationship between the Lads was skilfully developed'. However, some people felt there was a 'sameness and predictability' about the show.

Reviewing the Success

At its peak, over 16 million people watched the sitcom. With an appreciative audience and, most unusually, a warm embrace from TV journalists, it's a show that has earned its reputation as one of the nation's classic comedies. As Peter Black reported in the *Daily Mail*, Clement and La Frenais' sitcom was 'character comedy at its best.' He added: 'Not a gag in sight, every laugh springing with perfect naturalness out of the truth of the characters.'

Meanwhile, Philip Purser in the *Sunday Telegraph* said: '*Whatever Happened to...?* is the best-written, best-performed, best-produced comedy to be seen just now.' He also felt that it was 'a feeling commentary on changing fashions, changing landscapes and ordinary growing up.'

Resurrecting the kind of magic the public were attracted to in *The Likely Lads* was no easy task, but many critics felt that *Whatever Happened to...?* was better than the original series. Its wry study of behaviour and life was helped along by the more expansive canvas Clement and La Frenais now had to work with.

But one person who disagrees that the sequel was better than the original is Rodney Bewes. 'The sequel was good and we had a ball, but I always thought the black and white episodes were fab. And it was better when the episodes lasted just 25 minutes. I always thought the extra five minutes was padding; we didn't need it.'

Focusing on realism in both humour and storylines meant the show appealed across the spectrum. Everyone seemed able to identify with the characters, as Bernard Thompson explained: 'Friends would admit to being like Bob or Terry.' He also felt nostalgia played a part in the success. 'A lot of people remembered their youth as being like Terry and Bob's. When we look back we all think our younger days were wonderful; we all believe we had greater success with the opposite sex than we actually did.'

The importance of nostalgia is something Ian La Frenais also sets store by. 'It's like people rediscovering the music of their youth, the clothes and the references. At the time, *Whatever Happened to...?* had a legacy from when the original series was transmitted, so it had a built-in captive loyalty, which gave it a tremendous kick-start.'

Ian also knows the viewers' recognition of the Lads' characters was fundamental. 'The feeling that you could walk into any pub and see a Bob or Terry was important.'

The sitcom's success was ultimately a result of excellent scripts and a good cast. It is not unusual to amend scripts prior to recording; often days are spent rewriting scenes. But that never happened with *Whatever Happened to The Likely Lads?* as Jimmy Gilbert points out. 'There were certain series where I had to make a big contribution, but with the quality of Dick and Ian's scripts you'd have to be pretty second-rate to muck them up.'

Jimmy also acknowledges the part Rodney Bewes and James Bolam played. 'The chemistry between the two characters was magical, and the fact it's one of the few series that still works on television has got a lot to do with that.' Newspapers have often questioned Bewes and Bolam's relationship, suggesting they didn't get on. But Jimmy Gilbert never saw them as anything but professional in the way they approached their work. 'Any feelings they may or may not have had never got in the way of working together,' he's keen to point out. 'I wouldn't have allowed it. They were professional colleagues and always acted as such.'

Actor Donald Gee – who played a vicar in three episodes of the sequel, and a shop steward in the original series – agrees that the show's success was built on the quality of acting and writing. 'Someone once asked John Gielgud what style was, and he said it's knowing what play you're in. And that's exactly what we did. Everyone knew where they were with the writing; we knew how far to go, and how restrained we had to be – that's why it worked so well. Most of it was funny, but you knew there would be some barbs in there hitting home and making you think.'

As far as Bernard Thompson – who became something of a specialist in North-country comedy, also working on *Last of the Summer Wine*, *I Didn't Know You Cared*, *The Brothers McGregor* and *Rosie* – was concerned, there wasn't anything better than *Whatever*

Happened to The Likely Lads? 'It was good working-class humour, containing a certain intelligence that gave it scope for a wider audience. It was a show that could be appreciated by all classes of society. It had the conservative, straight line with Bob, and the drop-out in Terry, a great combination.'

27 shows, we didn't know what else to do with the Lads. Terry couldn't carry on like he was, he would have to develop and that would mean leaving and, probably, getting married. We just felt there was nowhere left to go.'

The two series were a big success for the BBC.

All Good Things Come to an End

By the time the final episode was transmitted during Christmas 1974, Dick Clement and Ian La Frenais – who received a joint fee of £1,100 per script – had made up their minds to pension off Bob and Terry. After writing 46 episodes, a Christmas Special, a film and a sketch for *Christmas Night with the Stars*, it was now the time to move on. 'We wrote 13 for the first *Whatever Happened to…?* series and then the BBC asked for another 13. It felt like we'd just come down from Everest only to go back up again. Being asked to write that many half-hour shows is very flattering but a lot of work,' explains Dick, who feels writing more could have proved detrimental. 'If we'd continued the storylines would have become repetitive; there are only so many plots you can create with "bad boy" Terry pulling "good boy" Bob off the rails.'

His writing partner echoes Dick's justifications for drawing the Lads' lives to an end. 'In the first series each episode led very nicely into the next, whereas the second series was more episodic,' says Ian. 'After

Although the corporation reluctantly acknowledged that the second series was likely to be the last, it was keen that Clement and La Frenais – by now in heavy demand – continued writing for the Beeb. Before he left his post as Head of Comedy, Duncan Wood suggested to the BBC hierarchy that they be given their own series of pilots, 'a sort of Clement and La Frenais Playhouse', with the hope that one or more of the pilots would be picked up for a full series. Sadly, Wood's idea never came to fruition.

Bernard Thompson produced the final episode and remembered it as rather sad, although only a few tears were shed. 'There weren't many tears because working together had been such a happy time. After the last show we had a big slap-up meal and drank lots of vino.'

It's often rumoured that Bob and Terry will be brought out of mothballs for a further set of adventures, something producer Jimmy Gilbert believes could work. 'I told Dick and Ian that it could be a social documentary right up until the geriatric ward!'

Because the series had such a strong social content, he felt it was a shame it couldn't be revisited every decade. 'It's a social history of England, really. If it had gone on into the 1980s, presumably Bob would have been made redundant, or found himself with negative equity, while Terry's fortunes would be much rosier and he'd be in a position to sub his old friend; the whole thing could be turned on its head.'

But realistically Jimmy Gilbert feels a revival would be difficult. 'It's probably too late now; although I feel it would be a brilliant idea, I'm not sure the actors and writers would be so keen.'

The writers dismiss talk of another revival. 'We've all moved in such different directions, so it's very unlikely it would ever happen,' says Dick. 'But we always joked that if we brought them back for another series, this time focusing on their middle age, Bob would have gone into the building trade and become bankrupt, while Terry, who'd never done a hard day's work in his life, would win the lottery. It would be the ultimate example of how unfair life is.

'There's an element of this in 'The Ant and the Grasshopper', which reveals Terry doesn't have any moral fibre, or the sort of work ethic that Bob possesses. Another revival would have been interesting, but I don't think we'd ever get it together.'

Someone else who felt there would be merit in pursuing the possibilities of a revival was Bernard Thompson, who wasn't surprised when recent repeats attracted a new following of fans.

'It was so beautifully written and beautifully performed, and a lot of the attitudes explored still persist. Without doubt, it's this timeless element that has made the show just as accessible today as 35 years ago,' he says.

THE NOVELIZATIONS

When writer Patrick Tilley was offered the job of adapting selected scripts into novel-form, it couldn't have come at a better time. 'It was a life-saver because I was short of money. When Dick and Ian asked me to do it, I jumped at the chance,' says Patrick, who'd given up a career in graphic design to write full-time. 'For two years I'd been working on my first book, so the £500 I was paid came in very useful.'

Patrick was happy with the result. 'I think Dick and Ian were, too.' Typing the final word of the manuscript had a significant impact. 'I had written 80,000 words in five weeks, and adapting the TV scripts into prose made me realize that I could finish a book, so I settled down and completed my own.'

***Whatever Happened To The Likely Lads?* (ISBN: 056312569) was adapted from the TV series by Patrick Tilley. It was published in 1974 by the BBC, but is now out of print. An earlier novelization, *The Likely Lads* (ISBN: 0853910677), was adapted from the series by Clement and La Frenais. Long out of print, it was published by Rapp and Carroll in 1967.**

BRIGIT FORSYTH • THELMA FERRIS

Thelma, a librarian, wants married life to be as orderly as the bookshelves in the library, but that is asking too much seeing she marries Bob, whom she has known since class 4b at Park Juniors.

Her father's business success – he trained as a brickie before setting up his own building firm – and her mother's haughtiness has sometimes led people, especially Terry, to view Thelma as snooty and dour, which is unfair. Although she often nags Bob, it is understandable considering everything she puts up with. All Thelma wants was a straightforward marriage, with all the goals and dreams newlyweds aspire to — namely a comfortable and successful lifestyle.

A keen badminton player and active member of the local sewing circle, Thelma has already dated Bob for some years before they get married.

Even though her relationship with Bob can be volatile – at one point she ditches him for Billy Potter – she is happy with her lot, but would be even happier if she could get shot of Terry Collier's unwanted influence, and the memory of the 1967 supporters' club outing to Blackpool, where she ended up on the back seat of the coach with Terry, earning herself a two-star rating in the process!

Halfway through the first series of *Whatever Happened To The Likely Lads?* Brigit Forsyth discovered she was using the wrong accent. 'I'm very instinctive, quickly adopting a particular style of character because it feels right,' she says, 'and I used a slightly posh Manchester-style accent for Thelma – it was also the only

Northern accent I could do!' It was only after several episodes she learnt that her character actually lived further North. 'One day during rehearsals Jimmy Bolam said: "A Newcastle lass would never say that." I asked what that had got to do with it, and he replied: "Well you're from Newcastle!"

'I was absolutely stunned. I don't know why, but I thought it was in Manchester. So what I regarded as my posh Manchester was coming out as posh Newcastle, possibly because of the mix with my Scottish accent; but whatever it was people didn't notice, so I just carried on.'

Brigit had watched *The Likely Lads* back in the Sixties, so when her agent mentioned auditioning for the part of Thelma, she already knew the show well. In fact, she had a vested interest in the earlier black and white episodes: she studied at RADA with Sheila Fearn, who played Audrey. 'I'd left drama school and was in rep by the time the first episode was shown in 1964. But I watched as many episodes as possible, because Sheila was in it, and I liked the show.'

Although Brigit remembers her audition was 'very daunting', her nerves were eased by the quality of the script. 'It was wonderful; all the scripts were. It was like being given gold; you couldn't go wrong. But the audition was still terrifying because Dick Clement, Ian La Frenais, James Bolam, Rodney Bewes and Jimmy Gilbert were all there.'

She didn't hold out much hope of securing the role. 'I remember thinking it was such a good part I wouldn't get it because everybody would be up for it. But the audition went well, and I knew I'd done my best.' Brigit's husband, director Brian Mills, who was her boyfriend at the time, was a great deal more optimistic. 'He felt sure I stood a good chance, and that getting the part would send my career in a completely different direction.'

When she was finally offered the job, Brigit was very excited, welcoming the chance to appear in a sitcom; she'd just completed *Holly*, Granada's tense six-part psychological thriller, in which she played the name part. 'It was about schizophrenia and incredibly complicated, but I learnt a lot from it. So it was welcome relief to do some comedy.'

Whilst preparing for any new role or audition, Brigit likes finding out as much as possible about the character. 'I can't remember being told anything about Thelma, and don't think I saw any scripts beforehand. Usually you're not told enough, so end up working in the dark. I always like to know whether a character is middle-class, working-class, Scottish, Irish, or doesn't it matter? But often you can never find out.'

When she finally received scripts for *Whatever Happened to …?* she spent an entire afternoon laughing uproariously. 'I was sitting on the balcony of my flat – well, it was a garage roof overlooking the railway

line – on a lovely, sunny day. In those days it wasn't unusual to receive a funny script, whereas now it's rare to read one and laugh out loud.'

Classing herself primarily as a theatre actress, Brigit has vivid memories of recording the first episode, 'Strangers on a Train'. 'It was very scary, almost a schizophrenic feeling because when I heard the audience, a part of me was thinking: "Oh, people, it must be theatre," while the other side was saying: "No it isn't, it's for the camera," which drives you completely mad because you don't know what path to follow.

'I'd been doing theatre and some TV prior to playing Thelma, but as it was all drama it wasn't in front of a live audience. The powers that be are convinced that filming in front of a live audience makes a show funnier. I don't know why; it drives a lot of actors crazy because your instinct as an actor is to play up to the audience, and you mustn't because it's for the camera and the people at home.'

Brigit's fine portrayal of the prissy Thelma soon earned the character the nickname 'Dreaded Thelma', a label that still bewilders her. 'I don't understand it,' she says. 'The first time I read about it I didn't know what was meant because I'd always felt so sorry for her.' As far as Brigit is concerned, her character was the unfortunate piggy in the middle, caught between Bob's desire to better himself and settle down, and his reluctance to relinquish ties with his youth. 'Thelma may have been a person of some social pretension, but really she just wanted to have a lovely life and progress, all the things a young married girl aspires to.

'It should have been the "dreaded boys" or, else,

perhaps, the "dreaded Terry", who was constantly distracting Thelma's husband, so I was a little hurt, to be quite honest. I remember thinking: "That's awful, it's not Thelma's fault." Overall she was very caring, and wanted to be something more than just a little Northern girl.'

Without a doubt, playing Thelma is one of the highlights of Brigit's career, and she's not surprised the show was a success. 'Dick and Ian are brilliant writers,' she says. 'They're talented people and have both got a wonderful sense of humour. They also have an ear for everyday sayings and events, and the ability to pick them up and use them in their work.'

Another aspect of the show Thelma liked was its reliance on character studies instead of being a gag-driven comedy. 'The whole thing was based on the way the people acted towards each other, something we don't see very much in today's offerings.'

One of the qualities of Clement and La Frenais' creation was the gentle mix of humour and drama, with many episodes containing a degree of pathos. 'In those days, you weren't expected to laugh all the way through a show. You were given time to get to know people, to understand the plot and sympathize with characters. Bob questioning whether he regrets marrying Thelma is so real; people do.

'And because life is like that, the most wonderful humour comes from it. It's based on reality, which is something else that made it successful. Nowadays, people think the audience has got to laugh all the time. But it's not realistic; life's not like that.'

Many people will always remember Brigit for her role as Thelma Chambers, but her extensive career also features successful excursions into all strands of the profession. However, the theatre will always be her first love. 'I prefer working in the theatre, especially now I feel I can just about do it,' she smiles. 'I have been given some tremendous parts during the last few years – they've been very satisfying to play. I love the camera and I love television for different reasons, but working on the stage is my favourite; it's what I came into the profession for. Every night you're in front of a different audience, and you've got to try and get it right for two hours – there's no stopping and starting.'

When considering her numerous stage roles, Brigit struggles to pick a particular favourite, so many are special. 'I suppose one of the highlights would be Lady Bracknell in *The Importance of Being Earnest* at the Royal Exchange, Manchester. That was just thrilling. Amanda Wingfield in *The Glass Menagerie* was very good and, of course, I've just had the part of all-time: Betty in Kay Mellor's *A Passionate Woman*. It was the most wonderful experience and I got standing ovations, which I'd never had before and could become addicted to!'

At school she played the cello, but later switched to the guitar. For years she was involved with amateur orchestras and wrote her own songs. 'My family were very musical, and I thought seriously about becoming a professional musician,' she says.

With a year to occupy before joining drama school, her father insisted she trained for another career, because he knew that acting was a precarious job. Brigit enrolled herself on a secretarial course while nurturing her musical talents during the evening. 'I played the cello and was told I was capable of following a musical career, but decided against it because it would have meant spending hours on my own each day practising – it would have been awfully lonely.'

Brigit also has a respectable singing voice, and for a short time she earnt some extra cash singing in a London café. 'It was around the time I was trying to break into TV,' she explains. 'I was working with another actress, Anne Raitt, who was a childhood friend of mine, in *Macbeth* at the Edinburgh Festival in 1966, and discovered that we both played the guitar. We started singing together and to our surprise, got work.'

As well as an appearance on Scottish TV, they also sang at the Festival. 'We did a late night show; I don't know how we arranged that, but I carried on when I returned to London. I worked in a café in Earls Court, singing for about five hours and earning £2.50, which I thought was brilliant.'

In between acting jobs she would earn money from secretarial work and her singing. 'I loved doing it; I think I saw myself as Joan Baez because I had long black hair in those days and learnt all her songs.'

But it appears the long hair had a detrimental effect on her career, because as soon as she cut it her career took off. 'I began taking Alexander lessons and started to relax,' says Brigit, who had just appeared in *Oh! What A Lovely War*, at Liverpool. 'I think I may have been hiding behind my hair. As

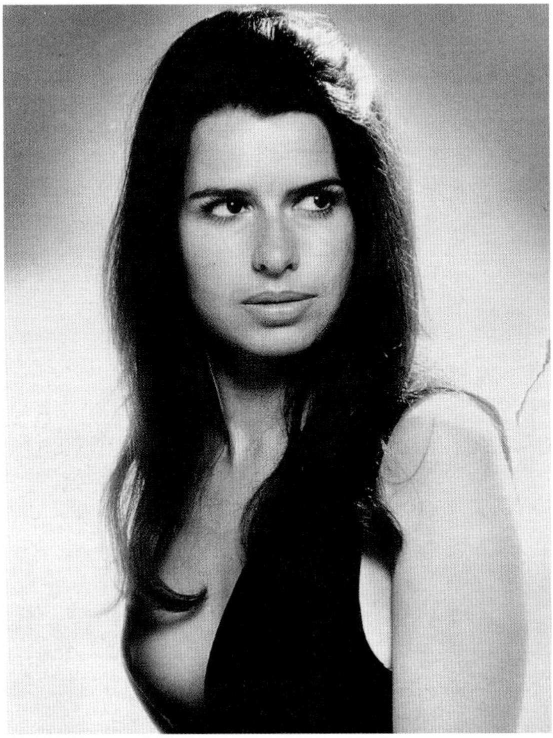

soon as it was cut short I went from having no work at all to getting lots of parts, especially on telly, starting with an Irish part in ATV's *Look Out, it's Margaret Mitchell's Solicitors*, in which I played a strongman's daughter in a circus, and the Irish series *The Sinners*.'

Born in Edinburgh, one of five children, Brigit studied at RADA, graduating in 1961, after winning the Emile Littler Award for outstanding aptitude for the professional theatre. Six years of rep followed at numerous venues around the country, including her first job in Edinburgh, Lincoln's Theatre Royal for 14 months, where she first worked with Rodney Bewes in a play called *Caught Napping*. She also appeared in Salisbury, Aberdeen, Folkestone, Cheltenham and Hornchurch. 'It was fantastic training,' she enthuses, 'because you were allowed to learn and test yourself. I feel such sympathy for young actors today, who don't have the sort of opportunities rep work provided.'

After several years in theatre, Brigit decided it was time to branch out and try breaking into the world of TV. 'I'd done theatre for ages, and much as I loved it I was fed up earning very little money. I gave myself a deadline to get my first television job, and I succeeded by securing a small part in *Dr. Finlay's Casebook*, and things developed from there. I remember that first role vividly: I played a receptionist and had one line, "Doctor Finlay's out; he won't be back until later today."'

Being a novice in television, it took a while before Brigit adapted her performance to suit the medium. 'I'd been doing theatre for six years, so I proclaimed my line at the top of my voice. Everyone was very sweet and helped me adjust to working in television, but it was such a shock at first.'

After her role in the medical drama, she appeared in plenty of small roles, and was regularly cast as Irish women. 'For some time people thought I was Irish. In fact, I was very pleased because it meant I got plenty of work. My first Irish role was in a show for ATV, playing a strongman's daughter in a circus. It was a super part, and meant I was able to work with some great Irish actors.'

More Irish roles followed, all for Granada. Then in 1972 she was offered the part of Annie, the wayward student daughter in *Adam Smith*, a religious drama series about the Reverend Adam Smith, played by Andrew Keir, the parish minister of a tiny Scottish village. 'It was my first Scottish part and one of the few in my whole career,' says Brigit.

But she was playing an Irish character when spotted by director Jimmy Gilbert, who was responsible for casting her as Thelma. 'It was a fantastic short story by Frank O'Connor, called *The Sinners*, and I had a wonderful part.'

Whenever *Whatever Happened to ....?* is repeated, Brigit watches with interest. 'It's very strange seeing it,' she says. 'It's just like watching somebody else. My daughter, Zoe, is 19, and although I thought we had similar personalities, I never realized we were alike in looks until I watched some recent repeats. It

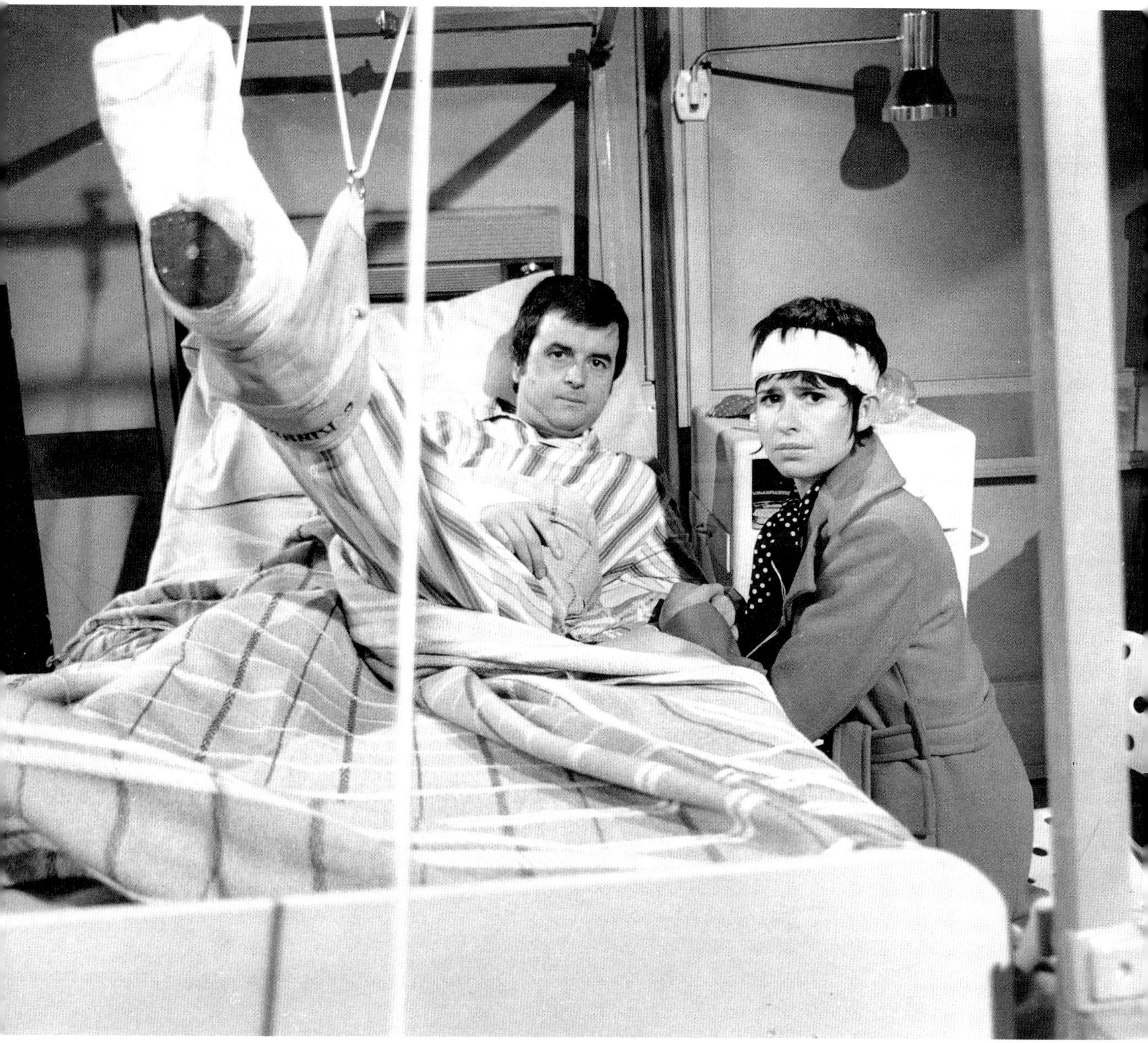

may have been simply a turn of the head, but it reminded me of Zoe – it was quite spooky!'

As well as continuing a busy stage career, Brigit has not been a stranger in the world of TV. She has appeared in many shows, including two series of *Playing the Field, The Ward, Tom, Dick and Harriet, Sharon and Elsie, The Practice* and *Stanley's Vision* with Ben Kingsley for Channel 4.

As far as Brigit is concerned, playing Thelma has been advantageous to her career. 'Because it was just two series of *Whatever Happened to....?* as well as a Christmas special and the film, it worked well because it gave me an identity; people knew who I was. But it can also work against you in that people always have a particular image of you in their head: they don't think you can do anything else. Luckily, it hasn't worked out that way for me.'

Brigit holds nothing but happy memories of her time spent working on the show. 'I couldn't be anything but positive; I've had so much work since

Thelma. It's really nice to see people enjoying the reruns. People come up to me with beaming faces, saying: "Oh, we're enjoying them so much." How can you be anything but pleased with that sort of reaction? I think it's a great compliment.'

Recent repeats have also generated lots more fan mail, something that pleases Brigit. 'It's been wonderful, especially as people still recognize me – even after all these years!'

Brigit, who has two children, Ben and Zoë, both studying at university, enjoys the outdoor life when she's not working. 'I enjoy swimming, walking, or doing the gardening,' she says. 'I've been working virtually non-stop for two years, so now that I have a little more time I will attack the garden, and perhaps take up the cello again – who knows?'

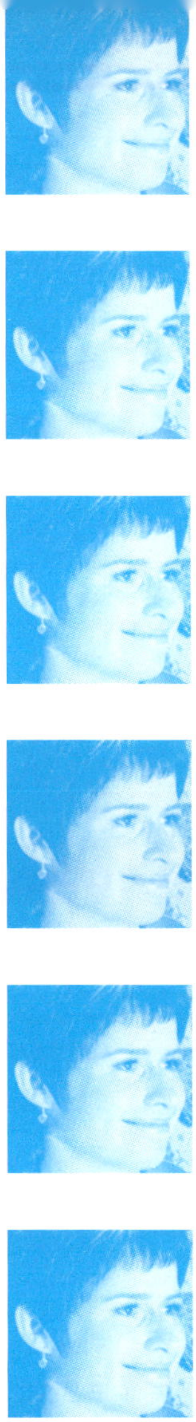

TV CREDITS INCLUDE:

The Sinners
Adam Smith (Annie Smith)
Call My Bluff
The Master of Ballantrae (Mistress of Ballantrae)
The Ward (Sylvia Dickinson)
Jackanory
Tom, Dick and Harriet (two series as Harriet)
Sharon and Elsie (two series as Elsie)
The Practice (two series as Dr. Vincent)
Boon (13 episodes as Helen Yeldon)
Graham's Gang
Spark (Mrs Wells)
The Visit
My World
Glamour Girls
Holding the Fort
Bizarre and Rummage (Play for Today)
Poirot (first episode)
Running Wild
Nice Town
Waiting
Stanley's Vision (Hilda Spencer)
Playing the Field (two series as Francine Pratt)
Wycliffe (Ella Jones)
Dangerfield (Linda Barton)

THEATRE CREDITS INCLUDE:

The Merchant of Venice (Jessica)
Importance of Being Earnest (Lady Bracknell)
Little Murders (Marjorie)
The Norman Conquests (Annie)
The Glass Menagerie (Amanda Wingfield)
You Must Be the Husband (Alice)
Tom and Viv (Viv)
The Price (Esther)
Dusa, Stas, Fish and Vi (Dusa)
My Fat Friend (Vicki)
A Passionate Woman (Betty)

FILM CREDITS INCLUDE:

The Likely Lads (Thelma)
The Wrong Side of the Blanket
The Roadbuilder
The Crystal Stone

Clement on Forsyth

'Imagine how difficult it was for Brigit to walk into a series which had previously been about two lads, and literally come between them. If she hadn't brought humour and believability to the role, the series would have been a disaster. But from the start Thelma was funny, precisely because of her predicament. How hard she tried to be fair. And how hard we tried to be fair to her, until Clive James, in a review, dubbed her 'the dreaded Thelma'.

'I think Brigit would have been slightly hurt by that adjective, but would also have seen the funny side of it. She took the role very seriously, which is the only way to play comedy well. Not that she didn't have moments of stress. There was a famous occasion when she tried to strangle Rodney. She stopped, not because of a sudden pang of conscience, but because, as she later put it, "I simply didn't have the strength."

EPISODE GUIDE

WHATEVER HAPPENED TO THE LIKELY LADS?

PRODUCTION TEAM

(Unless otherwise stated, the people mentioned performed the job throughout the two series.)

SCRIPTS: Dick Clement and Ian La Frenais

PRODUCER: James Gilbert (series 1); Bernard Thompson (series 2 & episode 27)

PRODUCTION ASSISTANT: Bernard Thompson (series 1); Evan King (series 2 & episode 27)

COSTUMES: Roger Reece (credited on episodes 12 & 13); Mary Woods (episodes 16 & 21); Michael Burdle (episodes 24 & 26); Elizabeth Waller (episode 27)

MAKE-UP: Sylvia Thornton (credited on episodes 12 & 13); Penny Delamar (credited on episodes 16 & 21); Lee Smith (episode 24 & 26); Susan Rothwell (episode 27)

SOUND: Trevor Webster (series 1, except episodes 3 & 9–13); Malcolm Johnson (episode 3); Lance Andrews (episodes 9–13, 19, 20, 23, 24 & 26); Richard Partridge (series 2, except episodes 19, 20, 23 & 24); Alan Machin (episode 27)

LIGHTING: Robbie Robinson (episodes 1,2 & 3); James Purdie (episodes 4–8, 10–13, series 2 & episode 27); Richie Richardson (episode 9)

FILM CAMERAMAN: Alan Featherstone (series 1); Len Newson (series 2)

FILM EDITOR: Bill Harris (series 2); Bob Rymer (episode 27)

DESIGN: Tim Gleeson (series 1, except episodes 2, 4, 6, 8, 10 & 11, episodes 16 & 8–20, 24 & 27); Gloria Clayton (episode 2); Allan Anson (episodes 4, 6, 8, 10 & 11); Peter Kindred (episodes 15, 17 & 21); John Hurst (episodes 23 & 26)

GRAPHICS/TITLES: Mic Rolph

SIGNATURE TUNE: Written by Mike Hugg and Ian La Frenais

SERIES ONE

(Rodney Bewes and James Bolam appeared in every episode)

1. STRANGERS ON A TRAIN

Original transmission: Tues. 9/1/73, BBC1, 8.30p.m.
First repeat: Mon. 2/12/74, BBC1, 7.40p.m. (not Scotland or Wales. BBC Wales repeated episode on 4/12/74, same time.)
(Original viewing figures = 13.1 million)

CAST:

Thelma . . . . Brigit Forsyth
Woman on Train . . . . . Deirdre Costello
Steward . . . . James Mellor
Stripper in Club. . . . . . Angelique Ashly

It's five years since the Lads parted, so they're both shocked when they meet unexpectedly on a Newcastle-bound train. Bob's been to London on business, while Terry's heading home after his stint in the army.

All is forgiven when they discuss the mess-up that led to Terry swapping civilian life for the Forces. While Terry regrets wasting five years of his life, things couldn't be better for Bob, who's secured a good job, is onto his second set of wheels, smokes cigars, plays tennis and is marrying Thelma Chambers in six weeks.

For Terry, returning home is worrying because life has left him behind, with all his mates settled down and having mortgages and kids. Thelma, meanwhile, sees his return as a threat to her future with Bob.

2. HOME IS THE HERO

Original transmission: Tues. 16/1/73, BBC1, 8.30p.m.
First repeat: Mon. 9/12/74, BBC1, 7.40p.m.
(Original viewing figures = 10.8 million)

CAST:
Thelma . . . . Brigit Forsyth
Audrey. . . . . Sheila Fearn
Stan . . . . Derek Etchells

Thelma's suffering delayed shock, induced by Terry's homecoming. She's concerned his influence on Bob will have serious ramifications for their forthcoming marriage. Bob also feels life is less than rosy now his old pal has arrived back again.

Terry, however, wonders whether returning to the area was such a good move, especially as his parents are attending a funeral, leaving the house feeling cold and empty.

Adapting to civvy street is no easy task for him: old friends have either left for pastures new or are married. Bob makes him feel worse by reminding him that he's homeless, jobless, carless and also still single.

But Terry drops a bombshell: he married a German girl while serving in the army, but as she didn't speak English, and he wasn't prepared to learn German, they separated.

3. COLD FEET

Original transmission: Tues. 23/1/73, BBC1, 8.30p.m.
First repeat: Mon. 16/12/74, BBC1, 7.40p.m.
(Original viewing figures = 14 million)

CAST:
Thelma . . . . Brigit Forsyth
Audrey. . . . . Sheila Fearn
Vicar. . . . . Donald Gee
Verger. . . . . John Barrett
Barman . . . . Shay Gorman
Man in Waiting Room . . . . Roy Denton

Pressures associated with the impending marriage are taking their toll on Bob, but the invites have been posted so there is no backing out. Even though he's fancied Thelma since childhood, their relationship has been up-and-down, and he feels rather socially inferior to his fiancee.

Another tiff strains the relationship to the point where Thelma even stops knitting Bob his fawn cardigan for weekend use, so Terry – who feels his bitter experience of wedlock makes him suitably qualified – tries advising his mate on the dangers of marriage. But deep down, Bob knows she's the right girl for him – at least he thinks so!

4. MOVING ON

Original transmission: Tues. 30/1/73, BBC1, 8.30p.m.
First repeat: Mon. 6/1/75, BBC1, 7.40p.m.
(Original viewing figures = 9.6 million)

CAST:
Audrey. . . . . Sheila Fearn
Ernie . . . . Ronald Lacey
Landlady. . . . . Effie Morrison
Wendy (Bob's Secretary) . Elizabeth Lax
Hughie . . . . Iain Blair

Time stands still for no one, especially Terry Collier, who can't believe his eyes when Bob shows him how all their old haunts have been flattened, or turned into high-rise flats.

On the job front, the labour exchange send Terry – who's reluctant to grab any old opportunity of work – to see Frank Busby at an electrical contractor's, but when he's out his assistant – who turns out to be Bob – gives him an interview.

Feeling proud – or simply foolish – Terry won't admit, especially to Bob, that he needs help finding a job and kick-starting his life. Instead, he heads for pastures new, namely Berwickshire, where he falls into a dead-end job. But it's not long before his long-time friend catches up with him.

5. I'LL NEVER FORGET WHATSERNAME

Original transmission: Tues. 6/2/73, BBC1, 8.30p.m.
First repeat: Mon. 13/1/75, BBC1, 7.40p.m.
(Original viewing figures = 10.3 million)

CAST:
Thelma . . . . Brigit Forsyth
Jackie Norris . . . . Margaret Nolan
Glenys Roberts . . . . Sandra Bryant
Pub Manager . . . . Norman Mitchell
Barmaid. . . . . Lorna Wilde

In a desperate attempt to cling onto the past, Terry – in search of female companionship – tries tracking down a few old flames, thanks to some faded telephone numbers scribbled in his 1967 diary. A glance through the well-thumbed pages reveals a myriad of memories from days long gone when Terry and Bob were lads about town.

They reminisce about their sexual conquests, and the likes of Wendy Thwaites and her pink sequined dress. Bob calls Jackie Norris on Terry's behalf and sets up a date, with Bob and Thelma making up a foursome.

But digging up the past can prove embarrassing, as Bob and Thelma find when Jackie airs romantic memories of Bob, including of a 'quick snog behind the blacksmiths'!

6. BIRTHDAY BOY

Original transmission: Tues. 13/2/73, BBC1, 8.30p.m.
First repeat: Mon. 20/1/75, BBC1, 7.40p.m.
(Original viewing figures = 10.2 million)

CAST:

Thelma . . . . Brigit Forsyth
Janey Freeman . . . . Sandra Downes
Hugh. . . . . Michael Ralph
Podge . . . . Christopher Biggins
Barman . . . . Norman Mitchell
Deborah . . . . Shirley Steedman
Clare . . . . Elissa Derwent
Mrs Collier . . . . Olive Milbourne
Colin . . . . Brian Grellis
Mary. . . . . Stephanie Turner
Stan . . . . Derek Etchells

It's Terry's birthday and no one seems to care, not even Bob, who's more interested in getting a present for Thelma to celebrate their engagement anniversary. Terry has hit rock bottom: no job, no friends and no social life, unlike in the good old days when life was full of girls and hopes.

Unbeknown to him, Bob's arranged a surprise party, virtually filling the room with ex-girlfriends. A dejected Terry drinks alone until Bob rescues him from his deep depression, trying hard to convince him he does have friends. But at the party it's not long before insults start flying!

7. NO HIDING PLACE

Original transmission: Tues. 20/2/73, BBC1, 8.30p.m.
First repeat: Mon. 27/1/75, BBC1, 7.40p.m.
(Original viewing figures = 11.5 million)

CAST:

Audrey. . . . . Sheila Fearn
Flint . . . . Brian Glover
Vicar. . . . . Donald Gee
TV Announcer. . . . . . . Corbett Woodall
Barmaid. . . . . Lorna Wilde
Dallas . . . . Bernard Douglas
Garry . . . . Brian Godfrey
Rita . . . . Katy Allan
Sonia . . . . Drina Pavlovic

The Lads are desperate to avoid hearing the score of England's football match with Bulgaria. They're intent on watching the evening highlights but because there are eight hours to go someone's bound to blab the result – especially with people like Flint around. When they bump into him at the pub, they lay a bet that they'll somehow survive the day without unintentionally overhearing the score.

At Audrey's, Bob and Terry switch the radio off and prevent her answering the phone, just in case the score is mentioned. They resort to seeking refuge in the local church, but even that isn't safe from Flint.

With hours to go, the Lads help kill time by trying flower arranging with the WI and donating blood. They survive their longest and most agonising day, only to collapse in front of the TV and discover the match was postponed due to a waterlogged pitch.

8. GUESS WHO'S COMING TO DINNER?

Original transmission: Tues. 27/2/73, BBC1, 8.30p.m.
First repeat: Mon. 3/2/75, BBC1, 7.40p.m.
(Original viewing figures = 11.5 million)

CAST:

Thelma . . . . Brigit Forsyth
Audrey. . . . . Sheila Fearn
Mrs Collier . . . . Olive Milbourne
Alan Boyle . . . . Julian Holloway
Brenda Boyle . . . . Jacquie-Ann Carr

Terry still believes that serving his country in the army is good enough reason to take life easy, but Bob tries getting his mate's life back on track by inviting him to a dinner party at the home of Bob's workmate, Alan, and his wife, Brenda.

Terry recognizes the uppish Brenda from her younger days, before she adopted airs and graces, and spends the entire evening reminding her of her working-class roots. But Brenda retaliates, pointing out that his reluctance to leave the past behind is because he has little to look forward to, other than the pub and billiard hall: it's certainly an evening to remember!

9. STORM IN A TEA CHEST

Original transmission: Tues. 6/3/73, BBC1, 8.30p.m.
First repeat: Mon. 10/2/75, BBC1, 7.40p.m.
(Original viewing figures = 12.1 million)

CAST:

Thelma . . . . Brigit Forsyth
Police Sergeant . . . . . . Robert Gillespie
Vicar. . . . . Donald Gee
Policemen . . . . Michael Stainton
. . . . and John Owens

Bob and Thelma buy their first home, but when Bob moves his belongings in, Thelma complains that old comics, spinning tops and Rupert annuals are useless reminders of his past and banishes them from the house. Bob hates the thought of throwing them away, so Thelma does it for him, donating everything to the vicar's jumble sale.

When she feels sorry for Bob and regrets her actions, she suggests he reclaims them from the church, even though it costs him £5. But having earlier reported the toys missing, the Lads get themselves arrested for possessing stolen property.

10. THE OLD MAGIC

Original transmission: Tues. 13/3/73, BBC1, 8.30p.m.
First repeat: Mon. 17/2/75, BBC1, 7.40p.m.
(Original viewing figures = 11.6 million)

CAST:

Susan . . . . Anita Carey
Norma . . . . Brenda Cavendish
Mrs Ferris . . . . Barbara Ogilvie
Waiter . . . . Gertan Klauber

Terry is recovering from Chilean flu and is disappointed no one, especially Bob, has kept in touch. Eventually Bob pops round and invites him out to dinner at a fashionable new restaurant. He also informs Terry that he's not going to be best man at the wedding, because Frank Clarke was asked before his homecoming. Terry feels it's because his working-class roots now embarrass Bob. But before the day is out, Bob hears Frank has fallen ill, and ends up offering the job to his old friend after all.

At the restaurant the Lads relive the old days, discussing various of their previous relationships. After the meal and a few drinks, they try their luck with a couple of girls – Norma and Susan – sitting at a nearby table, just to see if the old magic is still there. Bob suggests they return to his house, but Susan doesn't like the idea, especially as she happens to be Thelma's sister, who is newly returned from Canada!

11. COUNTDOWN

Original transmission: Tues. 20/3/73, BBC1, 8.30p.m.
First repeat: Mon. 24/2/75, BBC1, 7.40p.m.
(Original viewing figures = 12 million)

CAST:

Thelma . . . . Brigit Forsyth
George Chambers . . . . Bill Owen
Mrs Chambers . . . . Joan Hickson
Shop Assistant . . . . . . Robin Parkinson
Susan Chambers . . . . Anita Carey
Barmaid. . . . . Lorna Wilde

With 150 guests attending the wedding, the day requires meticulous planning, so Bob, Thelma, Susan, Mrs Chambers and Terry discuss arrangements. When it comes to the suit fitting, Terry is embarrassed at being expected to wear top hat and tails, another sign of Bob's social climbing.

Later, Terry has a drink with the more down-to-earth Mr. Chambers and they decide to make a stand for men's lib. They return their morning suits, but their act of defiance backfires when the women go to collect the pageboy's outfit. It's all getting too much for Bob and Thelma, especially when young Dean sets fire to his kilt!

12. BOYS' NIGHT IN

Original transmission: Tues. 27/3/73, BBC1, 8.30p.m.
First repeat: Mon. 3/3/75, BBC1, 7.40p.m.
(Original viewing figures = 14.3 million)

CAST:

Police Sergeant . . . . . . Robert Gillespie
Policeman . . . . Michael Stainton

To avoid a drunken booze-up, Bob decides against the traditional stag night, much to Terry's amazement. Preferring a cup of tea and game of ludo to meeting his pals at the Black Horse, Bob tells Terry he's having problems sleeping because he's worried about his speech. Even fantasizing about a naked woman coming out of the sea riding a horse doesn't cure the problem. But his troubles worsen when he spills ink over his wedding trousers and spends the night in jail.

13. END OF AN ERA

Original transmission: Tues. 3/4/73, BBC1, 8.30p.m.
First repeat: Mon. 10/3/75, BBC1, 7.45p.m.
(Original viewing figures = 13 million)

CAST:

Thelma . . . . Brigit Forsyth
Audrey . . . . Sheila Fearn
George Chambers . . . . Bill Owen
Mrs Chambers . . . . Joan Hickson
Susan Chambers . . . . Anita Carey
Mrs Ferris . . . . Barbara Ogilvie
Aunt Beattie . . . . Daphne Heard
Usher . . . . Christopher Biggins
Jutta . . . . April Walker

It's the wedding day and everyone is suffering pre-marital nerves, while Mrs Ferris is tearful after serving Bob his final cup of tea under her roof. Every minute seems like an hour for Bob and Terry as they wait to go to church. Before they leave Bob shows his appreciation of Terry's lifelong support and friendship by giving him a prized possesion: his photo album.

Arriving early at church, Terry passes the time imitating birds and Guatemalan spiders, but it's not long before a nervy groom with shaky legs is swapping wedding vows and wondering what his best man has included in the long-awaited speech!

SERIES TWO

(Rodney Bewes and James Bolam appeared in every episode)

14. ABSENT FRIENDS

Original transmission: Tues. 1/1/74, BBC1, 8.30p.m.
First repeat: Mon. 17/3/75, BBC1, 7.40p.m.
(Original viewing figures = 12.3 million)

CAST:
Thelma . . . . Brigit Forsyth
George Chambers . . . . Bill Owen
Susan Chambers . . . . Anita Carey
Chauffeur . . . . Terry Scully
Hotel Porter. . . . Constantin De Goguel

Bob and Thelma head off for their Norwegian honeymoon, while Terry has been eyeing up Susan Chambers, even though she's engaged. Unbeknown to Thelma, Bob has asked Terry to look after the house while they're away – and it is the ideal place in which to entertain Susan.

When Thelma discovers what Bob has done, she's very annoyed. As far as she's concerned they can never rid themselves of Terry's influence even though they're hundreds of miles from home. As expected, things don't run smoothly for either of the Lads.

15. HEART TO HEART

Original transmission: Tues. 8/1/74, BBC1, 8.30p.m.
First repeat: Mon. 24/3/75, BBC1, 7.40p.m.
(Original viewing figures = 12.8 million)

CAST:
Thelma . . . . Brigit Forsyth
Susan Chambers . . . . Anita Carey
Mrs Chambers . . . . Noel Dyson
Jack . . . . Norman Mitchell
Gloria . . . . Lorna Wilde

The newly-weds return from their honeymoon, with Bob sporting a plaster cast on his leg: after enduring air turbulence, he disembarked feeling giddy and fell down the aircraft steps.

Terry, meanwhile, is still seeing Susan but is melancholic when he visits Bob and Thelma. Head bowed and very dispirited, he explains that staying at their house and spending time with Susan has made him realize that he wants more from life.

But he has to sort out his future with Susan first and, after enjoying tea with Mrs. Chambers, Bob and Thelma, the couple go for a walk to discuss their situation. They decide it's best for Susan to return to Canada; they've enjoyed spending time together but know their futures lie elsewhere. But they have a shock in store for Mrs Chambers!

16. THE ANT AND THE GRASSHOPPER

Original transmission: Tues. 15/1/74, BBC1, 8.30p.m.
First repeat: Mon. 7/4/75, BBC1, 7.40p.m.
(Original viewing figures = 12.1 million)

CAST:
Thelma . . . . Brigit Forsyth
Brenda . . . . Jacquie-Ann Carr
Alan . . . . Julian Holloway
Wendy . . . . Elizabeth Lax
Madelyn. . . . . Vicki Michelle
Gloria . . . . Lorna Wilde

Over a lunchtime drink the hardworking Bob – who faces a 30-mile journey across the moors to a potential building site – meets Terry, whose afternoon consists of visiting the billiard hall and the pictures. Life couldn't be busier for Bob: when he's not working he's studying for exams, which entails evening classes, as well as trying to enjoy married life with Thelma.

Terry feels Bob's pursuit of success is likely to bring him ulcers at 30 and a coronary at 40 and the only future Thelma can look forward to is his life insurance coughing up.

Later, Bob reflects on the additional responsibilities married life has brought: studying, filling in forms, digging borders, planting daffodils, buying insurance, painting the garage and laying lino – it's all taking its toll. Perhaps Terry's philosophy of living for today is the solution?

17. ONE FOR THE ROAD

Original transmission: Tues. 22/1/74, BBC1, 8.30p.m.
First repeat: Mon. 14/4/75, BBC1, 7.40p.m.
(Original viewing figures = 11.6 million)

CAST:
Thelma . . . . Brigit Forsyth
First Police Sergeant . . Robert Gillespie
PC in Patrol Car. . . . . James Mellor
Dr. McKae . . . . Leonard MaGuire
Second Police Sergeant . . Michael Beint
Barman. . . . . Norman Mitchell
Waiter . . . . Gertan Klauber
Glaswegian. . . . . Phil McCall
Doorman. . . . . Brian Vaughan

Bob and Thelma dine out at the Ridley Arms, but on the way home they're pulled over by the police. Bob fails a breath test and is taken to the station, where he meets Terry, who's been arrested for football hooliganism.

For Bob, losing his licence will mean the ruination of his entire social life: he'll have to catch a bus to and from work and won't be able to enjoy his little weekend drinks up the coast. Terry concocts a plan to get Bob off the hook, but it backfires and Bob is charged with disorderly conduct and fined £10. But there is a further shock in store for Mr. Ferris.

18. THE GREAT RACE

Original transmission: Tues. 5/2/74, BBC1, 8.30p.m.
First repeat: Mon. 21/4/75, 7.40p.m.
(Original viewing figures = 15.7 million)

CAST:

Audrey . . . . Sheila Fearn
Station Master . . . . Bert Palmer
Lorry Driver . . . . Roy Pattison
Gloria . . . . Lorna Wilde
Barmaid . . . . Patti Dalton
Picnicker . . . . Roger Bourne
The Boys . . . . . Sean Flanagan and Clive Warwick

The Lads discuss the virtues of staying in shape and leading healthy lifestyles now they're getting older. Arguing over who's the fittest, they challenge each other to a cycle race to Berwick, with £25 to the winner.

Drink containers full of beer, Terry dons his peaked cap and heads off, while Bob's sporting shorts and cycle gloves help him look the part. When Bob secures a 12-minute lead, the tactics get dirty with back wheels being loosened, brakes tampered with and lifts being cadged on lorries.

Saddle-sore and physically shattered, Bob and Terry submit to the rigours of the challenge, but upon discovering they've missed the last train home, pedal power seems the only alternative.

19. SOME DAY WE'LL LAUGH ABOUT THIS

Original transmission: Tues. 19/2/74, BBC1, 8.30p.m.
First repeat: Mon. 28/4/75, BBC1, 7.40p.m.
(Original viewing figures = 8.5 million)

CAST:

Thelma . . . . Brigit Forsyth
Audrey . . . . Sheila Fearn
Mrs Collier . . . . Olive Milbourne
Sandra . . . . Helen Cotterill
Milkman . . . . Anthony Haygarth

Bob and Thelma are off skiing in Scotland, and Bob leaves Terry in charge of their new home on the understanding he clears a few of the outstanding household jobs. But when Mrs Chambers catches Terry at the house, news of what is happening soon filters through to an unhappy Thelma.

When she returns and finds the house looking shipshape and lots of jobs completed, she wonders whether she's been harsh on Terry – that's until Bob falls through the ceiling, dropping the sitting-room light on her head.

20. IN HARM'S WAY

Original transmission: Tues. 26/2/74, BBC1, 8.30p.m.
First repeat: Mon. 5/5/75, BBC1, 7.40p.m.
(Original viewing figures = 9.1 million)

CAST:

Thelma	Brigit Forsyth
Wendy	Elizabeth Lax
Miss Dixon	Claire Nielson
Sister Kennedy	Pamela Duncan
Vic	Alan Hockey
Frank	Louis Mahoney
Old Lady	Hilda Barry
Workman	James Garbutt

Bob is in plaster again, this time nursing damaged ligaments after crashing through the ceiling. He feels Bob is the source of all his troubles, and tells him so.

Terry pops in to see Miss Dixon at the benefits office and receives bad news: due to a string of broken interviews and unwillingness to take jobs, his money will be stopped unless he bucks up his ideas. So he takes a temporary job as a hospital porter.

When Bob arrives to have an X-ray, Terry is given the job of transporting him in a wheelchair to the appropriate department. Not wanting Bob to see him, he dons a mask and speeds along the corridors like a mad man, only to lose control and see Bob go crashing into a tea trolley.

21. AFFAIRS AND RELATIONS

Original transmission: Tues. 5/3/74, BBC1, 8.30p.m.
First repeat: Mon. 12/5/75, BBC1, 7.40p.m.
(Original viewing figures = 10.1 million)

CAST:

Thelma	Brigit Forsyth
George Chambers	Bill Owen
Valerie	Carole Ann Ford
Beryl Atkins	Ann Hamilton

Bob is away on a weekend's fishing trip with Terry, but no sooner has he arrived at the hotel than he's on the phone to Thelma, guilt-ridden that he's left her behind.

As the weekend progresses, so his guilt worsens and he spends more time in the phone box than on the river. Things get so bad Thelma joins her husband, only to find her father spending a dirty weekend at the same hotel with his secretary, after visiting a trade fair in Edinburgh.

To top it all, confusion involving Valerie, the sexy barmaid, and Beryl, the secretary, causes a row between Thelma and Bob.

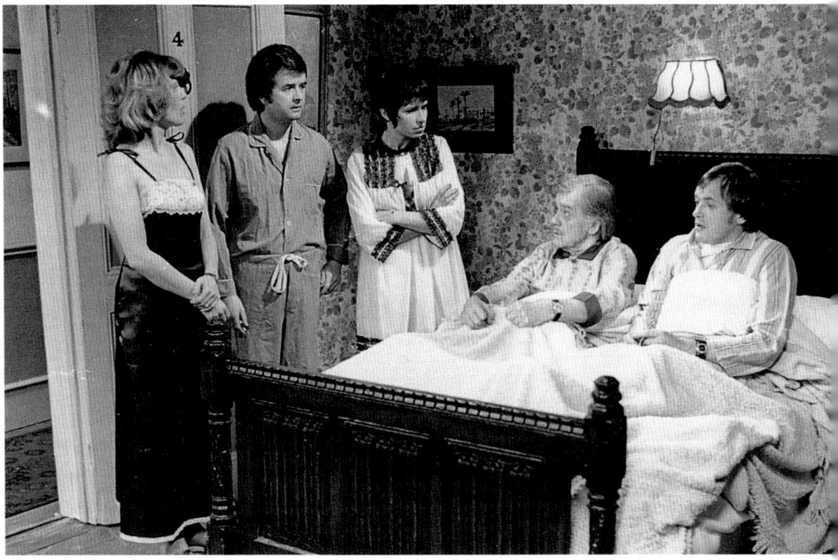

22. THE EXPERT

Original transmission: Tues. 12/3/74, BBC1, 8.30p.m.
First repeat: Mon. 19/5/75, BBC1, 6.55p.m.
(Original viewing figures = 12 million)

CAST:

Thelma . . . . Brigit Forsyth
Anthea . . . . Juliet Aykroyd
Mrs Greenlands . . . . Bay White
Neighbour . . . . Rose Power

As a result of her recent row with Bob, Thelma moves back to live with her mother. Initially, Bob discards Terry's offer of help, but eventually agrees that his suggestion to stay calm and do nothing is the best course of action. However, this strategy doesn't seem to be working when Thelma returns to the house to collect her clothes.

Underneath his cool exterior Bob is riddled with worry, and matters aren't helped when Norman – his teddy bear – smells of Thelma's cologne.

When he ends up locking the cleaning lady in the bedroom – mistaking her for Thelma – it's obvious a change of tack is required if he is going to patch up his marriage.

23. BETWEEN OURSELVES

Original transmission: Tues. 19/3/74, BBC1, 8.30p.m.
First repeat: Mon. 26/5/75, 6.30p.m.
(Original viewing figures = 11.8 million)

CAST:

Thelma . . . . Brigit Forsyth
Audrey . . . . Sheila Fearn
Anthea . . . . Juliet Aykroyd
Wendy . . . . Elizabeth Lax
Les, the Milkman . . . Anthony Haygarth
Vivienne . . . . Elizabeth Day
Moira . . . . Nova Llewellyn

Bob's off his food and not sleeping: Thelma leaving after accusing him of having an affair has hit hard. Terry moves in with Bob, prepared to stand by his friend during this emotional crisis – even though the promise of an electric blanket might have had something to do with it.

Bob spends hours mulling over what he'll say when Thelma finally comes home. When Terry visits the library and delivers a letter Bob has written to her, and she rips it up, it seems Bob will have to suffer more heartache before his marriage is back on track.

24. THE GO-BETWEEN

Original transmission: Tues. 26/3/74, BBC1, 8.30p.m.
First repeat: Mon. 2/6/75, BBC1, 7.40p.m.
(Original viewing figures = 11.9 million)

CAST:

Thelma . . . . Brigit Forsyth
Audrey . . . . Sheila Fearn

Terry is still living with Bob, but with fags stubbed out in the rubber plant flower pot, the house looking like a tip and Terry beginning to resemble an archetypal housewife, Bob gets fidgety, especially when his pal breaks the toaster trying to defrost chops in time for Bob's dinner.

Bob loves Thelma and wants her back. He blames Terry for his current crisis, believing he's had a destructive effect on their marriage. Terry has had enough when Bob accuses him of frittering away the housekeeping, and decides to leave his mate to run his own life.

But before the night is out, Terry plays Good Samaritan and visits Thelma. He talks her into getting back together with Bob, which is just as well because he's got his head in the oven!

25. CONDUCT UNBECOMING

Original transmission: Tues. 2/4/74, BBC1, 8.30p.m.
First repeat: Mon. 9/6/75, BBC1, 7.40p.m.
(Original viewing figures = 13.8 million)

CAST:

Thelma	**Brigit Forsyth**
Magistrate	**James Cossins**
Scaife	**Alun Armstrong**
Anthea	**Juliet Aykroyd**

Terry finds himself in front of the magistrates, charged with disorderly conduct, rowdyism and brawling at the Drift Inn. After being fined £25, which Bob pays, the Lads discuss their forthcoming night out with Thelma and Andrea, who also works at the library.

When his name appears in the paper, Terry is proud, until he notices they've spelt his name wrong. During the evening out, Bob and Thelma do their utmost to prevent Andrea knowing about the unsavoury incident, and how Terry is a 'common criminal'. Their scheme fails, but Andrea shocks everyone when she admits to having read the article in the local rag and liking a good 'punch-up'.

As far as Terry is concerned, the fight isn't over, and he intends finalizing the matter the following evening at The Ship. But a pint and a fag does wonders for peace and he calls a truce with Scaife, his opponent. Then Bob puts his foot in it.

26. THE SHAPE OF THINGS TO COME

Original transmission: Tues. 9/4/74, BBC1, 8.30p.m.
First repeat: Mon. 16/6/75, BBC1, 7.40p.m.
(Original viewing figures = 9.5 million)

CAST:

Audrey	**Sheila Fearn**
Mrs Collier	**Olive Milbourne**
Joe Hargreaves	**Jack Woolgar**
Mrs Hope	**Eve Pearce**
Nurse	**Rosalind Bailey**
Aunt Rose	**Olive Mercer**
Aunt Kitty	**Helena McCarthy**

Over a plate of greasy fish and chips at Terry's place, the Lads become nostalgic, remembering bygone days when they were carefree and regular visitors to the 'warm, sweaty cavern' known as The Roxy. It isn't long before Bob becomes woeful about how life is ebbing away.

Just as Bob starts blaming Terry for continuing to lead him astray, making him drink too much, eat too much, filling him up with carbohydrates, Mrs Collier and Audrey arrive with news that Great Uncle Jacob has died, aged 81. Since his wife, Marjorie, died, he's moved from one OAP's home to another, causing mayhem wherever he's gone. But Terry defends his uncle, classing him as a great character.

Mrs Collier has different views: she remembers him as a liar and a drifter who never did an honest day's work in his life; any money he did have was spent on booze or horses. He ruined his best friend's marriage as well as his own and was simply a cantankerous, bigoted old so and so.

Suddenly, Bob sees the shape of things to come. In his view, Mrs Collier's description of Uncle Jacob fits Terry exactly, and if he doesn't make a stand, his life will be ruined, too.

CHRISTMAS SPECIAL

27. CHRISTMAS CRACKERS

Original transmission: Tues. 24/12/74, BBC1, 7.45p.m.
First repeat: Thursday, 18/12/75, BBC1, 7.45p.m.
(Original viewing figures = 16.1 million)

CAST:

Thelma . . . . Brigit Forsyth
Sylvia Braithwaite . . . . . . Lilian Verner
Andrea. . . . . Joanna Ross
Police Constable . . . . John Crocker
Jack . . . . Norman Mitchell
Man in Pub . . . . John White
Woman in Pub. . . . . Betty Bowden

Thelma is determined to organize Christmas well in advance so she can enjoy the festive period. Terry, meanwhile, passes his car test and finally leaves the dole queue, driving fork-lift trucks and taxis.

On Christmas Eve, Bob and Thelma – dressed as Captain Hook and Peter Pan – are off to a fancy dress party, and their taxi driver for the night is none other than Terry. When the party turns out to be a wife-swapping night, and Bob sneaks off with Sylvia Braithwaite – one of his exes – Thelma asks Terry, who's invited in to the party, to take her home. Trouble is, Captain Hook has pinched his cab!

FAMILIAR FACES

Whatever Happened to The Likely Lads?

JULIET AYKROYD
(b. India)
Role: Anthea
(episodes 22, 23 & 25)

Anthea was seen in three episodes of the second series. She worked with Thelma in the library, and was Juliet Aykroyd's first comedy role on TV. 'Theatre was my true love, and I'd been working in London's fringe theatres prior to playing Anthea,' she says. 'My TV debut was playing Derek Jacobi's girlfriend, but Anthea was early on in my career.'

Before moving to England in her late teens, Juliet had lived in India and Italy, where her father worked as a scientist.

With her heart set on a stage career, she gained valuable experience, which helped towards this goal, while she was studying English at university. After graduating she spent eight months in a publishing company before joining RADA, where she was spotted in a drama school production and invited to join Birmingham Rep upon leaving in 1969. Six months later her run of good fortune continued when she was accepted by the RSC. She stayed with the company three years, returning later on to teach.

On TV Juliet appeared in many small parts, including the role of an art student in *Open All Hours*. She also made several commercials, and worked on the stage whenever it was possible, her last job being at Newbury.

Juliet gave up acting to raise a family, and now concentrates on writing, specializing particularly in theatre plays.

CHRISTOPHER BIGGINS
(b. Oldham)
Role: Podge
(episodes 6 & 13 – when Podge was credited as an 'Usher')

Podge, originally played by Geoffrey Hughes in *The Likely Lads*, is an old friend of Bob and Terry. For Christopher, it was one of his first TV roles. 'I think I was offered the job because I was cheap!' he laughs. 'The first thing I ever did was play a thief in *Paul Temple*, but this was certainly early on. I enjoyed it enormously; Rodney and Jimmy were great, and Brigit Forsyth was especially nice, quite enchanting.'

When it came to portraying the character, Christopher decided to base it on his own personality. 'It was just an extension of me: bright and bubbly. When I watch the episodes now, they're terribly funny; it's nice getting the repeat fees but it wasn't any great role – it's not as if it was *Hamlet*.'

Christopher, who went on to play the character 'Lukewarm' for Clement and La Frenais in *Porridge*, has no doubts as to why *Whatever Happened to…?* was so successful.

'The two main characters were wonderful; they were like every man in the street, which meant everybody could identify with them and the things they did. The writing was wonderful: usually when you do a sitcom you spend the first two days rewriting everything, but that never happened. Reading the scripts during rehearsals was hysterical.'

Christopher, who's also a director, grew up in Salisbury and attended elocution lessons whilst at school. His teacher introduced him to the theatre, and he joined the local rep. Initially he intended staying two weeks but remained for two years, by which time he'd earned his Equity card. Wishing to receive formal training, Christopher attended Bristol Old Vic Theatre School before joining Derby Rep. Shortly after he made his West End debut in *The Owl and the Pussycat Went to Sea*, playing Head Jumbly.

Other TV credits include: Adam Painting in *Rentaghost*, Brian Reeves in the BBC sitcom, *Watch this Space*, Nero in *I Claudius*, a student in *Some Mothers Do 'Ave 'Em*, *Upstairs, Downstairs*, *Five's Company*, *Poldark*, *Jackanory*, *Kidnapped* and *Surprise, Surprise*.

He's also appeared in a handful of films, including *Eskimo Nell*, *The Rocky Horror Picture Show*, *Applause* and *The Tempest*, and remains busy in the theatre, recently appearing in *School for Scandal* and the musical, *Guys and Dolls*, playing Nathan Detroit.

JACQUIE-ANN CARR
(b. Birmingham)
Role: Brenda Boyle
(episodes 8 & 16)

Brenda Boyle, who is married to Alan, is a typical working-class girl until she adopts all the airs and graces of a middle-class snob, so it's no surprise when Terry brings her down a peg or two during a dinner party. Jacquie-Ann based the character on her own mother!

'When my mother actually saw the programme, she said: "No one talks like that." We had such a ball making the programme, and Dick and Ian were lovely to work with.'

Jacquie-Ann feels the vein of realism running through the show is an important factor in its continued success. 'The association of actually knowing someone like one of the characters makes it very funny; it's also cleverly written.'

Although born in Birmingham, Jacquie-Ann grew up in North Yorkshire, and always wanted to follow a career in entertainment. By the time she joined the Guildhall School of Music and Drama, she was a trained dancer. Upon graduating in 1966 she took up a position in rep at Leatherhead. During her first year as a professional actress she gained valuable experience in several strands of the profession, such as *Four People*, a TV series for ATV, lots of theatre and a film, *Privilege*.

In 1971, Jacquie-Ann – who has appeared in lots of musicals over the years – joined the original cast of the rock musical, *Godspell*. Two years later, while

MEMORABLE SCENES

EPISODE

Strangers on a Train

(Terry and Bob meet up, unexpectedly, on a train. Terry has just left the army, a period of life he regrets.)

TERRY: It's ironical that when this country goes through a social transformation I'm not here to see it. It's ironical that while everybody over here is having the best time they've ever had since the roaring Twenties, I'm stuck in a Nissen hut in BFPO14 – I missed it all. Swinging Britain was just hearsay to me: something I read about in the overseas edition of the *Daily Mail*. Death of censorship, a new morality, *Oh! Calcutta!*, topless waitresses in see-through knickers.

BOB: They never caught on – uh, topless waitresses.

TERRY: Well that's a crumb of comfort. At least I'd like to have been here to see them not catching on. Permissive society, I missed it all. I get back and it's Malcolm Muggeridge, Lord Longford and the Jesus revolution.

BOB: Well it wasn't all that much.

TERRY: It has to be better than Monchengladbach.

BOB: Where?

TERRY: Exactly! Monchengladbach.

BOB: Where's that?

TERRY: Monchengladbach is the West Hartlepool of West Germany – you get the picture?

on Broadway, she was offered a part in the stage show *Grease*, opposite Richard Gere, and came back to London with the production. Then she returned to the small screen.

'A huge love of mine is sitcoms, and I was given the part of the lady doctor in the *Doctor* series,' says Jacquie-Ann, who played Kate Wright in two series of *Doctor on the Go* in the mid-Seventies. 'I was in loads of sitcoms: *Sink or Swim*, *In Loving Memory*, *The Dick Emery Show* – lots of one-offs in various shows, and I loved it.' But when it comes to picking a favourite, Jacquie-Ann has no doubts. 'It's *Whatever Happened to The Likely Lads?* Obviously I enjoyed the *Doctor* series because I carried the character all the way through, but appearing as Brenda was special.'

Jacquie-Ann's TV career hasn't been limited to comedies: she's also appeared in numerous dramas, such as *Dempsey and Makepeace*, but it's for her sitcom and theatre work – including a spell with the Welsh National Theatre – that she's best remembered.

Nowadays she leads a busy life teaching business people presentation skills, as well as working in drama schools, teaching singing, voice projection and doing plenty of voice-overs. A talented singer, Jacquie-Ann recently spent a year as the cabaret star on a luxury cruise liner, and three years in Menorca.

NOEL DYSON
(b. Newton Heath)
Role: Mrs Chambers
(episode 15)

When ill-health forced Joan Hickson to give up playing Mrs Chambers (Thelma's mother), Noel was recruited for episode 15. Well-known for her roles as 'Nanny' in *Father, Dear Father* and Aileen Potter in the BBC sitcom, *Potter*, Noel trained as a secretary upon leaving school. But realizing her interests lay elsewhere, she quit to attend RADA in 1936, despite strong opposition from her father.

Her first professional engagement was at Frinton-on-Sea in a pre-war farce, before securing other small jobs around the country; but a thyroid problem forced her to retire from the business for four years, during which time she served as a nurse at a RAF convalescent home in Torquay.

During the war she worked for ENSA, performing around the country at hospitals and nursing homes. She continued working for the association after the war, embarking on a tour of European cities. When she returned to home soil she appeared at Oxford Rep, before further appearances in the West End and moving into films and TV.

But it wasn't until her 1960 appearance in *Coronation Street* as Ida, Ken Barlow's mother, who was later knocked down by a bus, that she became well known to TV audiences. Other small screen credits included *Bergerac*, *Executive Stress*, *May to December*, *Prime Suspect*, *Never the Twain*, *Z Cars*, *Casualty*, *The Randall Touch*, *The Ronnie Barker Yearbook* and *Joan and Leslie*. She also spent six months Down Under in the late 1970s, where she recorded an Australian version of *Father, Dear Father*.

Noel made over 20 films, including: *Carry On Constable*, *Press for Time*, *Please Turn Over* and *Three Crooked Men*.

She died of liver cancer in 1995, at the age of 79.

DONALD GEE
(b. Manchester)
Role: Godfrey
(episode 17 of *The Likely Lads*);
Vicar in *Whatever Happened To...?*
(episodes 3, 7 & 9)

Donald will never forget playing a shop steward in *The Likely Lads* episode, 'The Razor's Edge', because his son was born on the day when he was recording! 'It was certainly a fraught day, I was dashing about everywhere,' he says. 'I remember having an argument with the man running parking control at Television Centre. I was late for rehearsals and he told me I couldn't park in the space I'd chosen, so I said to him abruptly: "I'll tell you what, I'll go back to the

MEMORABLE SCENES

EPISODE

Home is the Hero

(Bob thinks Terry dislikes Thelma, and confronts him.)

BOB: You've never liked Thelma, have you?

TERRY: It's the other way around, mate...

BOB: No, no, you've always resented her...oh God, I can just see my life stretching ahead of me: my marriage is going to be like a tennis match with you and Thelma serving for advantages over each other. I'll just be the ball that's bashed from one to the other, trying to love all. I might as well make plans for the divorce now. No point in wasting time; mental cruelty I suppose you'd come under.

TERRY: Well it's certainly not going to be adultery.

hospital and you can call me when you need me!"' Finally, the car park attendant relented.

Donald, who'd already worked with Bolam in a play at Hammersmith, admits it was difficult keeping his mind on the acting. When his wife and newly-born son came out of hospital, a Rolls Royce was waiting for them. 'She was looking for our Morris 1000 Convertible,' says Donald. 'I hired a chauffeur-driven white Roller, thanks to some of the money from the show.'

During *Whatever Happened to The Likely Lads?* Donald was seen a little more regularly, playing a vicar, a role he enjoyed. 'I was a straight actor who could do comedy, so it was nice being asked back. It was a funny series, and the vicar was a nice character to play.' So authentic was his acting, it was suggested he became a man of the cloth! 'We were filming outside this church, and the incumbent vicar came up to me and said: "You do this very well; you ought to take over the job." The show was great fun and I enjoyed working with everyone, particularly Brigit, she really was excellent.'

After leaving school, Donald served an apprenticeship in electrical engineering for several years, before joining the army for six months. When he returned to civvy street prematurely – upon discovering he had flat feet – he went back to the factory and joined a local amateur dramatics society, the Experimental Theatre Group in Manchester. 'We did some wonderful plays and it was an exciting time.'

Whilst attending voice lessons at the Northern School of Music, his tutor suggested he join the Bristol Old Vic School and become an actor. He won a scholarship in 1961, which meant his fees were paid and he was given £5 weekly to live on.

After graduating, his first job was at Manchester's Library Theatre, followed shortly by his TV debut driving a dumper truck. Next he was playing a policeman in *Z Cars*, but his favourite job will always be *On the Move*, with Bob Hoskins.

Donald continues to work in the theatre and TV, his last role being a roué in Lynda La Plante's *Trial and Retribution*. He has also recently appeared in *Burning Light*, a film recorded in France.

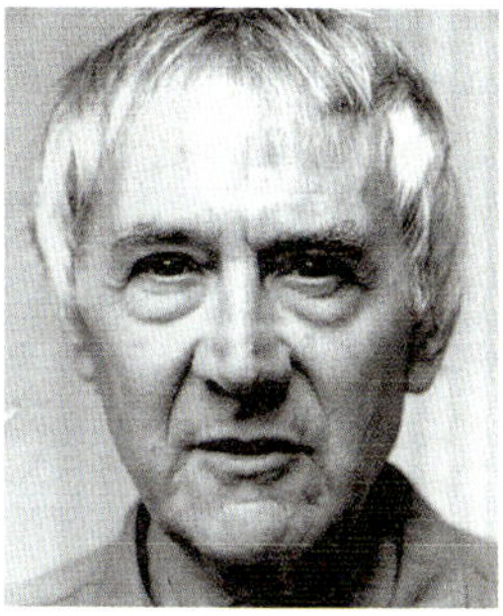

ROBERT GILLESPIE
(b. Lille, France)
Role: Police Sergeant
(episodes 9, 12 & 17)

Robert has played lots of policemen in his career, starting off as a Moroccan bobby in *Hugh and I Spy*. Although he feels his lack of height prevents him playing a policeman on stage, it's not a problem on TV. 'It doesn't matter on television because you're usually shoved behind a desk. But I ended up being hired because I got the laughs, and it didn't matter what I looked like.'

When he read the script, Robert knew the part was going to be rewarding. 'The character had a very downbeat, flat, cynical attitude, which comically, I thought, was very tricky and daring, largely because it's non-animated and reactive.

'Of course, the Lads were doing all the work, but between us it was such a marvellous example of the balance required in comedy. They were the active part of the combination and I was the passive, but we needed each other. It was terrific.'

It wasn't long before Robert found himself being asked to exercise his skills playing similar characters in other productions. 'Sometimes the scripts weren't good enough, which caused a few problems. But appearing in Dick and Ian's show was wonderful. Their writing was exceptional – in fact, it was a period of exceptional comedy.'

Robert spent his early years in Nantes, until his parents moved to Manchester. He eventually began performing as a semi-professional at the city's Library Theatre, before joining RADA. After graduating he worked at the Old Vic until he was offered the role of Matthew in the TV production of *Jesus of Nazareth.*

Although Robert is normally cast in comedy roles, such as the gas man in *Rising Damp*, five series of *Keep It in the Family*, *The Fall and Rise of Reginald Perrin*, *Robin's Nest*, *Butterflies*, *George and Mildred* and *Dad's Army*, he's appeared in numerous dramas, including: *Maigret*, *Crane*, *New Scotland Yard*, *The Sweeney*, *Van Der Valk*, *The Professionals* and *Secret Army*.

Robert, who also writes and directs, has made a handful of films, and has appeared regularly on stage, including two years with the RSC.

MEMORABLE SCENES

EPISODE

Guess who's Coming to Dinner

(Bob invites Terry along to a dinner party being held by his work colleague, Alan, and his snooty wife, Brenda. He has little in common with the couple. Alan enquires about his interests.)

TERRY: Oh, I've got a wide range of leisure activities.

BOB: *(sniggering)* He does jigsaws.

TERRY: I do hundreds of things. That's one thing I got out of the army; I've done more sports in the last five years than you've ever heard of: football, cricket, tennis, swimming...pole-vaulting.

BOB: You never done any pole-vaulting.

TERRY: Yes, I have. We had this Polish fella in our hut and we used to tie him to the bed and vault over him!

JOAN HICKSON
(b. Northampton)
Role: Mrs Chambers
(episodes 11 & 13)

Joan Hickson's face popped up in so many British post-war movies that it seemed a film wasn't made without her presence. But for many people she'll always be remembered for her portrayal of Agatha Christie's detective, Miss Marple, whom she played for eight years.

Joan, who was the uppish Mrs Chambers, Thelma's mother, for two episodes before ill health forced her retirement from the show, wanted to act from childhood. During the Great War she sang for wounded soldiers at home, while her mother played the piano. Joan joined RADA aged 19.

She made her first appearance on the London stage in *The Tragic Muse*, followed by two years in numerous West End comedies and three seasons of Oxford rep. By the mid-1930s, she was appearing in movies, early credits including *Widows Might*, *Love from a Stranger*, *Freedom Radio*, *This Was a Woman* and *The Guinea Pig*.

During a career spanning nearly six decades, Joan notched up over 100 film appearances. Other notable credits include *Carry On Constable*, *Seven Days to Noon*, *Doctor in the House*, *The Man Who Never Was*, *Angels One Five*, *Murder She Said* and *Clockwise*.

On TV, she appeared as Mrs Pugsley in BBC's sitcom, *Bachelor Father*, ITV's *Confidentially*, Mrs Morrow in *Good Girl*, *Mincemeat*, Mrs Pearce in the sitcom *Our Man at St. Mark's*, *Sinister Street*, *A Policeman's Lot*, *A Ferry Ride Away* and Lady Harriet in Granada's *Poor Little Rich Girls*.

Joan worked until her death in 1998, aged 92.

ELIZABETH LAX
(b. Oldham)
Role: Wendy, Bob's secretary, (episodes 4, 16, 20 & 23)

Elizabeth Lax – who died of a heart attack in 1996, aged 46 – didn't think she'd make it to her audition at Television Centre. 'She got lost in the BBC building, so when she finally arrived at the audition, she was in a bit of a state,' explains her widower, Chris Buckley. 'Because she didn't have time to get nervous, she came across as very natural, which she felt helped her get the job.'

While her parents worked for the Post Office, Elizabeth harboured dreams of being a dancer or actress, and from an early age was involved in amateur dramatics. After leaving grammar school she wanted to pursue her dream, but her father insisted that she must have something to fall back on if her acting career didn't work out, so she joined a local engineering company.

Elizabeth hated the job and swiftly left. Through her training at a local dancing school, she was given the opportunity in the late 1960s to appear in panto with performers like Harry Worth in Bradford, Sheffield and other venues. At the same time she worked part-time at Oldham's Coliseum as an ASM. By the time she was 18 she had earned her Equity card and was performing with the Black and White Minstrels on stage and TV.

'She worked with the Minstrels in the early Seventies, after which she started getting more opportunities,' says Chris. Those opportunities were roles like Carol Webb in *Coronation Street* in 1972, a pilot by Brian Finch titled *A Week on an Island*, which was recorded in Majorca, James Ellis' girlfriend in *Z Cars* and *The Liver Birds*. Elizabeth also appeared in La Frenais' production of *Billy Liar*, playing Billy's girlfriend, but, sadly, didn't continue the role when the show entered the West End.

A couple of years later she suffered a feeling of déjà vu when she completed the provincial tour of *My Fair Lady* with Anna Neagle and Tony Britton, only to be dropped when the show moved on to the West End.

Elizabeth's first love was always dancing, and she began working as a choreographer for a company staging shows around the country and on cruises. In the 1980s her career declined, and her last professional job was in panto at Sunderland's Empire Theatre in 1985, playing the Good Fairy in *Sleeping Beauty*. The following year she gave up the business to raise a family.

NORMAN MITCHELL
(b, Sheffield)
Role: Jack, the pub manager of the Black Horse (episodes 5, 6, 15, 17 & 27)

Veteran actor and scriptwriter Norman Mitchell, who's now 80, has built a career out of small parts in film, TV and theatre. He particularly enjoyed being in charge at the Black Horse, a pub regularly frequented by the Lads. 'I knew James Bolam well, and had worked for Jimmy Gilbert and Bernard Thompson quite a lot, so it was a nice part to play.'

The pub became an important element in the series, a focal point for Bob and Terry. Norman wasn't unfamiliar with the role of barman. 'I've played a lot of landlords during my career, including one in *Potter*. I don't know why, it's not as if I've ever been a landlord; but I am a big, fat bloke and I suppose they thought landlords were like that,' laughs Norman, who couldn't appear in *The Likely Lads*' movie.

Norman studied medicine at Sheffield University for three years before embarking upon an acting career at the local rep. Other than a six-year spell in the Royal Army Medical Corps during World War Two, he has led a busy career, and since his screen debut in the 1950s, has clocked up over 2,000 TV credits, including *Crossroads*, *All Creatures Great and Small*, *Yes, Minister*, *Beryl's Lot*, *One by One*, *You Rang*

M'Lord? and *Worzel Gummidge*, as well as over 100 films, such as *Barry Lyndon*, *Revenge of the Pink Panther*, *A Night to Remember*, *Invasion*, *Oliver!*, *Mess Mates*, *Carry On Spying*, *Carry On Cabby*, *Carry On Cleo*, *Carry On Screaming*, *Legend of the Werewolf* and *Goodbye Mr. Chips*.

His numerous stage appearances have included Anthony Quayle's production of *The Clandestine Marriage* in the West End, *A View from the Bridge*, *The Visit* and *Shadow of Heroes*. He was also a member of the RSC for three years, touring Australia.

Norman continues to work, and has just finished a film, *The Lighthouse*, in which he plays Brownlow, a lighthouse keeper. 'I also did a voice-over for an advert the other day. I have to keep working because I haven't been in the big earning class; I did get £4,000 a week when I was in a production of *William Tell* in France during the late 1980s, but that's the best I ever did.'

BILL OWEN
(b. London)
Role: George Chambers (episodes 11, 13, 14 & 21)

For many people, Bill Owen is best remembered as Compo, the dishevelled OAP in *Last of the Summer Wine*, but he was well cast as Thelma's father, whose hard work in establishing his business has led to a more affluent style of living. Bill was already a fan of the sitcom when he joined the show. 'I liked it very much, particularly because of the relationships. Its success depended so much on the artistry as well as the writing, and I think Jimmy and Rodney got it off to a tee. I enjoyed being in it very much.

'When you're making guest appearances in a show, especially if it's an established show, you don't always get to know the regulars, and sometimes it's not a pleasant experience. But with *Whatever Happened to The Likely Lads?* it was never like that and one was always made welcome.'

Bill, who wrote and directed for the theatre, received no academic training before going straight into rep as a teenager. He spent over seven decades in the profession, covering all strands of the business, including songwriting.

He began his career as a holiday camp entertainer, but after World War Two started acting in films, frequently in cockney roles. His film credits include *Perfect Strangers*, *The Way to the Stars*, *Daybreak*, *Easy Money*, *Trottie True*, *The Square Ring*, *The Ship that Died of Shame*, *Carry On Sergeant*, *Carry On Nurse*, *Carry On Regardless*, *The Comeback* and *Davy*. On TV he's appeared in *Three Piece Suite*, *The Challengers*, *Coppers End* as Sgt. Short for ATV, *Treasure Island*, *Brideshead Revisited*, *Tales of the Unexpected* and many other programmes. Bill died of cancer in 1999, aged 85.

LORNA WILDE
(b. Maesteg)
Role: Barmaid (episodes 5, 7 & 11); Gloria, the same character (episodes 16 & 18)

Lorna Wilde very nearly missed out on playing Gloria, the barmaid who pulls the pints at the Black Horse. 'Jimmy Gilbert knew my work because he was responsible for giving me my TV break,' says Lorna. 'When he phoned my agent and asked if I was available to do the part, my agent said the role was too small.' But as soon as Lorna found out, she reversed the decision.

The contribution Lorna made to the overall series was a little bigger than the recorded episodes suggest because lines were chopped. 'If we were overrunning, Dick and Ian would come up to me, and I knew immediately what they were going to tell me. They'd say: "We're sorry, darling, but we have to make some cuts." That was because my scenes were not an integral part of the plot. So a lot of banter with the Lads would end up with a red line running through it!' smiles Lorna. 'But I didn't mind because it was such a joy to work with them. Anyway, I wanted to do it as a thank you for Jimmy Gilbert because by then I was more interested in working behind the scenes.'

It was left to Lorna to decide how to play Gloria, which turned out to be her final TV part; the only brief given stated she was a 'busty, good-looking barmaid'. 'It didn't take much thinking about when deciding how to play the character.'

Lorna still enjoys watching the series. 'I think it's great. It stands the test of time because the scripts and characters were excellent, but also it can be applied to society now: we still have the same sort of problems and resolve them in very much the same way. It was witty and everyone gelled together well.'

Originally Lorna had ambitions of becoming a ballet dancer, and attended classes at Bridgend before having to give it up when a joint problem developed in her foot.

After leaving school she attended Cardiff's College of Music and Drama. But due to lack of funds, she never graduated, moving to London instead to establish her acting career via the Actors' Workshop and modelling Marks and Spencer underwear and swimsuits. Her first TV role was a walk-on in a show with Jimmy Edwards.

This quickly led to parts in films and TV, such as *The Heroes of Telemark* and *The Comedy Man*, before moving on to leading roles in *Under Milk Wood*, *The Canterbury Tales* and *The Saint*, with Roger Moore. She was also seen in the Norman Wisdom film, *A Stitch in Time*, playing a girl in the dentist's chair.

Her first starring role in a feature movie, *The Body Stealers*, with George Sanders and Maurice Evans, didn't quite turn out as Lorna had hoped. 'The film turned out so bad that it didn't even make it into the top ten of worst pictures ever made,' admits Lorna, 'I was so disappointed I swore I was never going to make another film!'

Lorna began concentrating on her writing career, specializing in books about the war. She then wrote some comedy and a documentary, *Around the World in Seven Minutes and Four Times on Saturday*, a history of the golden age of cinema and newsreel, shown on BBC2 in 1986. 'I also co-wrote a comedy series for Frankie Howerd: it was his last ever sitcom for BBC, called *Then Churchill Said to Me*. It was scheduled to go out in 1982 but was withdrawn because of the Falklands' War.' But the show was finally transmitted. 'I re-edited it, got it down to half an hour, and it was shown during the week of UK Gold's launch in 1994.' She has been involved in several other shows, including *My Favourite Nosh*, a BBC series with Angela Rippon in 1996.

Now involved in production – she runs her own production company, Big Ben Entertainment Ltd., with a partner – she was partly responsible for *Best of British*, the archival programme narrated by Sir John Mills and Sir Anthony Quayle. 'I'm now a behind the scenes editor and writer, and must say I prefer it!'

MEMORABLE SCENES

EPISODE

I'll Never Forget Whatsername

(Terry's old 1967 diary reveals that on a coach trip to the Blackpool illuminations, which Bob missed due to an abscess, he's marked a girl with two stars. To Bob's horror, Miss Two Stars is Thelma. Bob turns to his own diary.)

BOB: *(reading from diary)* Just after that trip Terry came round wearing his new hipsters and a smug face; he knows something.

TERRY: It will never stand up in a court of law.

BOB: I shall never be able to get on a bus again.

TERRY: Oh, it's a bad thing that, shudders of doubt.

BOB: I think she could've told me, don't you? Some time after we were engaged she could've told me; or better still years ago, just after it happened, she could've told me. I would have understood. I would have been mature and forgiving, and adult about it. I would have gone round to your house, taken back your Christmas box, kicked your head in and all would have been forgiven.

TERRY: If only everyone could be that reasonable.

THE LIKELY LADS – THE MOVIE

CAST

Rodney Bewes	Bob
James Bolam	Terry
Brigit Forsyth	Thelma
Mary Tamm	Christina
Sheila Fearn	Audrey
Zena Walker	Laura
Anulka Dubinska	Dawn
Alun Armstrong	Milkman
Judy Buxton	Iris
Vicki Michelle	Glenys
Penny Irving	Sandy
Michelle Newell	Alice
Susan Tracy	Edith
Gordon Griffin	Cyril
Edward Wilson	Les
Roger Avon	Joe the Landlord
Ronald Lacey	Ernie
Elizabeth Lax	Bob's Secretary
Linda Robson	Marcia
Ian McDiarmid	Vicar
Eric Mason	Truck Driver
Hugh Turner	Mr. Chipchase
Christian Rodska	Pump Attendant
Eddie Silver	Fireman
Barbara Elliott and Stephanie Lawrence	Demonstrators
Bob Ritchie	Passer-by
Jim Rushton	Demolition Worker
Olga Anthony	Boutique Saleslady
Alan Smell	Taxi Driver

First showing on British TV: Sun. 8/6/80, 7.15 p.m. – 8.45 p.m. (Audience: 11.1 million)

PRODUCTION CREDITS

Conceived by Dick Clement and Ian La Frenais

Producer	Aida Young
Director	Michael Tuchner
Production Executive	Philip Collins
Director of Photography	Tony Imi
Art Director	Robert Jones
Editor	Ralph Sheldon
Production Supervisor	Christopher Sutton
Production Manager	Donald Toms
Assistant Director	Kip Gowans
Continuity	Renee Glynne
Camera Operator	Tony White
Sound Recordist	Kevin Sutton
Assistant Art Director	Tim Hutchinson
Dubbing Editor	Frank Goulding
Dubbing Mixer	Trevor Pyke
Costumes	Emma Porteous
Make-Up	Neville Smallwood
Hairdresser	Jan Dorman
Music	Mike Hugg

'Remember When' lyrics by Ian La Frenais, music by Mike Hugg. Made at EMI Elstree Studios, England and on location in Newcastle and Whitley Bay. An Anglo-EMI Production, distributed by EMI Film Distributors Ltd. Presented by Nat Cohen for EMI, 1976

Running Time: Approximately 86 minutes. Colour by Technicolor (Available on video)

The passage of time leaves the Lads in a melancholic mood, two helpless victims realizing their pasts are nothing more than fading memories. Life is slipping away fast, and when the Fat Ox – one of their favourite haunts – is razed to the ground in the name of modernisation, Bob and Terry use

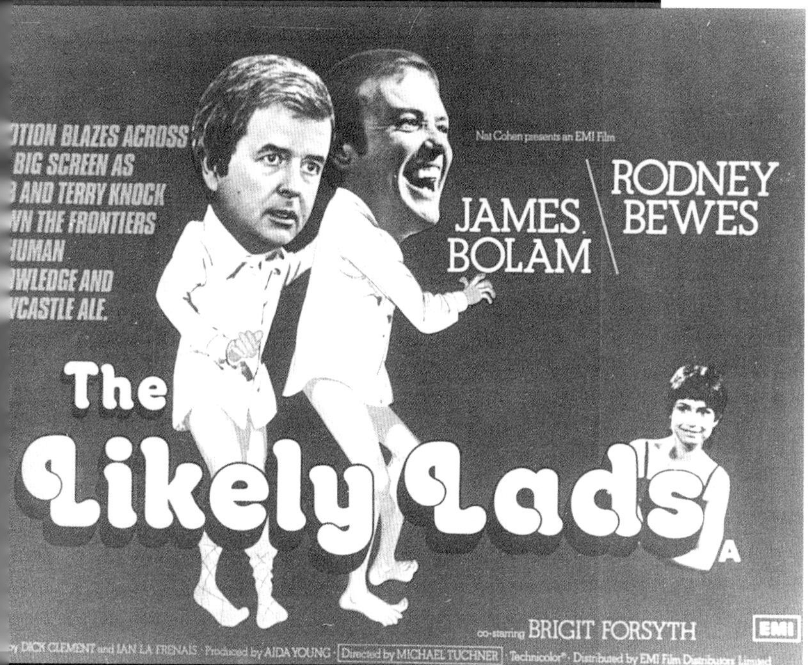

feeble excuses to skip work and down their final pint at the pub.

Thanks to his divorce, new flat and new job, Terry is more sanguine about the future, while Bob feels bogged down in life, summed up beautifully by his profound statement: 'In the chocolate box of life, the top layer's already gone, and someone's pinched the orange cream from the bottom!'

Straining under the rigours of marriage, he desperately misses the sexual freedom and sense of adventure enjoyed whilst single – pleasures which are being savoured, once again, by Terry, whose new lifestyle also forces the demise of the weekly boys' night out, depressing Bob further.

When Thelma suggests Terry and his new girlfriend, Christina, spend a weekend with her and Bob caravanning, Terry is convinced there is an ulterior motive for the invitation – namely that Thelma is trying to marry him off, and in the process rid Bob of his final link with a life involving Terry Collier.

As expected, the weekend is full of chaos and disappointments: Bob and Terry, who pop out for a quick drink before dinner, get lost returning to their caravan and end up with nothing but burnt offerings; everyone oversleeps, which means Christina misses the chance of visiting Holy Island, while an arduous hike to see Roman remains leaves them drenched when rain sets in.

Fed up with his new fitness-crazed girlfriend, Terry proudly proclaims that an ideal weekend consists of nothing but 'sport, sleep, slippers and sex'. So early next morning, with the girls still sleeping in the back, the Lads cunningly decide to head home. But before the day is out Terry and Bob manage to pick up two female hitch-hikers, lose their nightdress-clad partners at a set of traffic lights and career right out of control into the back of another caravan!

The rows that ensue result in Bob dossing down at Terry's flat, and before long his usual bouts of regrets and depression return. Taking a brief holiday together – a way of keeping Bob's mind off matrimonial affairs – the Lads end up staying with a randy housekeeper and her daughter.

Their evening escapades see them heading home trouserless, but when Thelma, who has magnanimously decided to forgive Bob for their previous quarrel, arrives at Terry's flat with Audrey to await the boys' return, she can't believe her eyes.

After being exposed to Bob's blues for too long, Terry begins realizing his life adds up to nothing. As a last ditch attempt to put some meaning and value into his existence, he joins the crew of a merchant ship, destination unknown.

But even before the boat has left port he foresees feelings of homesickness and seasickness, and jacks in his plans to sail the oceans. However, he fails to rescue Bob, who's en route to Bahrain!

When EMI approached Dick Clement and Ian La Frenais about making a movie of their TV hit, the writers had just moved to the States. 'It meant we ended up writing the script in America,' says Dick, who was disappointed he couldn't take a more active role. 'We weren't around during the filming, which was a pity; it's always better when you're more involved than we were because occasionally you can fine tune things. But it was fun to write.'

Jimmy Gilbert, who'd produced the first *Whatever Happened to…?* series, was asked to direct the movie, but turned down the offer.

'It was just bad timing,' he explains. 'I'd recently taken on a new job, as Head of Comedy at the BBC, and although they raised no objections, I realized I wouldn't be able to give either job 100 per cent.'

Given the job of directing the picture was Michael Tuchner, an experienced film and TV director. 'I'd done a couple of films for EMI – who were putting up the money – including *Villain* with Richard Burton, and it was during this time that I got to know Dick and Ian, who had rewritten the script,' he says. 'We became friends, and being persona grata as far as EMI were concerned, I was offered the chance to direct *The Likely Lads*.'

Transferring a successful sitcom into a hit film is no easy feat: the movie world is littered with failures, projects that failed to maintain the character, strength, hilarity and overall flavour of the small-screen original. Jimmy Gilbert believes *The Likely Lads* adaptation worked reasonably well, although he acknowledges the difficulties involved. 'Television adaptations are not entirely satisfactory,' he admits. 'Dick and Ian are absolute masters of construction, but making a 90-minute film out of a TV series was going to be very different.'

Director Michael Tuchner was well aware of the task he faced. 'A 90-minute production gobbles up ideas and materials, so extending a compact, polished half-hour script into a sustainable and funny film is difficult. What you're trying to do is take something that is an essay in weight and turn it into a novel.'

Another factor sent to try directors facing such a challenge is a tight budget. Michael experienced such financial restraints on this project. 'Money for a director translates into time, and because I've been around the block a few times, I know that if you're given the chance of seven weeks to shoot a film as opposed to six, it will always take seven.

'Time pressures can deny you the chance to take something away to the cutting room, to pause and make it even better. Instead, you find yourself accepting material that, ideally, you'd like to work on further, purely because of the tight schedule. But to be honest, every film is made on a tight budget: directors would always prefer more money and time to play around with.'

Inevitably, some scenes take time to get right, and Michael remembers one particular day when James Bolam got so cold it affected his lines. 'We were filming a scene where Terry is fishing off a pier. It was supposed to be summer, but we shot the scene in winter, and it was horribly cold. Yet the sky was blue, the sun shining, so on celluloid it looked like a perfectly warm, summer's day.

'James was so cold he was having trouble with a long speech. We did a take but he couldn't finish his words, so we gave him a hot cocoa and a duffle coat to help warm him up.

'After an unusually large number of takes, James was OK, but then to my horror I realized we'd have to do it again. Although about 50 people were standing around, including cameramen and continuity girls, no one saw he was still wearing his duffle coat!'

One aspect of making the film that Michael Tuchner particularly enjoyed was going on location. 'It's great fun. I'm from Manchester and love the North a lot. Over the years I've done plenty of work in the region; for a while I was viewed as a bit of a Northern specialist, probably because I was doing Brian Glover plays, and others such as *Sling Your Hook* and *Keep Your Eye on Albert*. My background is in documentaries, and I used to film a lot of them up in that area.

'I just love the Northern grit; the place is very atmospheric and strengthening. There's something about London actors going to the studios which isn't the same as when they're staying in some crummy hotel in Blackpool being reminded of their roots, which are often provincial. There is a process of osmosis whereby just being in this sort of location, with the people surrounding you every minute of the day, creeps into the film, giving it an unstuffy, unsnobby, folksy feel.'

Although all the main performers appeared in the film, one face nearly missing was Brigit Forsyth's, because she was busy appearing in the West End as Annie in Alan Ayckbourn's *The Norman Conquests*. 'Everyone kept telling me a film was being made about *The Likely Lads* and that I'd be in it,' she says, 'but I would reply: "Oh no, I probably won't." When I didn't hear anything I assumed they'd checked with my agent and I wasn't available. I felt a little sad but I thought I had moved on.'

Appearing in *The Norman Conquests* at The Globe theatre meant a heavy workload, with three different plays rotating each week, but it was a production that Brigit enjoyed.

With just a few weeks to go before the cameras starting filming in the North-East, Brigit's agent was finally contacted by the production team responsible for adapting the hit comedy series. 'It was rather embarrassing,' Brigit admits, 'but all I could do was thank them for asking.'

The thought of another actress stepping into Thelma's shoes was unthinkable. After frantic negotiations, Brigit was temporarily released for filming. 'I didn't particularly want to do the film because I felt Thelma was in the past, but no one believed me!'

Director Michael Tuchner understood. 'I loved her in the role of Thelma, and will always remember her in that way,' he says, 'but everybody, including myself, wants to be versatile and do lots of different jobs rather than be labelled for one character.'

Eventually Brigit agreed to make the film, once a few details had been finalized. 'Initially they were offering peanuts,' she says, 'so I was able to persuade them to pay more, as well as arranging a car to pick me up and take me back to the theatre. This was vital because without it, I would have been so tired I couldn't have done it.' An understudy stepped in while Brigit travelled North for a week's location work, but a hectic schedule during the period of studio recording saw her filming at Elstree during the day and appearing on stage in the evening!

This gruelling timetable lasted six tiring weeks, and Brigit readily admits it would be beyond her today. But looking back, she's pleased she agreed to appear in the film. 'I enjoyed it, and wouldn't have missed it for the world. I liked working for Michael Tuchner; he was wonderful and made a good job of the film.'

Brigit has two particular memories of making the movie: having to wear a wig and giggling a lot. 'I'd grown my hair for the part of Annie in *The Norman Conquests*, so when it came to being Thelma again, I needed a wig. Working with Mary Tamm, who played Terry's girlfriend, was fun, and we all had hysterics filming the scene where we're playing bridge inside the caravan. The temperature rose to about 120 degrees. We all felt we were going to melt, and suddenly became hysterical, I don't know why!'

The scene, which sees Terry pop outside the caravan to spend a penny, but in earshot of Bob, Thelma and Christina, is a favourite of Dick Clement. 'I was told this story while serving with the RAF, and it was enormously gratifying to finally discover the perfect place to use it in a script,' he laughs.

Among the other scenes there is one that sticks in many people's memories, and Brigit is still stopped in the street to be reminded of it. 'It's when Thelma wakes up in the caravan and steps out in her nightie outside a church, in front of the minister and his congregation. So many people have told me it's one of the funniest scenes they've ever seen.'

One advantage of making the film after the last episode of *Whatever Happened to The Likely Lads?* had been screened was that the actors knew their characters inside out. For Rodney Bewes this was a blessing. 'I didn't have to give a thought to how Bob would react, or say a line; I knew him so well.'

There's one moment that sticks in Rodney's mind when he thinks back to the making of the movie: the occasion when he was mistaken for a sales assistant. 'We were filming in a high street in Wallsend, near Newcastle, and I was using a shoe shop as a place to rest in between shots. When a huge delivery of shoes arrived, I helped the shop staff carry boxes into the shop. Then a little old lady asked if she could have a pair of slippers, so I ended up by serving her; it was very funny.'

The film was premiered in Newcastle, an occasion Brigit Forsyth remembers well. 'Michael Tuchner came up to me afterwards and asked what I thought. I told him I didn't like seeing myself, and he joked about actors all being the same, only interested in looking good. I felt so ashamed because he'd been talking about my performance.

'He was really pleased with what I'd done and thought I'd be as well, but all I could think about was this awful face blown up on the big screen; every time I came on I just winced and died, desperately trying to disappear into my chair! It was only later, when I could watch in a much more detached way, that I could relax and enjoy the film.'

Michael Tuchner enjoyed the premiere. 'It was a rip-roaring success; the Newcastle audience just loved the TV show. In fact, that particular audience should have travelled round the country with the film because they were real suckers for *The Likely Lads*, and saw it as their series. It was a wonderful place at which to open the film because everyone just laughed their heads off – I was very pleased.'

The local press was equally commendatory. Peter Mortimer wrote in the *Newcastle Journal*: 'What may, in concentrated episodes, and in the comfort of the living room, look like sparkling humour, mostly flounders in the more demanding venue of the cinema.' However, *The Likely Lads* was an exception. 'The North-East locations here are more accentuated...the material is all new, and the flair for situation humour well sustained.' Mortimer felt the film's plot was never far from the television formula. 'It's a friction which the authors exploit well.'

Although most of the national critics also lauded the movie, David Robinson, writing in *The Times*, reminded readers of the difficulties associated with adapting small screen successes for the movies. 'The big screen, extending the action and increasing the concentration, exposes the limitations of television series comedy, in which it is a basic requirement that characters should not develop, but be left suspended and crystallized.' He added that even television's best characters are 'of necessity like cut-out dolls, on whom each week's new adventures are amusingly hung like paper dresses.' Robinson thought that 'the

Most of the newspaper critics complimented the movie, and director Michael Tuchner feels much of the film's success was due to Clement and La Frenais' script writing.

dialogue...is still amusing and the Lads retain their charm even if the big screen reveals the actors' own maturity. But the ups and downs of marital and extra-marital adventures prove very thin, spun out to 90 minutes.'

Whatever the critics felt, Michael Tuchner certainly enjoyed making the film, and proudly admits that he 'laughed at the result, perhaps because I'm a sucker for my own material.' But he's the first to point out that the success was largely due to Clement and La Frenais' script. 'Dick and Ian's stuff reads well and is very funny, so I couldn't wait to get my hands on the script. Of course, there's always a difference between how a script reads on the page and how it plays; it's what I call the staying power of the idea. But, in my view, Dick and Ian's idea certainly had that.'

Although pleased with the end result, Ian La Frenais wasn't too sure about making a film when EMI first suggested the idea. 'Making films of television shows is very difficult,' he admits, 'but I think it turned out quite well. There are some nice moments in it, and we managed to get a bit serious as well.

The series had contained some flat, little scenes and sets, and the film allowed us the opportunity to open it up somewhat.'

Dick Clement, meanwhile, is fond of the movie. 'The location work gave us the chance to touch on the fact that the world was changing: buildings being knocked down, including the pub, were an example of these changing times,' he explains.

'One or two bits are a little creaky, but there are many lovely moments, too. On the whole I'm pleased with the result: I think it's got the essence of what the TV series was all about. And Michael Tuchner did a good job. It's always tough when you're inheriting something from somebody else – it's very hard to impose a completely fresh style.'

But Michael didn't feel the need to stamp his own style on the film. 'I didn't want to change it,' he says. 'It was all about taking some well-loved characters and putting them in a different context in terms of screen and dimension. And that was made easier because everyone was an accomplished actor and knew how to gear themselves for a different medium.

MICHAEL TUCHNER

(Director of *The Likely Lads* movie)

Born in Berlin in 1934, Michael was five when he came to England at the outbreak of the Second World War. After finishing his education at Manchester Grammar School and University College, London, he had made up his mind to work in the film industry.

But it was no easy task, and whilst he struggled to achieve his aim, he taught English and PE at Wolsey Grammar School, until joining the BBC in 1958, initially as an editor. His first taste of directing came with short documentaries for the *Tonight* series, of which he directed over 300 for the programme.

Tuchner moved on to full-length documentary-making, many with Alan Whicker, before getting involved in plays for TV, including *Summer Season*, *Sling Your Hook*, *The One and Only Phyllis Dixey* – for which he received a BAFTA nomination – and *Barmitzvah Boy*, which won him a BAFTA for Best Director in 1979.

By the 1970s, he was directing films, both for TV and the big screen, such as the 1971 feature film *Villain*, starring Richard Burton and Ian MacShane, followed a year later by EMI's *Fear Is The Key*, from the Alistair MacLean novel.

Since 1977, Michael Tuchner has been directing films all over the world, especially America, where his credits include *Haywire* for CBS TV, *Summer Of My German Soldier* for NBC, *Adam* for NBC TV, *At Mother's Request*, *Internal Affairs* and *Desperate For Love*.

'I enjoyed working with everyone involved,' says Michael, 'especially James, Rodney and Brigit. I think Thelma is a wonderful character, and I was very fond of Brigit and the way she played her part. They were all experts in their own characterizations. This meant I didn't have to do the hard direction of exploring a character with an actor. Overall it was a nice script with nice people, and it was an easy and enjoyable time.'

PRESS REVIEWS

Although the occasional reviewer wasn't enthused by the big screen adaptation of *The Likely Lads*, the majority heaped nothing but praise on the production, as the following sample shows.

'Director Michael Tuchner senses the need for episodic humour, and while it rarely sends us into paroxysms of laughter, neither does it have that self-conscious silliness which hallmarks so much recent British cinema humour.'
PETER MORTIMER, *NEWCASTLE JOURNAL* (9/4/76)

'Bewes and Bolam, aided by yet another brilliant script from Dick Clement and Ian La Frenais, are certain to win new friends. Marvellous fun.'
NEWS OF THE WORLD (18/4/76)

'It still retains the quality of living so well illustrated in the TV comedy series: the awful realization that in the end, you settle for what you are and what you've got, rather than strive for what you'd like to be and can't have. Bewes and Bolam act together like clockwork ...'
MARGARET HINXMAN, *DAILY MAIL* (17/4/76)

'*The Likely Lads* ...succeeds because the characters from the TV series are clearly defined and its script is written with wit and perception. Rodney Bewes and James Bolam play the two Newcastle chums with style, and the accidents that befall them...are nicely handled by director Michael Tuchner. Good support, too, from Brigit Forsyth as Bewes' wife and Mary Tamm as Bolam's girlfriend.'
KEN CHRISTIE, *DAILY EXPRESS* (15/4/76)

'The contrast of characters is amusing; and the supporting performances are good. The script, however,...is uneven – rich comedy here, sheer farce there, and mere nonsense somewhere else. The naturalistic lower-middle class setting is fine but it won't fit fantasy, and from time to time it seems as if the film, for want of stricter writing, splashes aimlessly about in both camps, as if the pressures of sustaining a series from week to week had caused the authors to slacken. Or is the fun simply funnier in short doses?'
ERIC SHORTER, *DAILY TELEGRAPH* (15/4/76)

'....this well-judged film adaptation.'
DAVID CASKIL, *SUNDAY TELEGRAPH* (18/4/76)

'Films based on TV series rarely transfer successfully to the big screen. *The Likely Lads* ...is an exception. Scriptwriters Clement and La Frenais have come up with a fresh crop of warmly-amusing situations for Bob and Terry...It has crisp dialogue and it's a treat for fans.'
DAILY MIRROR (15/4/76)

'Stretched to feature length and padded out Alfie-style with a series of abortive sexual encounters, the escapades lose their colour and individuality and end up just another pre-packed product on the assembly line of low-budget British comedy.'
NIGEL ANDREW, *FINANCIAL TIMES* (15/4/76)

THE RADIO VERSIONS

The Likely Lads and *Whatever Happened to The Likely Lads?*

Rodney Bewes and James Bolam were present throughout

Original script by Dick Clement and Ian La Frenais
Adapted for radio by James Bolam
Produced by John Browell
Pre-recorded at the Paris Studios, Lower Regent Street, London SW1

THE LIKELY LADS

SERIES ONE

1. WHERE HAVE ALL THE FLOWERS GONE?

Original transmission: Sun. 6/8/67, The Light Programme, 2p.m. (Audience = 5.3 million)
Repeated: Mon. 7/8/67, 8.15p.m. (Audience = 0.7 million)

CAST:
Audrey . . . . Sheila Fearn
Mrs Collier . . . . Olive Milbourne
Uncle Walter . . . . John Gazabon
Auntie Peggy . . . . Betty Hardy
Cyril . . . . Le Roy Lingwood
Elaine . . . . Carol Marsh
Beryl . . . . Rosalind Shanks

2. THE SUITOR

Original transmission: Sun. 13/8/67, The Light Programme, 2p.m. (Audience = 5.7 million)
Repeated: Mon. 14/8/67, 8.15p.m. (Audience = 0.6 million)

CAST:
Audrey . . . . Sheila Fearn
Mrs Collier . . . . Olive Milbourne
'The Suitor' . . . . George Layton

3. ROCKER

Original transmission: Sun. 20/8/67, The Light Programme, 2p.m. (Audience = 5.3 million)
Repeated: Mon. 21/8/67, 8.15p.m. (Audience = 0.8 million)

CAST:
Stacey . . . . Reginald Jessup
Nurse . . . . Cheryl Molineaux
Carol . . . . Rosalind Shanks

4. OLDER WOMEN ARE MORE EXPERIENCED

Original transmission: Sun. 27/8/67, The Light Programme, 2p.m. (Audience = 5.9 million)
Repeated: Mon. 28/8/67, 8.15p.m. (Audience = 0.6 million)

CAST:
Mrs Winsor . . . . Rhoda Lewis
Jack . . . . Donald McKillop
Cloughy . . . . Bartlett Mullins
Sheila and Elsie . . . . Madeleine Mills

5. BABY, IT'S COLD OUTSIDE

Original transmission: Sun. 3/9/67, The Light Programme, 2p.m. (Audience = 6.4 million)
Repeated: Mon. 4/9/67, 8.15p.m. (Audience = 0.9 million)

CAST:
Audrey Collier . . . . Sheila Fearn
Jack . . . . Donald McKillop
Margaret . . . . Dorothy White
Jane and Baby . . . . Shirley Jaffe
Rose . . . . Kate Story
June . . . . Janet Kelly

6. OUTWARD BOUND

Original transmission: Sun. 10/9/67, The Light Programme, 2p.m. (Audience = 6.7 million)
Repeated: Mon. 11/9/67, 8.15p.m. (Audience = 1 million)

CAST:
The Scoutmaster . . . . Peter Hawkins
The Postmistress . . . . Kathleen Helme
Jack . . . . Donald McKillop
Valerie . . . . Janet Kelly
Susan . . . . Kate Story
The Man . . . . David Brierley

7. THE TALK OF THE TOWN

Original transmission: Sun. 17/9/67, The Light Programme, 2p.m. (Audience = 6.8 million)
Repeated: Mon. 18/9/67, 8.15p.m. (Audience = 0.7 million)

CAST:
Jack . . . . Donald McKillop
Cloughy . . . . John Henderson
Audrey . . . . Sheila Fearn
Mrs Ferris . . . . Kathleen Helme
Elsie . . . . Madeleine Mills
Thelma . . . . Susan Jameson
Big Duggie . . . . Michael Kilgarrif
Blakey . . . . Douglas Hankin

8. ANCHORS AWEIGH

Original transmission: Sun. 24/9/67, The Light Programme, 2p.m. (Audience = 7.2 million)
Repeated: Mon. 25/9/67, 8.15p.m. (Audience = 0.8 million)

CAST:
Mum . . . . Julie May
Sally . . . . Sara Kestelman
Denise . . . . Madeleine Mills
Sam . . . . Wilfred Carter

THE LIKELY LADS

SERIES TWO

1. FRIENDS AND NEIGHBOURS

Original transmission: Sun. 19/5/68, Radio 2, 2.31p.m. (Audience = 2.4 million)

CAST:
Grandad . . . . Bert Palmer
Mrs Perrin . . . . Noel Dyson
Mr. Perrin . . . . Glenn Melvyn
Lorna Perrin . . . . Angela Lovelln

2. THE OTHER SIDE OF THE FENCE

Original transmission: Sun. 26/5/68, Radio 2, 2.31p.m. (Audience = 3 million)

CAST:
Jack . . . . Donald McKillop
Cloughy . . . . Bartlett Mullins
with . . . . Richard Moore, Michael Sheard
. . Eric Dodson, Anneke Wills, Didi Sullivan

3. ENTENTE CORDIALE

Original transmission: Sun. 2/6/68, Radio 2, 2.31p.m (Audience = 2.5 million)

CAST:
Audrey . . . . Sheila Fearn
Mrs Collier . . . . Olive Milbourne.
Jack . . . . Donald McKillop
Cloughy . . . . Erik Chitty
Louise and Waitress . . . . . . Anna Gilchrist
Colette . . . . Bettine Le Beau

4. DOUBLE DATE

Original transmission: Sun. 9/6/68, Radio 2, 2.31p.m. (Audience = 2.8 million)

CAST:

Audrey . . . . Sheila Fearn
Deirdre . . . . Dilys Watling
Pat . . . . Susan Jameson

5. LOVE AND MARRIAGE

Original transmission: Sun. 16/6/68, Radio 2, 2.31p.m. (Audience = 2.2 million)

CAST:

Jack . . . . Donald McKillop
Cloughy . . . . Bartlett Mullins
Duggie . . . . Derek Newark
Helen . . . . Helen Fraser
Archie . . . . Roger Avon
Podge . . . . Geoffrey Hughes
Mrs Foster . . . . Doris Rogers

6. BRIEF ENCOUNTER

Original transmission: Sun. 23/6/68, Radio 2, 2.31p.m. (Audience = 2.6 million)

CAST:

Ursula . . . . Isobel Black
Jack . . . . Donald McKillop
Cloughy . . . . Bartlett Mullins
All other male parts . . . . . Peter Hawkins
All other female parts . . . Jennifer Croxton

7. CHANCE OF A LIFETIME

Original transmission: Sun. 30/6/68, Radio 2, 2.31p.m. (Audience = 2.5 million)

CAST:

Audrey . . . . Sheila Fearn
Jeffcock . . . . Garfield Morgan
Ralph . . . . Barry Linehan
Jack . . . . Donald McKillop
Cloughy . . . . Bartlett Mullins
Cecile . . . . Veronica Lang
Blakey . . . . George Layton

8. GOODBYE TO ALL THAT

Original transmission: Sun. 7/7/68, Radio 2, 2.31p.m. (Audience = 2.1 million)

CAST:

Mrs Collier . . . . Olive Milbourne
Mrs Ferris . . . . Irene Richmond
Audrey . . . . Sheila Fearn
Jack and the Sergeant . . . Donald McKillop
Cloughy . . . . Bartlett Mullins
George, New Youth and Recruit . . . .
. . . . Melvyn Hayes

WHATEVER HAPPENED TO THE LIKELY LADS?

Original scripts written by Dick Clement and Ian La Frenais
Adapted for radio by Patrick Tilley (episodes 1 – 8),
John Browell (episodes 9 – 13)
Produced by John Browell
(Rodney Bewes and James Bolam appeared in every episode)

1. STRANGERS ON A TRAIN

Original transmission: Wed. 30/7/75, Radio 4, 6.15p.m. (Audience = 0.3 million)
Repeated: Fri. 1/8/75, Radio 4, 12.27p.m. (Audience = 0.5 million)

CAST:

Thelma Chambers . . . . Brigit Forsyth
Woman on Train and
Station Tannoy Voice . . . . Lois Daine
Steward . . . . Peter Whitman

2. HOME IS THE HERO

Original transmission: Wed. 6/8/75, Radio 4, 6.15p.m. (Audience = 0.8 million)
Repeated: Fri. 8/8/75, Radio 4, 12.27p.m. (Audience = 0.9 million)

CAST:

Thelma Chambers . . . . Brigit Forsyth
Audrey . . . . Sheila Fearn
Stan . . . . Peter Whitman

3. COLD FEET

Original transmission: Wed. 13/8/75, Radio 4, 6.15p.m. (Audience = 0.6 million)
Repeated: Fri. 15/8/75, Radio 4, 12.27p.m. (Audience = 0.6 million)

CAST:

Thelma . . . . Brigit Forsyth
Audrey . . . . Sheila Fearn
Vicar and Barman . . . . Michael Segal

4. MOVING ON

Original transmission: Wed. 20/8/75, Radio 4, 6.15p.m. (Audience = 0.8 million)
Repeated: Fri. 22/8/75, Radio 4, 12.27p.m. (Audience = 0.6 million)

CAST:

Thelma . . . . Brigit Forsyth
Audrey . . . . Sheila Fearn
Ernie . . . . Michael Segal
Hughie and House-owner . . . John Samson
Wendy . . . . Corinna Marlowe

5. I'LL NEVER FORGET WHATSHERNAME

Original transmission: Wed. 27/8/75, Radio 4, 6.15p.m. (Audience = 0.7 million)
Repeated: Fri. 29/8/75, Radio 4, 12.27p.m. (Audience = 0.7 million)

CAST:

Thelma . . . . Brigit Forsyth
Jackie Norris . . . . Lois Daine
Barmaid . . . . Lorna Wilde

6. BIRTHDAY BOY

Original transmission: Wed. 3/9/75, Radio 4, 6.15p.m. (Audience = 0.6 million)
Repeated: Fri. 5/9/75, Radio 4, 12.27p.m. (Audience = 0.7 million)

CAST:

Thelma . . . . Brigit Forsyth
Mrs Collier . . . . Olive Milbourne
Clare and Mary . . . . Elissa Derwent
Deborah and Janet . . . . Shirley Steedman
Colin . . . . Colin Jeavons
Podge . . . . Geoffrey Hughes
Wally . . . . Michael Ralph

7. NO HIDING PLACE

Original transmission: Wed. 10/9/75, Radio 4, 6.15p.m. (Audience = 0.5 million)
Repeated: Fri. 12/9/75, Radio 4, 12.27p.m. (Audience = 0.9 million)

CAST:

Audrey . . . . Sheila Fearn
Flint . . . . George Layton
Rita and Barmaid . . . . Jo Beadle
Garry . . . . Brian Godfrey
Vicar . . . . Donald Gee

8. GUESS WHO'S COMING TO DINNER?

Original transmission: Wed. 17/9/75, Radio 4, 6.15p.m. (Audience = 0.8 million)
Repeated: Fri. 19/9/75, Radio 4, 12.27p.m. (Audience = 0.8 million)

CAST:

Thelma . . . . Brigit Forsyth
Audrey . . . . Sheila Fearn
Mrs Collier . . . . Olive Milbourne
Alan Boyle . . . . Julian Holloway
Brenda Boyle . . . . Gretta Gouriet

9. STORM IN A TEA-CHEST

Original transmission: Wed. 24/9/75, Radio 4, 6.15p.m. (Audience = 0.6 million)
Repeated: Fri. 26/9/75, Radio 4, 12.27p.m. (Audience = 0.7 million)

CAST:

Thelma . . . . Brigit Forsyth
Police Sergeant . . . . Robert Gillespie

10. THE OLD MAGIC

Original transmission: Wed. 1/10/75, Radio 4, 6.15p.m. (Audience = 1 million)
Repeated: Fri. 3/10/75, Radio 4, 12.27p.m. (Audience = 0.8 million)

CAST:

Susan Chambers . . . . Anita Carey
Mrs Ferris . . . . Barbara Ogilvie
Norma . . . . Brenda Cavendish
Waiter . . . . Anthony Smee

11. COUNTDOWN

Original transmission: Wed. 8/10/75, Radio 4, 6.15p.m. (Audience = 0.6 million)
Repeated: Fri. 10/10/75, Radio 4, 12.27p.m. (Audience = 0.8 million)

CAST:

Thelma . . . . Brigit Forsyth
Mrs Chambers . . . . Joan Hickson
Mr Chambers . . . . Bill Owen
Susan Chambers . . . . Anita Carey
Assistant . . . . Robin Parkinson

12. BOYS' NIGHT IN

Original transmission: Wed. 15/10/75, Radio 4, 6.15p.m. (Audience = 0.5 million)
Repeated: Fri. 17/10/75, Radio 4, 12.27p.m. (Audience = 0.7 million)

CAST:

with . . . . Michael Stainton

13. END OF AN ERA

Original transmission: Wed. 22/10/75, Radio 4, 6.15p.m. (Audience = 0.5 million)
Repeated: Fri. 24/10/75, Radio 4, 12.27p.m. (Audience = 0.6 million)

CAST:

Thelma . . . . Brigit Forsyth
Audrey . . . . Sheila Fearn
Mrs Chambers . . . . Joan Hickson
Susan and Stewardess . . . . . . Anita Carey
Mrs Ferris . . . . Barbara Ogilvie
Aunt Beatie . . . . Daphne Heard

MEMORIES...

Actress Sheila Fearn had a good time recording the radio series. 'It was great fun, and very easy to do. One major advantage was not having to worry about how you looked. It didn't matter about hitting the mark for the cameramen, lighting, props or costumes. You just stood up in front of the microphone and read your scripts. It was good fun and the audience seemed to enjoy it as much as we did.'

After recording all the episodes for TV, Rodney Bewes went to the Paris Studios in Piccadilly thinking the radio shows would be 'a piece of cake'. But he was in for a shock. 'I felt I was smart enough by the time we did the shows on radio,' says Rodney. 'I remember not giving the matter as much thought as I should have. But when I stood up at the microphone, heard the signature tune being played and the blue light coming on to signal everything was ready, I noticed with horror that my script was shaking, and I mean really shaking! I thought to myself: "Rodney, you haven't thought this through."'

Of course, he survived and enjoyed recording the radio episodes, with audience figures peaking at just over seven million. Rodney experienced the programme's popularity first-hand while travelling back from Cornwall. 'I pulled in at a service station and decided to stretch my legs. As soon as I got out of my car this chap in the vehicle next to me opened his window and said: "We've just been listening to you on the radio."'

TERRY'S DATES

RITA
From Barrow-in-Furness. Met her on the Spanish holiday. She's all right.
('ENTENTE CORDIALE')

DEIRDRE
A hairdresser. Met her in a coffee bar. Part of the double date (Bob went out with Pat). Expensive date, so just a one-off. I spent about three quid – forget that for a lark!
('DOUBLE DATE')

FREDA (Mrs Winsor)
New manageress at works' canteen. Married to a staff sgt. in the army. Visit her place one evening, but she's got me there under false pretences. Spent the whole evening mending her immersion heater – and ruined my suit in the process!
('OLDER WOMEN ARE MORE EXPERIENCED')

SALLY ANNE
A friend of Judith Francis, who Bob fancies. Works in Personnel at the factory. She was with Roger at the drawing office do, but ended up going with me for a drink at the Black Horse. What a snobby bunch those white-collar workers are.
('OTHER SIDE OF THE FENCE')

ROSE
A nurse. She's been working at the local hospital, in the radiography dept. Not a successful night: agreed to baby-sit for Jack and Margaret, which meant we could entertain the girls at his place, but it was a nightmare. They found out there was a baby in the place and spent the whole night cooing over it – what a washout that was.
('BABY, IT'S COLD OUTSIDE')

ANGELA
Saw her demonstrating 'Miracle Mop' and 'Wonder Foam' at the local dept. store. Pretty. Bought some liquid floor cleaner so I could chat her up. She's staying in a Newcastle hotel – with her friend, Lynn – while in the area. Borrowed £4 off my Dad. Got expensive tastes, too expensive for my liking. Wanted to eat at a posh roadhouse, has all the expensive drinks, even wanted to go to a gambling club, all-night bowling. Relieved when two guys took them off our hands!
('LAST OF THE BIG SPENDERS')

EVA
Foreign. Works for someone called Mrs Seaford, looking after the house, picking kids up from school. Just got chatting to her, nothing serious.
('FARAWAY PLACES')

VALERIE
Met her en-route to a place on the coast where all the beatniks go. She was on her first camping trip, so Bob and I pitched our tent and got talking. Nice girl.
('OUTWARD BOUND')

URSULA
What a fiasco – she ended up dating Bob and me. Enough said about her!
('BRIEF ENCOUNTER')

JANEY (Freeman)
An old flame. Married to someone called Hugh, as I found out at my surprise party, which Bob organized.
('BIRTHDAY BOY')

SUSAN (Chambers)
Thelma's younger sister. She lives in Canada, but has been over for Thelma and Bob's wedding. Engaged to Peter, an accountant, originally from Luton. Susan is a bit of a rebel: when she was 13 she went off with a boy who looked after the donkeys on Whitley Bay sands. Spend two weeks with her, we have some fun, but she decides to go back to Canada. Never mind.
('HEART TO HEART')

MADELYN
Usherette at the Odeon Cinema. Only wanted me for my money. Spent every penny I had on her, then when nothing left, she decided to give me the elbow. Rotten cow!
('THE ANT AND THE GRASSHOPPER')

LINDA
Didn't take long to get over Madelyn. Linda works in the betting office – very nice, too.
('THE ANT AND THE GRASSHOPPER')

PAMELA
Works in the sweet factory as a rockbreaker, breaking all the rock into foot-long lengths. Not a bad girl.
('SOME DAY WE'LL LAUGH ABOUT THIS')

ANTHEA
Works with Thelma. Anthea has a nice little body for a librarian. Her father's secretary of the bowling club, and she likes a good punch-up – that's what she told me.
('CONDUCT UNBECOMING')

PENNY
She's 27. Has taught me to drive, while her husband's on an oil tanker in the Persian Gulf.
(SPECIAL CHRISTMAS EPISODE)

BOB'S DATES

LOUISE (Rogers)
My holiday romance. Fell in love with her in Spain. Mind you, never spoke to her, so was surprised when she came to visit me and Terry and turned out to be Welsh.
('ENTENTE CORDIALE')

COLETTE
A French au pair. Couldn't believe my luck when she turned up with Louise. Spent a few evenings with her. Terry had played a dirty trick and given Louise his address, not mine, so he missed out on meeting Colette when they both visited the area, because he ended up with Louise.
('ENTENTE CORDIALE')

FELICITY
Unofficially engaged to her, but she heard about the holiday romance, and was annoyed I didn't send her a postcard, so she dumped me – another failed romance.
('DOUBLE DATE')

PAT
Met her in coffee bar, a friend of Deirdre's. Spent money I didn't have when I took her out on a double date. Dined at a Chinese restaurant and had a good time. Terry ended up with sausage, egg and chips, again!
('DOUBLE DATE')

SHEILA
A small blonde. Had the biggest shock of my life when I found out she was only 14 and was the canteen manageress' daughter.
('OLDER WOMEN ARE MORE EXPERIENCED')

JUDITH (Francis)
Mr Holgate's secretary in the drawing office. Fell in love with her the first day in the dept. (I've been seconded to the drawing office.) Seems to go around with Bill Nesbit, a company rep.
('OTHER SIDE OF THE FENCE')

JUNE
A nurse. Has been working in the radiography dept. at the local hospital. A one-night date. Says her sole hobby is men! As she's only around for a few days, I thought my luck was in, but nothing of the kind – the evening wasn't a success at all.
('BABY, IT'S COLD OUTSIDE')

HELEN
Apparently I was drunk at the Clarksons' engagement party, stood on the sideboard and announced my engagement to Helen, before putting a ring on her finger. Had a dreadful hangover and can't remember anything about it. To make matters worse, rumours are spreading that she's expecting! Luckily, it sorted itself out and everything's off – not that it was ever on!
('TALK OF THE TOWN')

LYNN
Friend of Angela. Both in-store demonstrators. Went out with them, but their tastes are too expensive for my liking. Apparently they only agreed to the date to ease the boredom of staying at a Newcastle hotel. Went off with two other blokes at the gambling club – good riddance to them.
('LAST OF THE BIG SPENDERS')

SUSAN
She was tasting her first experience of camping. Had a friend, Valerie, who Terry liked. Met her en route to the coast. Terry suddenly thinks there's nothing better than a little camping out in the fresh air.
('OUTWARD BOUND')

LORNA (Perrin)
A classy bird. She's seventeen. She lives next-door to Terry's auntie. Her father's got an administrative job at the Co-op.
('FRIENDS AND NEIGHBOURS')

URSULA
Very tall. Danced with her at local dance. From Blackpool. Down for a few days to visit her sick auntie. Planned to meet her tomorrow, but discovered Terry had danced with her as well, and had walked her home.
('BRIEF ENCOUNTER')

BRIONY
Had a frantic scene with Briony, who went to a convent school. Wouldn't think it because I hear she broke her father's heart by dancing topless at a Sunderland disco.
('THE GO-BETWEEN')

JACKIE (Norris)
I'd forgotten about Jackie, until she poured out memories of our quick snog behind the blacksmiths on a rainy day in Wooler. Thelma not amused! And I was setting up a date for Terry – I wish I'd never bothered.
('I'LL NEVER FORGET WHATSERNAME')

SYLVIA (Braithwaite)
Saw my old ex, Sylvia, at the fancy dress party – she was dressed as Joan of Arc. Got into hot water with Thelma when she found out that we were together.
(SPECIAL CHRISTMAS EDITION)

NAME-DROPPING

It's surprising the number of writers who experience difficulties dreaming up apposite names for characters, often resorting to a quick flick through the local telephone directory for inspiration. When it came to writing *The Likely Lads*, Dick Clement and Ian La Frenais encountered their fair share of headaches, particularly when deliberating over names for the Lads. 'Names are terribly important because you live with them for such a long time,' says Dick, who recalls the night they eventually decided on Bob and Terry. 'We'd been kicking the names around for a long time, and just decided to go with them.'

Ian admits that naming characters doesn't get easier with experience. 'We always take ages over names, perhaps days just to decide on one. We'd used Bob and Terry in the revue sketch written for the Ariel Players, because we were looking for straightforward blue-collar names. So it seemed sensible to use the same names again.'

Although Dick and Ian don't recall being influenced directly by anyone they knew, they both have memories of a Terry. While Ian La Frenais knew a Terry in his teens, who was a 'bit of a lad', Dick is still good friends with old school mate, Terry Taylor.

'He was one of my best friends, and we still keep in touch. That may have influenced the use of the Christian name, but I can't be sure.' But there's one name Dick particularly likes. 'Thelma Chambers is a wonderful name,' he says, 'it's very evocative.'

Ian, meanwhile, is keen on the surnames given to Bob and Terry, even though, again, he has no recollection of their derivation. 'Ferris and Collier were brilliant. Terry Collier reminds me of words one would associate with a tin mine,' he says.

While some incidental names used during the series were fictional, many were borrowed from real life, perhaps old friends of Dick's, or from Ian's days back in the North-East; some even originated from Rodney Bewes' past. Thanks to Terry and Bob's busy social life in *The Likely Lads*, and their time spent reflecting on a bygone era in *Whatever Happened To….?*, a myriad of names was required, often for characters who are never seen.

As Dick's former wife, Jenny Clement, points out, Dick and Ian would deliberately drop in names of mutual friends from time to time. But the characters were never like their true-life counterparts – except for the time Jenny's friend, Brenda, found her name being used, because there were certain similarities between her and the snobby on-screen character, Brenda Boyle, who hosts a dinner party in 'Guess Who's Coming To Dinner?'

'The character and her husband were based very loosely on friends who gave very "proper" dinner parties; Dick was poking gentle fun at them,' laughs Jenny, who shared a flat with **BRENDA PUNSHON**, on whose personality the character of Brenda Boyle was based.

'Brenda always did things properly – not that there's anything wrong with that. It's just that we lived very differently, much more casual.'

Brenda Punshon trained as a dancer and arranged several dance numbers for the Ariel Players' Christmas review, the production which saw the birth of Bob and Terry, in 'Double Date'. She joined the Beeb as a production secretary, and it was there that she met Dick and Jenny, both BBC employees at the time. Brenda admits that some of the similarities between the true-life and fictional Brenda were accurate. 'I also gave a lot of dinner parties, and people have been known to comment that I come across as snooty and rather aloof. So from that point of view, I suppose I bore some resemblance to the character in the episodes,' she says, smiling. Brenda didn't mind her name being adopted. 'I just fell about when I saw the episode,' she says. 'Most of Dick and Ian's friends found their names appearing in the show at some point, even my husband, Richard Punshon.'

Another friend of Jenny Clement whose name popped up was **BRIONY HOOD**.

MEMORABLE SCENES

EPISODE

The Go-Between

(Bob and Thelma still haven't made up after their row, and Bob's missing his wife.)

TERRY: I suppose it's times like these when you miss Thelma the most – when you come home for a casserole and a cuddle. I noticed that when I left my wife; meal times and bed times are the hardest part, aren't they?

BOB: Yes, the bed times are the worst. It seems such a big bed without Thelma; it's got a kind of slope to it, I've never noticed that before. I keep rolling to the edge whereas before I'd just roll into Thelma. I'm not sleeping.

Whilst Terry talks to Thelma in the episode 'The Go-Between', it's mentioned that Bob had a 'frantic scene' with Briony. Thelma says she remembers the girl because she broke her father's heart. After being educated at a convent school she ends up dancing topless at a Sunderland disco, flaunting herself in front of the town's teenagers. 'I've never danced topless on a table, so it's all invented!' stresses Briony, who got to know Dick and Jenny via friends. 'Dick would never tell you when he was going to drop your name into an episode. I attended the recording of the show and was half delighted and half-embarrassed when I heard my name – it was certainly a shock! Thank goodness they didn't make me stand up or something, that would have been awful. But I didn't mind; it was quite a laugh really.'

Other names were borrowed for more specific reasons, as Rodney Bewes explains: 'We had fun with the story-lines. There was a guy working at the BBC who was renowned for never buying a round of

Ian La Frenais (third from left) attends Brian Flint's (far left) wedding in 1964.

drinks in the bar at Television Centre. So when writing one of the episodes, Dick and Ian thought they'd have a bit of fun. During a pub scene, Terry comes over from the bar to Bob, who is sitting at a table with two girls, and says something like: "Quick, so-and-so is buying a round." So we all go up to the bar and order lots of drinks.'

After the recording, Rodney bumped into the man to whom the scene was dedicated. 'I couldn't believe it when he thanked us for the mention; he was thrilled to have been part of *The Likely Lads*, even though it was the most derogatory mention you could ever think of!'

Another name that cropped up on more than one occasion, particularly as Bob had been the president of her fan club at school, was **DEIRDRE BIRCHWOOD**. In the *Whatever Happened to…?* episode, 'Guess Who's Coming To Dinner?', Terry claims Bob was in love with her, describing her as 'a nice girl, a year ahead of us, well advanced for her age. Someone who could answer all the questions about sex that no one else would.' Deirdre was the gardener's daughter who, Terry recalls, 'smelt of weedkiller'.

'I knew a Deirdre Birchwood when I was a little boy; she lived near me,' says Rodney. 'It was such a good name I suggested to Dick and Ian that they use it in the scripts.' He couldn't believe his eyes when the real Deirdre Birchwood turned up when he was the subject of *This Is Your Life*. 'It was amazing because I hadn't seen her since I was about ten.'

In the early episode, 'Older Women Are More Experienced', Bob Ferris informs his workmates that a certain 'Morrie Hardaker' told him the new canteen manageress, who everyone is eyeing up, is divorced. Again, the character never appeared in the series, but the real **MAURICE HARDAKER** appreciates the difficulties of inventing names. 'I've tried doing it myself and it's difficult because the name never sounds convincing, but if you use someone else's name, it's real and you feel confident about it.'

Maurice, who now lives in France, didn't mind his name being used. After all, he'd been a friend of Ian's for years. 'They didn't ask me, but that never worried me. I watched the show and enjoyed it.'

Someone who enjoyed waiting to hear all the old names was **HORACE JEFFCOCK**, who grew up with Ian in the North-East. But unlike most of the other names used, Jeffcock was adopted for an actual character. In the 1965 episode, 'Chance of a Lifetime', the Lads are persuaded by Wally Ralph to emigrate to Australia, until a policeman called Jeffcock breaks the news that Ralph is in fact a fraud. 'I didn't mind my name being used, it was a good laugh.'

But Horace was used to it because Ian had used his name before, after which he decided to seek revenge! 'Ian used to make up these little advertising slogans and jingles for TV commercials,' says Horace. 'He did one for a beer company and used my name in the jingle. The character being depicted drinking the beer was an idiot, so as a joke I rang the product manager at the advertising agency. I pretended I was angry, telling him my name was being vilified and intended suing. The company took it seriously and contacted Ian to ask what he was doing using my name. We were always playing jokes on one another like that.'

VIN WELCH and his wife, **ANN**, were also victims of Ian and Dick's name-dropping. Vin grew up a few streets away from Ian in Whitley Bay. The two were teenage friends, spending time together in the school holidays, exploring the local area and playing tennis at a nearby park. Vin was extremely 'chuffed' having his name used in the show. 'I used to travel around the North-East on business, and everyone watched *The Likely Lads*. Many of my customers would say: "I heard you mentioned last week." It was a bit of a novelty.'

But not everyone found the use of names so amusing. **BRIAN FLINT** – who used to play rugby with Ian for Rockliff, a club in the North-East – wasn't

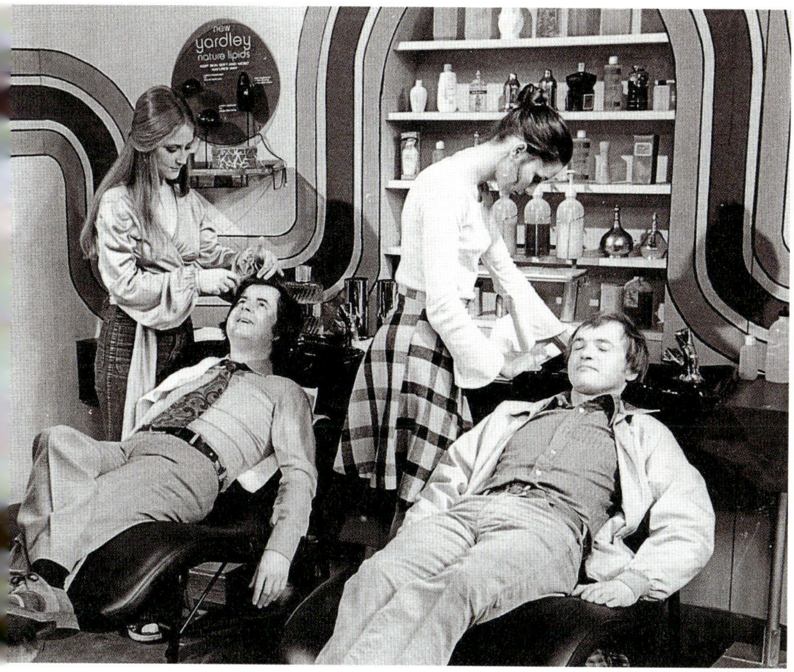

particularly happy when his name was given to actor Brian Glover's character in 'No Hiding Place'. Flint is the pain in the neck who tries his utmost to tell Bob and Terry the result of a soccer match, spoiling their evening's viewing of the match highlights. 'He used my name without asking, and for a character who wasn't very nice. What made it even worse was that my name was used in full. If he had asked me first, I would have said: "OK" – I'm not without a sense of humour.'

MEMORABLE SCENES

EPISODE

Chance of a Lifetime

(Terry and Bob are considering emigrating, and being stood up by their dates can only help them make up their minds.)

BOB: It might be this weather – the rain.

TERRY: What d'you mean – the rain? We're here.

BOB: Oh I know but I mean – they're women.

TERRY: So?

BOB: Well it's worse for them in the rain.

TERRY: What d'they do – shrink?

BOB: No, y'know what I mean – shoes and that.

TERRY: What d'you mean shoes?

BOB: *(vaguely)* Oh well y'know – they don't keep the rain out like ours do. And their hairstyles and that.

TERRY: Oh I see. So while they stay at home cleaning their shoes and keeping their hair dry, we have to borrow two quid to take them out, sit in damp clothes and spend the evening drinking flat beer at two and two a pint.

BOB: Yes it is a bit cloudy.

TERRY: Cloudy! It's like a sandstorm. Oh, I hate this place.

BOB: Well, we may as well shove off. Save the money. Pay day tomorrow.

An Appreciation of *The Likely Lads* by Stephen Wagg (Roehampton Institute)

Stephen Wagg teaches at Roehampton Institute in London and is editor of *Because I Tell a Joke or Two: Comedy, Politics and Social Difference* (Routledge, 1998)

WHAT BECAME OF THE PEOPLE WE USED TO BE?

Situation comedy is television's junk food: it's frequently consumed, but it rarely satisfies. Since the Second World War the best part of 700 sitcoms have been generated for British television. Among these there has, by common consent, been much dross (I recall a TV critic describing one sitcom of the 1970s as 'wince-inducing') while, every now and then, another gem has been placed in the national treasure house of Classic Sitcom. Here Tony Hancock fulminates alongside Harold and Albert Steptoe, Basil Fawlty, Edina and Patsy, Trotters Independent Traders and the bumbling, octogenarian soldiers of the classic *Dad's Army*.

Terry Collier, Bob Ferris and Thelma Chambers are, of course, indispensable members but, for me, even within this elite company something sets apart the characters of *The Likely Lads* (to which its cringe-making title is my only objection). In my judgement, when they returned for *Whatever Happened To The Likely Lads?* in 1973 and 1974 British sitcom reached its zenith and nothing approaching it was seen again until *I'm Alan Partridge* in 1997. Here are my reasons for saying so.

Firstly, there's the question of social class and, specifically, the working class, into which both Terry and Bob are born. In British suburban homes of the 1950s, like the one I grew up in, there wasn't much first hand experience of working-class people. They came to fix the sink, or to help your Mum round the house, or maybe they shouted something at you from 40 foot up some scaffolding, and that was about it.

Working-class people were similarly absent from the popular media. On the grainy black and white TV screens of the time they appeared mainly as Teddy Boys, questioned sternly by interviewers with plummy voices, or as women in pinnies and hair curlers, arms folded beneath large bosoms, chatting

across a fence. Of the real lives of working-class men and women little more was seen.

All this began to change in the late 1950s and early 1960s. There were the 'kitchen sink' dramas in the West End, novels of working class life, such as *Saturday Night and Sunday Morning* and *A Kind of Loving* were adapted for the cinema screen and, in 1960, the flawed men and strong women of *Coronation Street* were seen for the first time. *The Likely Lads* scripts, the first of which was televized in 1964, are among the very best of these popular fictions.

Bob Ferris and Terry Collier seem, in the original series, to inhabit a generalized 'up North'. There's the odd mention of Hull and Middlesbrough and the occassional 'Why, aye man, it's champion', but, on the whole, little specific reference to local culture or geography. Nevertheless, there is a richness and an authenticity in the drawing of Terry and Bob's social world that has no real parallel in British sitcom.

Few sitcoms have had working-class settings in any event and, of the ones that have, even fewer live in the memory. Most of these were exclusively domestic, as sitcoms tend to be, and seem rooted in nothing wider than the front parlour: *Till Death Us Do Part* comes to mind here, or *Bread.* Others, like *The Rag Trade* (BBC1 1961–63) and the low farce *On the Buses* are set largely in the workplace. But Terry and Bob live in a community, which is made up of relatives, friends, workmates (some of them never seen, like Morrie Hardaker and Ronnie Cooper in Maintenance) and shared experiences. Through the successive series the two continually mine their own past, recalling teachers, neighbours, people who were kids when they were: Miss Lundy, Celia Fletcher, 'Bugless Douglas', Ronnie Oliver...

The relationship of this invented community to the real ones that inspired it is hard to judge. As Bob's mother remarks at his pre-enlistment leaving do, 'there's more opportunities nowadays'.

But in 1964 the working-class communities themselves, and the smokestack industries that supported them, were already in decline. When the cast came back in *Whatever Happened to ...?*, they were sited more explicitly in the North-East of England – indeed, Terry and Bob meet up again on the London-Newcastle train. But, again, local ethnicity is not obtrusive. The language, too, is moderate, in keeping with the broadcasting conventions of the time: Terry and Bob's frequent disputes never involve any effing and blinding, as, in real life, they undoubtedly would have done.

Two years later *The Wackers* (Thames 1975), a sitcom featuring working-class characters in Liverpool, caused a hail of protest in the city and closed after one series. Whether *The Wackers* was a distortion of working-class life on Merseyside or simply a breach of the middle-class proprieties of the time is impossible to say. But it is difficult to think that *The Likely Lads* characters were not warmly embraced by the working-class people of the North-East. (This, in itself, is an interesting judgement: one would never think of asking whether the Steptoes were genuinely representatives of rag and bone men or if Basil Fawlty was really a believable representation of a down-at-heel hotelier.)

The characters, after all – both the principals and walk-ons – are so carefully drawn. Clement and La Frenais have a keen eye for detail and an ear for dialogue that compares with Alan Bennett's. In an early episode, for example, Terry's mother is fretting about a young French woman coming to visit: should they use the front room and what, she wonders, do you give a young French woman for her tea ('I was wondering if a ham salad…?').

And in *Whatever Happened to…?* in a comic subplot that involves the antics of the vicar who was to have married Thelma and Bob, who runs off with a woman, Terry chats with the verger outside the church where the banns are to be read: 'Hear about Reverend Norman?', says the verger. 'He'll lose his pension, you know.'

The central context for all this is the long-standing friendship between Bob and Terry, and the tensions that characterize it. These tensions have been common both to all working-class communities and to all classic situation comedies: between people who think they are better than all this and aspire to middle-class respectability and the people who remain doggedly themselves.

Pretension, of course, nearly always loses. Hancock was always trumped by the cackling laugh of the worldly Sid James, Captain Mainwaring's pomposity is lost on his bumbling platoon, Harold Steptoe will never escape the scrapyard, and so on.

But, of all these focal relationships, the one between Terry and Bob is perhaps the most finely drawn and delicately weighted. Both characters are extremely articulate and neither stays on top for long: sometimes the laugh's on Bob, sometimes it's on Terry and sometimes it's on them both. Bob is prissy but has more formal learning; Terry is a philistine, but more streetwise.

In the first series, on the pair's return from a holiday in Spain, Bob talks piously about how travel

broadens the mind; Terry chuckles that he's managed to give his address to the French girl Bob fancied, and she's coming to visit.

When the girl arrives, though, she turns out to be Welsh, meaning Terry will lose face down at the Working Men's Club, and only Bob has the necessary language skills to escort her friend, a beautiful French au pair.

So here, the person with O-Level French gets the prettier girl and the more sexually prolific Terry is temporarily eclipsed.

In another early episode, both young men founder, Terry failing to have his way with the new

Bob and Terry's friendship survived through thick and thin, and the tensions were adroitly explored by Clement and La Frenais.

canteen manageress and Bob finding that his date, the manageress's daughter, is only 14.

The return of the characters in 1973 is a *tour de force*. Now Bob is in management. He wears ludicrous blazers, he has a carefully sculpted helmet of hair and he has got himself engaged to the snobbish Thelma Chambers.

Emotionally and ideologically Bob shuttles between Terry, returned from army service and trading ruthlessly on an imaginary wound to his leg, and his betrothed. Around Terry he remembers the lads and the laughs and 'the people we used to be'. Around Thelma (whose portrayal by Brigit Forsyth

MEMORABLE SCENES

EPISODE

Entente Cordiale

(Bob and Terry return from their holiday abroad, and Terry admits it was better than Scarborough)

BOB: You what? You don't know you've been abroad. Did you eat Spanish food? You had roast beef and two veg. Did you drink the wine? Only when you couldn't get bottled British beer. And what about all those luscious foreign girls? French, Italians, Germans, the lot – and you spent two weeks chasing a *signorina* from Barrow-in-Furness.

TERRY: She was all right, Rita.

BOB: Yeah, but Barrow-in-Furness, I ask you.

TERRY: I went out with plenty of women.

BOB: Everyone an English subject. You could tell them a mile off: English girls abroad with their peeling shoulders and flowery dresses, like wallpaper on the march.

Thelma provided much needed strength and direction to a rudderless Bob in the sequel.

is, for me, one of the great performances of British situation comedy) he speaks the stilted language of suburban marital life: 'You wrong me with your assumptions, Thelma', he shouts through a door after one of their many rows.

He is attracted to Thelma's lower middle-class respectability (Terry: 'She can be quite poetic, your Thelma'/Bob: 'Well, she *is* an assistant librarian') and nervously tries to practise a leaden speech for their wedding reception: 'It's lucky that Thelma and I like toast – because we've got a toast rack for each day of the week!'

Thelma is the embodiment of all the fears young men have of domesticity. She will soften her voice when she wants to express doubts about the seaweed green décor they have chosen for their new living room and, although she may enjoy sex before marriage with Bob, she won't want the neighbours to see him leaving in the morning.

Bob and Thelma are at their most romantic sighing wistfully at a slide show of the building work on their new house: 'Ah,' they pant, 'the damp proof course!'

But, in truth, Thelma, is no more manipulative than Bob or Terry. Terry is the great threat to Thelma, and vice versa. Terry, whingeing and truculent by turns, is angry that all his mates are now married 'and saving their Green Shield stamps for a set of hock glasses'. He is contemptuous of Bob's new home – Bob: 'We haven't got a name for it yet'/ Terry (surveying a street of identical dwellings): 'Well, you'll certainly need one, won't you? Or you'll never find it again.' He wants Bob back and Thelma's constant fear is that he will take him.

Then after their marriage, in a beautiful dramatic device, Thelma leaves Bob and Terry takes her place. Rapidly this man's man *becomes* Thelma, exhorting Bob to drink his tea while it's hot and complaining that he's stood for 15 minutes at the butchers. And of course, like her, he storms out in a huff.

One final factor that makes *The Likely Lads* shows unusual is the nature and quality of the playing. There is a saying that all good comedy is played straight, but almost all the characters in British sitcom are played in some degree of caricature, with

booming voices and elephantine body movements announcing the arrival of a punchline. Here, though, the performances of Bolam, Bewes, Forsyth and the others are comparatively understated and the comedy emerges organically from the quality of the dialogue and the plotting.

The Likely Lads programmes were collectively, I think, the best British comedy about the dilemma that confronted many young working-class males of Bob and Terry's generation: whether or not to postpone gratification. What was it to be? A night on the ale with the lads, or change your accent and save for the deposit on a house?

Each, as Bob and Terry are aware, has its price. Bob Ferris chooses respectability and ends up wondering 'Oh, what happened to me?'

Nowadays, in sitcoms as in life, you can live in the suburbs and drop your 'h's, as the two leading characters in *Birds of a Feather* have shown. That's fine, but, for myself, I cherish the hope, however forlorn that may be, that we haven't as yet seen the last of Terry, Bob and Thelma.

MEMORABLE SCENES

EPISODE

One For The Road

(Bob and Thelma are enjoying a meal out, and the wine is going down well – as far as Bob's concerned.)

THELMA: Which in anybody's language, connoisseurs included, means you've knocked back a bottle and a half of wine.

BOB: Darling, wine is my hobby. I'm not drinking, I'm learning about it.

THELMA: Oh.

BOB: Not like some people: not like Terry Collier – he hasn't got beyond beer yet. His idea of sophistication is a pint of Newcastle Brown with a cherry in it.

THELMA: I take it all back: if your interest in wine will take you further away from Terry Collier in the Black Horse, you drink on, petal. *(She raises her glass)*

CROSSING THE ATLANTIC

It's a risky business predicting which British sitcoms will conquer the American television market, particularly as so many regarded as 'classics' have been spurned. Television companies opting for an Americanization of the original formula instead of simply transmitting the British version, often exacerbate failure rates. Sometimes cultural and social differences force such changes, but in the process much of the magic is often lost, leaving behind a pallid interpretation devoid of the characteristics that reaped the original success.

Dick Clement and Ian La Frenais have experienced their fair share of adaptations for the American market, with varying degrees of success. Not long after moving to the States they were negotiating an American version of *Porridge*. Titled *On The Rocks*, the series – set in the fictional Alamesa Minimum Security Prison – was screened on ABC, running to 23 episodes between 1975–76. Although the programme was generally well-received, Dick and Ian weren't pleased with the results, and the show came to an end.

Producing *On The Rocks* was John Rich, who first became involved with the writers when he was sent a script based on their sitcom, *Thick As Thieves*. 'Warner Brothers sent me a script written by an American, asking whether I'd do the pilot – but it was hopeless. It was about three people living together, yet there was a terrible flaw in it, and I told Warner Brothers so. When they asked what I meant, I replied: "These people are not related in anyway; where's the problem?"

'I asked to see the original script because I wondered if there was some element missing from the American version. As soon as I got it everything became clear: two of the characters were married – only a small detail!' laughs John. 'The original script intrigued me so much, I decided to track down the writers. Eventually I met up with them when they came over to America, and we had a dicussion about their work and in particular making an American version of *Porridge*.'

Dick and Ian's relationship with John Rich led to a subsequent pilot based on *The Likely Lads,* even though there had been an earlier attempt to introduce the Lads to the American public, as Dick explains. 'The rights were acquired by the late Sheldon Leonard, a very nice man, who's famous for playing Harry the Horse in *Guys and Dolls*, and countless other heavies. Sheldon told Ian that he envisaged *The Likely Lads* becoming the natural successor to *The Honeymooners,* the classic American sitcom.

'Another writer, Bob Klane, wrote a pilot, then we wrote one ourselves, back in the early Seventies – neither was shot. In both of them Bob and Terry were blue-collar guys working as luggage handlers at an airport. I think Bob's pilot was called *I Can't Hear You When the Planes are Flying*; the one we did was our first attempt at writing a script for America.'

The first script based on *The Likely Lads* that they developed with Rich was titled *What Are Friends For?*, altered to *Steubenville* on the second script in 1977. '*What Are Friends For?* barely resembled the script we eventually shot, where the Bob and Terry characters were brothers living with their dad. It was a long way from the original screened in the UK.'

Steubenville was recorded for ABC Television, starring Rick Hurst and Charles Thomas Murphy. The producer and the director of the pilot was Rich, who made a very definite point of never watching any episodes of the British version beforehand. 'First of all, Dick and Ian are wonderful at not throwing anything away, and I would have hated seeing a line they'd written for me, in its original formation. In fact, I've seen some of the jokes they'd written for my company turn up in movies later on. America is a different culture, and seeing a programme in its original form would colour my judgement regarding the new project.'

Disappointingly, Dick and Ian weren't very enamoured of *Steubenville.*

'The casting didn't gel and we were pushed towards slapstick,' says Dick. 'The best thing in it is the opening credits, shot in Steubenville, Ohio, chosen because it's one of the shittiest towns in America. We didn't like the show – and nor did the Network. It went to that graveyard in the sky where failed pilots go!'

Producer John Rich acknowledges that the production did have its fair share of problems. 'We tried retaining the original show's working-class background, but we had some difficulties in casting. One problem with American television is that TV companies aren't usually interested in casting new actors in main roles; they want established players. But we wanted to head off in the other direction, and it didn't work out.

'Certainly the writing was good, and the idea of setting it in a working-class neighbourhood worked well, but the Network didn't pick it up. There was nothing wrong with the concept, and if it had progressed to a series I strongly believe it would have made it, although it might have taken a while.'

Although the best of writers can't guarantee that every idea they generate will be given a chance, John Rich – who directed *The Dick Van Dyke Show*, produced and directed *All in the Family*, the hugely successful US version of *'Till Death Do Us Part*, and is currently working on the US version of *Fawlty Towers* – feels the British industry pays more attention to a writer's track record than the Americans. 'Here it's all about bottom line figures.'

Another factor that, perhaps, played a part in the pilot's fate is the importance of longevity in American TV. 'We can't just do 13 episodes,' John Rich explains. 'We have to make shows that will play for eight or nine years, otherwise it doesn't pay for the enormous expenses involved. One advantage in Britain is that writers can decide when they've had enough, whereas over here you just have to go on. And to sustain a series for so long, it needs many different elements, all of which must appeal to the general public – it's a very difficult task.

'Dick and Ian can do no wrong as far as I'm concerned,' says John. 'They're prolific and very clever. When I'm on the look-out for writers, I like people who aren't afraid to say something in literary English, creating a situation, comedy moment or a joke that is not necessarily understood by everybody: I call it a two per cent joke.

'If people don't understand something, it's harmless and goes straight by them. But for the small percentage of the audience who can acknowledge the writing, it's rewarding. Dick and Ian reach this level and I like that.'

Many writers would have been put off by *Steubenville*'s lack of success, but Clement and La Frenais' resilience led to the Lads being given another chance. 'In 1978, we tried again, still with John Rich," says Dick. 'This was actually entitled *The Likely Lads*, and was based much more closely on *Whatever Happened to…?* But it was never shot. Many pilots are written, some are shot, and a few, a very few, become series. I always liken it to baby turtles hatching and trying to reach the sea as seagulls swoop down on them from the skies.' A nice analogy, but, sadly, the baby turtles called *Steubenville* and *The Likely Lads* didn't make it into that vast and rich ocean, better known as the American TV Network!

STEUBENVILLE

Pilot Script

Written by Dick Clement and Ian La Frenais

Produced and Directed by John Rich

JOHN RICH PRODUCTIONS, INC.

5800 Sunset Boulevard

Hollywood, California 90028

SECOND DRAFT

February 2, 1977

STEUBENVILLE

(Pilot)

CAST

CAL LUKAS .... RICK HURST

RANDY LUKAS........... CHARLES MURPHY

BRENDA PEASLEY........... ANDREA ADLER

BEN LUKAS ....JACK GRIMES

MRS PEASLEY .... MARY GREGORY

SETS

LUKAS HOUSE

CAL'S NEW HOUSE

EXTERIORS

CAL'S NEW HOUSE

STEUBENVILLE

(Pilot)

ACT ONE

(FADE IN:)

INT. LUKAS HOUSE - DAY

(CAL COMES DOWN THE STAIRS IN BARE FEET AND PAJAMAS. HE SHIVERS AT THE EARLY MORNING CHILL OF THE HOUSE.

INSERT: A MOUSETRAP. A LARGE BARE FOOT COMES INTO FRAME.

THERE IS A HIDEOUS SNAP - AN INSTANT CRY OF PAIN FROM CAL.

HE HOPS TOWARDS THE KITCHEN TRYING TO REMOVE THE TRAP FROM HIS TOE. WE HEAR A VOICE FROM UPSTAIRS)

DAD (V.O.): What's going on?

CAL: It's only me, Dad.

DAD (V.O.): You got your foot caught in the mousetrap again?

CAL: No!

(HE PULLS IT OFF AND LIMPS INTO THE KITCHEN, SAYING:)

Why don't we get a cat...

DAD (V.O.): Because you kept standing on it.

(CUT TO THE FRONT DOOR. THERE IS THE SOUND OF A KEY IN THE LOCK AND IT OPENS TO ADMIT RANDY. HE IS CARRYING A SKATEBOARD AND THE NEWSPAPER.

HE CLOSES THE FRONT DOOR, CROSSES THE ROOM CASUALLY PUTS DOWN THE SKATEBOARD NEAR THE FOOT OF THE STAIRS CONTINUING ROUND TO THE ARMCHAIR READING THE PAPER AS HE MOVES.

CAL RE-ENTERS FROM THE KITCHEN. LOOKING UPSTAIRS HE CALLS:)

CAL: Coffee's on, Dad.

(AS HE SAYS THIS HIS FOOT CONTACTS THE SKATEBOARD WHICH PROPELS AN ALARMED CAL STRAIGHT ACROSS THE LIVING ROOM. THERE IS A TERRIBLE CRASH.

RANDY WITHOUT LOOKING UP FROM THE SPORTS SECTIONS SAYS:)

RANDY: Morning, Cal.

(AN ENRAGED CAL PICKS HIMSELF UP HOLDING THE SKATEBOARD.)

CAL: Where did this come from?

RANDY: Oh, that stupid kid from next door left it out front. I brought it in in case someone had a nasty accident.

(A TAKE FROM CAL)

CAL: Somebody has just *had* a nasty accident.

RANDY: You don't count. You have them all the time.

(RANDY SEES THE MOUSETRAP ON THE TABLE WHERE CAL HAS PUT IT)

RANDY: Mousetrap get you again this morning?

CAL: No!

RANDY: What are you doing up so early?

CAL: I'm going to work, of course. Question is, what are *you* doing up so early?

RANDY: I'm not up early, I'm just home late.

CAL: That says everything about you and me, doesn't it? I get up early so I'll be the first at the office. So I'll get on in the world and help my family. While my brother's been on the town. Probably been out all night with a girl whose name he can't remember.

(RANDY GETS INDIGNANTLY TO HIS FEET)

RANDY: That's typical, isn't it? Typical of the attitude of this house towards me. No one figures that maybe I've taken a night job. No one figures maybe I've been tending the sick in a hospital or serving soup to the poor.

(CAL IS HALF TAKEN IN BY THIS. COULD IT BE?)

CAL: Have you?

RANDY: No, I spent the night with a girl whose name I can't remember.

(RANDY MOVES THROUGH TO THE KITCHEN, CAL FOLLOWING. HE OPENS THE ICEBOX AND TAKES OUT A BEER)

RANDY: Want a beer?

CAL: How can you drink beer at six o'clock in the morning?

RANDY: Like this.

(HE DEMONSTRATES. THEY MOVE BACK INTO THE LIVING ROOM)

CAL: And I suppose while I'm at work you'll be sleeping all day, right?

RANDY: So, I have a few late nights. I'm entitled, I've been in the Army five years. You should come out *with* me. Live a little.

CAL: I have a job to go to, I have night school and I'm getting married in a few weeks. I haven't time for living!

RANDY (INVITINGLY): Tonight. You and me. The old team. What d'ya say?

CAL: Can't.

RANDY: Why?

CAL: I have to do some work on my new house.

RANDY: You're no fun anymore. You're still young. What are you doing rushing into marriage?

CAL: Rushing? I've been engaged to Brenda 11 years.

RANDY: I'm just saying don't be too hasty. You know, there's more to life than a tract house, night school, a white collar job and three ballpoints in you top pocket.

CAL: There's nothing wrong with improving yourself, Randy. Nothing wrong with trying to get out of those mills and plants and mines.

RANDY (NOBLY): There is a dignity about the working man's honest toil.

(DAD ENTERS DOWN THE STAIRS. HE IS DRESSED IN OVERALLS)

DAD: That kind of bull can only come from someone who's never done an honest day's toil in his life.

CAL & RANDY: Morning, Dad.

DAD: Let me tell you, there ain't nothing dignified about workin' in a Steubenville steel mill. There ain't nothing dignified about going to work before the sun's come up and getting back when it's gone down already.

RANDY: Listen, Dad, he may be pushing

to better himself but we working men know that we're the backbone of this nation.

DAD: Well, if that's true then *we* should get *you* a job at the plant.

RANDY (QUICK RECOVERY): I will, Dad. Soon. But, you know, the Army took a lot out of me.

(HE PATS HIS THIGH AND SIGHS)

Combat.

DAD: Combat! You were a *pastry* cook in Germany.

CAL: He did get into a lot of fights, Dad. People had to eat that pastry.

RANDY: That's right, gang up on me.

DAD: All I'm saying is you should knuckle down. Cal's got the right idea. He wants that white collar. He knows what's needed in life is not brawn, it's brains. Right, son?

CAL: (SHADES OF CLEAVER)

Hhmmm?

DAD: That's my boy.

(DAD SHAKES HIS HEAD AND GOES INTO THE KITCHEN)

RANDY: You were always his favorite.

CAL: Not that again.

RANDY: No, no. Childhood was very humiliating for me. D'you know any other family where the oldest son wore the kid brother's hand-me-downs?

CAL: That's because I was always bigger than you.

RANDY: You know why, don't you. They *fed* you.

CAL: Knock it off, Randy.

RANDY (SELF PITY): No, no. Mom and Dad never wanted me.

CAL: Don't be crazy. If they didn't want children, how come after you they had another one? *Me.*

(DAD RE-ENTERS HOLDING A MUG OF STEAMING COFFEE)

DAD: That's because after Randy was born I turned to your Mother - God rest her soul - and I said, 'Grace, we have to try again'.

(HE MAKES FOR THE STAIRS)

RANDY: Listen, Dad, you feel that way I could walk out of this house tomorrow.

(DAD STOPS ON THE STAIRS AND TURNS.

CUT TO CAL WHO LOOKS AT BOTH ANXIOUSLY.

CUT TO RANDY, SATISFIED THAT HIS REMARK HAS CUT THEM TO THE QUICK.

RESUME DAD)

DAD: Son, never put off till tomorrow what you can do today.

(HE LEAVES)

RANDY: Okay, that's settled. Soon as I've got some bread together, I'm out of this house.

CAL: Well, don't ask me for the money.

RANDY (INDIGNANTLY): When did I ever ask you for money?

CAL: Yesterday. And the day before.

RANDY: Oh, you're counting that!

CAL: And don't you ever tell Brenda that I loaned you the money put aside for our dishwasher.

RANDY: If that horse had come in you could have had a dishwasher in every room.

CAL: I don't want a dishwasher in every room. And you're getting nothing more out of me...

(AT THAT MOMENT CAL NOTICES RANDY'S FOOTWEAR)

You're wearing my shoes!

RANDY: What?

CAL: My best shoes.

RANDY: Oh, are these yours?

CAL: You know very well they are. And why are they covered in mud?

RANDY: Oh, I got that walking across the city dump.

CAL: The city dump? What were you doing there?

RANDY: It was a short cut home from where the car broke down. I had a blow out.

CAL: Oh, that's too bad.

(HE MAKES HIS WAY TO THE STAIRS, THEN TURNS)

Wait a minute - you don't have a car.

RANDY: Of course I don't. It was yours.

DISSOLVE TO:

INT. CAL'S NEW HOUSE - EVENING

(OPENING SHOT IS OF BRENDA ON A CHAIR MEASURING THE WINDOW FOR BLINDS. WE HEAR MRS PEASLEY'S VOICE)

MRS PEASLEY (V.O.): Look Brenda? I've cleaned this.

BRENDA: Yes, Mother.

(MRS PEASLEY ENTERS CARRYING WHAT LOOKS LIKE A TIFFANY LAMP)

BRENDA (NOT TOO ENTHUSIASTIC): Oh, it's going to look beautiful.

MRS PEASLEY: I hope Cal appreciates it. It's been in our family for forty years.

(CAL ENTERS, COLD AND BREATHLESS)

CAL: Hi, Brenda. Hello, Mrs Peasley.

(HE KISSES BRENDA)

Sorry I'm late. I had to take a bus.

BRENDA: Why?

CAL: 'Cause I didn't have time to pick up the car.

BRENDA: Where is it?

CAL: Where Randy left it. He had a blow out.

BRENDA: Oh, you didn't loan Randy the car.

CAL: Of course I didn't. He took it.

(CAL NOTICES THE LAMP WITH DISTASTE)

Where did *that* thing come from?

(MRS PEASLEY STIFFENS)

MRS PEASLEY: I'll make some coffee.

BRENDA (QUIETLY): Mom gave us that. It's been in the family forty years.

CAL: Oh...

(THEN LOUDLY)

What a beautiful lamp, boy, aren't we lucky!

BRENDA: So we have no car. Couldn't Randy have changed the tire?

CAL: Well, it wasn't just the tire. You see, the blow out caused him to swerve which is how the fire hydrant ran into the front fender.

BRENDA: And of course, *you're* gonna have to pay for it.

CAL (ADAMANTLY): Certainly not. He will.

BRENDA: With what?

CAL: The money I loaned him.

(A THOUGHT STRIKES BRENDA AND SHE SAYS ACCUSINGLY)

BRENDA: You didn't loan him the deposit for the new dishwasher?

CAL: Hmmmm?

BRENDA: You did.

CAL: I didn't.

BRENDA: You did.

CAL: Well, I did and I didn't.

BRENDA: What does that mean?

CAL: I didn't loan it to him... today.

BRENDA: So we now have no dishwasher.

(MRS PEASLEY RE-ENTERS)

MRS PEASLEY: What's this?

BRENDA: We've lost that dishwasher. The one that's in the sale with the thirty percent discount.

MRS PEASLEY: You think my daughter should wash the dishes herself and ruin her hands like I have?

CAL: Mrs Peasley, you have beautiful hands. They're two of your nicest features.

MRS PEASLEY (TO BRENDA): Is he being rude?

BRENDA: No, Mother. And he's wild about the lamp.

MRS PEASLEY (RAPIDLY): I suppose you think that Mr. Peasley and I should buy you a dishwasher. Besides paying for the entire wedding and the honeymoon. Not that we're keeping count. Even though it *is* sixteen hundred and forty eight dollars so far.

BRENDA: There's no need to keep reminding us, Mother.

MRS PEASLEY: I'm only reminding you that you're starting out with far more than your father and I ever did.

CAL: Didn't you have the lamp?

(BRENDA KICKS CAL. HE SUPPRESSES A CRY OF PAIN)

MRS PEASLEY: We only had each other and our love of ballroom dancing. Of course, all that's behind us now - the glamor, the glitter, the trophies - since Mr. Peasley's leg.

CAL: (OH, THAT AGAIN)

Ah yes, the leg.

MRS PEASLEY: But what Mr. Peasley always says, Cal, and this is my point - 'Even if a man has only one good leg, he can still stand on his own two feet.'

(WITH AN AIR OF FINALITY, MRS PEASLEY RETURNS TO THE KITCHEN)

BRENDA: I'm sorry, Cal. I didn't mean to get Mother on your back, but you know, dear, we just can't afford to subsidize your brother.

CAL (WEARILY): I know, I know. But blood is thicker than dishwater.

BRENDA: I try to be fair to Randy. But he's always been a bad influence on you, Cal, and some things I can never forgive him for.

CAL: Like what?

BRENDA: Like the night we decided to... well, you know... put the seal on our love for each other.

CAL: Yes? What about it?

BRENDA: It was Randy who took the Polaroids.

CAL: Yes, but...

BRENDA: And pinned them on the school bulletin board.

(CAL SMILES, A FOND MEMORY)

CAL: At least the fellas knew I wasn't lying.

BRENDA: It took me a long time to get over that. Why do you think I never go to class reunions?

CAL: Randy has his good points.

BRENDA: He does?

CAL: Oh yes. He's very kind to animals.

BRENDA (INCREDULOUSLY): Really?

CAL: Yeah. Especially if they win.

BRENDA: Why do you put up with him? He borrows your money, your car, your clothes. He embarrasses you. He leads you astray. He threatens everything you've ever worked for and you keep coming back for more. Why?

CAL (SIMPLY): He's my brother.

BRENDA: Sometimes I feel you like him more than you love me.

CAL: Oh, come on, sweetheart. Our love has survived eleven years which proves what we've got is a many splendored thing.

BRENDA: Eleven years and still not married only proves there's a lot of doubt.

CAL: No, it doesn't.

BRENDA: I know you. I know how indecisive you are. I have this secret dread that when we finally reach the altar and the minister says, 'Do you take this woman to be your lawful wedded wife' you're going to say, 'Can I think it over for a minute?'

(CAL, OFFENDED AND INDIGNANT, COMES ON VERY STRONG)

CAL: You're wrong, Brenda. That was the old me. Let me tell you something about the new me. The new me is not indecisive. The new me knows what he wants. *You* are what I want. *This* is what I want. And of that I am one hundred percent certain.

(BRENDA MELTS, TOUCHED BY THIS REAFFIRMATION OF CAL'S LOVE AND DEVOTION)

BRENDA: Oh, honey, are you sure?

CAL: Well, I *think* so...

DISSOLVE TO:

INT. THE SAME (LATER) - NIGHT

(OPEN ON NEWLY ERECTED BOOKSHELVES.

CAL STEPS BACK PROUDLY TO ADMIRE HIS HANDIWORK. AS HE DOES SO, HE KNOCKS OVER AND BREAKS THE TIFFANY LAMP. HE REACTS IN DISMAY AND BENDS TO CLEAR THE PIECES UP.

WE HEAR A KNOCK AT THE DOOR AND RANDY'S VOICE AS HE ENTERS)

RANDY: Cal?... Oh, what happened?

CAL: I don't know. It was just lying there and it... broke.

(LAMELY)

It was forty years old. What'll I tell Brenda?

RANDY: You're lucky it wasn't new.

CAL: It's *supposed* to be old. That's what makes it valuable. Just like that vase.

(RANDY PICKS UP THE VASE INDICATED AND LOOKS AT IT SKEPTICALLY)

RANDY: This is valuable?

CAL: Don't touch it.

RANDY: Hey, I'm not the one who breaks things.

(HE REPLACES IT)

Listen. I just came around to...

CAL: No!

RANDY: What?

CAL: Whatever it is you want, or want to borrow, the answer's no.

RANDY: I was going to offer to...

CAL: No, no, no, no!

RANDY: Cal...

CAL (VERY LOUDLY): NOOOO!!!

(THE RESONANCE OF HIS REFUSAL CAUSES THE VASE TO SHATTER. BOTH BROTHERS STARE AT IT IN ASTONISHMENT)

CAL: Now look what you made me do! You just walk into a room and something bad happens.

RANDY: It's not me, it's you. You're accident prone. Always were. *You* walk into a room and something breaks, falls, splinters or caves in.

CAL: Oh, yeah. And who's just put up those bookshelves?

(RANDY TURNS TO EXAMINE THEM)

RANDY: They don't look too secure to me.

CAL: Sure they are. Test them.

(RANDY GIVES THEM A GOOD THUMP AND SEEMS A LITTLE DISAPPOINTED WHEN THEY REMAIN INTACT)

CAL (TRIUMPH): See!

RANDY: I don't think they suit this room.

CAL: Well, they will. They're all empty at the moment. They have to be personalized. With photographs, momentoes, books.

(HE PICKS UP A BOOK FROM A PILE ON THE FLOOR AND PLACES IT ON THE SHELF. IT COLLAPSES. CAL WHEELS ROUND, CATCHING RANDY SMIRKING)

CAL: Get out!

RANDY: I didn't do nothing.

CAL: You did. You weakened it when you hit it! They weren't designed for that. Any shelf will collapse if you go round banging it.

(TO ILLUSTRATE HIS POINT, HE BANGS ANOTHER SHELF. THE WHOLE UNIT COLLAPSES LIKE A PACK OF CARDS.

CAL GIVES UP, DEFEATED AND SLUMPS INTO A CHAIR. RANDY LOOKS AT HIM SYMPATHETICALLY)

RANDY: Cal... Cal, you've been overworking. What you need is a break.

CAL: Haven't I broken enough?

RANDY (SWEET REASONABLENESS): You need to relax. Look, tonight take Brenda out. Take her to dinner and leave all this to me.

CAL (SUSPICIOUSLY): Why?

RANDY: I'll level with you. This girl I took out last night...

CAL (DISAPPROVINGLY): The one whose name you can't remember?

RANDY: Sure I remember. Her name's Sharon. Thing is, living with you and Dad, I don't have a place to... give expression to my feelings.

CAL: And you want to express them here, I suppose.

RANDY: Not until later on. Not until I've fixed everything. She won't be here for hours. Okay?

CAL: You really would fix all this?

RANDY: Sure. Get out and enjoy yourself. On your way.

(HE IS HELPING CAL TO HIS FEET, GETTING HIS COAT AND STEERING HIM TOWARDS THE DOOR)

CAL: Do you know where everything is?

RANDY: At the moment, everything is on the floor. Tomorrow it'll all be in its rightful place.

CAL: I'll see you then.

RANDY: Have a good time.

(CAL GOES)

(RANDY WATCHES HIM GO. THEN HE TURNS, KICKS THE WOODEN SHELVES OUT OF THE WAY, THEN TAKES THE DUST SHEET OFF THE SOFA. THEN HE OPENS THE KITCHEN DOOR)

RANDY: The coast is clear.

(A RATHER SEXY BUT NOT TOO CLASSY GIRL ENTERS. SHE LOOKS AROUND THE ROOM)

GIRL: Not too many creature comforts.

RANDY: Everything we need, Sharon.

GIRL: Karen!

(FADE OUT)

END OF ACT ONE

ACT TWO

(FADE IN:)

INT. LUKAS HOUSE - NIGHT

(A HAPPY, MELLOW BRENDA KISSES A HAPPY, MELLOW CAL. THEY ARE SEATED.

BRENDA: It's been a lovely evening. Super restaurant.

CAL: It's the best Armenian food in Steubenville.

BRENDA: I'd like to wait till Randy gets back. Just to thank him.

CAL: Oh, he'll be at it all night.

(BRENDA SNUGGLES UP TO CAL AND KISSES HIM ON THE EAR. HE SQUIRMS)

CAL: Don't do that.

BRENDA: You love that. You know you do.

CAL: That's the problem. That particular ear is one of my erroneous zones.

BRENDA: Darling, you mean erogenous. Erroneous means a mistake.

CAL: It would be if you did it again 'cause Dad's awake.

BRENDA: When we're married we won't have to worry about people upstairs or people in the next room.

CAL: Just your Mother at the window.

BRENDA (GENTLY REPROVING): Oh, Cal... I know she gets in our hair but she means well. And she does help. I wasn't supposed to tell you this because it was going to be a surprise but...

CAL: What?

BRENDA: She was going around to the new house tonight to hang all the drapes.

(A LOOK OF TERRIBLE DOUBT CROSSES CAL'S FACE AS HE DIGESTS THIS INFORMATION)

CAL: She was?

BRENDA: I'll bet she was surprised to find Randy working around there.

CAL: I hope she wasn't too surprised.

(RANDY ENTERS ASHEN FACED.

BRENDA RISES TO GREET HIM WARMLY)

BRENDA: Randy!

RANDY (INSTANTLY DEFENSIVE): What?

BRENDA (UNCERTAINLY): Hello.

RANDY: Oh.

BRENDA: And thank you.

RANDY: It was nothing.

(CUT TO CAL'S ANXIOUS, QUESTIONING LOOK)

BRENDA: There's some coffee made. Would you like some?

RANDY: What? Well... why not?

(SHE MOVES INTO THE KITCHEN.

THE TWO BROTHERS LOOK AT EACH OTHER FOR A LONG MOMENT BEFORE CAL ASKS:)

CAL: Brenda's Mother?

RANDY: Yes.

CAL: She didn't?

RANDY: She did.

CAL: When you were...

RANDY: Yes.

CAL (CLUTCHING AT STRAWS): Putting up bookshelves?

RANDY: No.

CAL: Not when you were with Sharon?

RANDY: Karen.

CAL: Who's Karen?

RANDY: Karen is Sharon.

CAL: Okay, tell me the worst. When Mrs Peasley arrived, what point were you at?

RANDY: I guess you could say... the point of no return.

(BRENDA RETURNS HAPPILY WITH COFFEE. SHE LOOKS BETWEEN THE TWO OF THEM)

BRENDA: What's going on?

CAL: You should have told me, Brenda. You should have told me!!

DISSOLVE TO:

INT. CAL'S NEW HOUSE - EVENING (The Following Day)

(THE ROOM IS IMMACULATE. THE SHELVES HAVE BEEN REPLACED. EVEN THE LAMP HAS BEEN REPAIRED. RANDY IS IN THE PROCESS OF FINISHING PAINTING ONE OF THE DOORS.

CAL ENTERS AND IS SURPRISED TO FIND HIM THERE)

CAL: What are you doing here?

RANDY: I've been here all day.

CAL: I don't want you here. I don't want you to ever set foot across my door ever again.

RANDY: Hey, hey! Just take a look around, will you. Notice the shelves. Attached to the wall. Notice the Tiffany lamp. Attached to the ceiling. Notice the freshly painted door...

(CAL TOUCHES THE DOOR TO SEE IF THIS IS TRUE)

... attached to your hand.

(CAL WITHDRAWS HIS HAND LOOKING AT THE PAINT ON IT)

CAL: Oh...

RANDY: Don't touch anything! Just stand perfectly still in the middle of the room. Don't move and don't wave your arms around.

(CAL IS IMPRESSED IN SPITE OF HIMSELF)

CAL: Hey, you really have done some job here.

RANDY: Thank you. How's... Brenda?

CAL: Not speaking to me, thank you.

RANDY: How's her Mother?

CAL: Not speaking to anyone. She's still in shock.

RANDY: Why don't you get yourself over there. Pour oil on troubled waters. If you hang around here you'll only break something.

CAL: What are you going to do?

RANDY: Gonna do the kitchen. Then I'll sleep here, make an early start in the morning.

CAL (KNOWINGLY): Oh, yes! With her I suppose. Karen or Sharon.

RANDY: No way. D'you think she ever wants to see me again? A nice girl like that embarrasses easy.

CAL: Promise? No more girls?

RANDY: Scout's honor.

CAL: You were kicked out of the scouts when you were twelve.

RANDY: I was framed. Look, I'm just trying to make amends.

(CAL SURVEYS THE ROOM)

CAL (GRUDGINGLY): You have done a good job. You could sleep on that, it converts into a bed.

RANDY: I know.

CAL: Oh, yes, I'm sure you do.

RANDY: And I'll bet I'm not the first person to use it.

(A SLIGHTLY COMPLACENT GRIN FROM CAL)

CAL: Well, sometimes Brenda and I stay over when we're working late. That kind of thing.

RANDY: I see. A little premarital decorating goes on, does it?

CAL: None of your business.

RANDY: Make the most of it. That'll all change when you're married.

CAL: Why?

RANDY: In the suburbs sex is a reward for cutting the grass.

CAL: Is it?... Brenda wants to concrete the yard.

RANDY: You and Brenda will be fine. Come on, get out of here. Go see her.

(CAL OPENS THE DOOR, THEN PAUSES)

CAL: Okay, Randy... and thanks.

RANDY: For what?

CAL: For all this!

(HE GESTURES EXPANSIVELY KNOCKING OVER A PIECE OF BRIC A BRAC.

RANDY ALERTLY CATCHES IT)

RANDY: Get out of here. While all this is still intact.

(CAL LEAVES, SLAMMING THE DOOR. THE TIFFANY LAMP FALLS FROM THE CEILING AND SMASHES.

RANDY SHRUGS HELPLESSLY)

DISSOLVE TO:

EXT. CAL'S NEW HOUSE - NIGHT

INT. CAL'S HOUSE - NIGHT

(RANDY IS ASLEEP ON THE SOFA. ALMOST INVISIBLE UNDER BLANKETS. HE SNORES.

CUT TO THE FRONT DOOR AS BRENDA ADMITS HERSELF WITH HER KEY.

WE FOLLOW HER INTO THE DARKENED ROOM WHERE SHE REGISTERS THE SLEEPING FIGURE IN THE BED AND SMILES FONDLY)

BRENDA: Cal?

(NO REPLY. JUST HEAVY BREATHING)

I came to say 'sorry'. I realize last night wasn't your fault.

(THERE IS A RESTLESS GRUNT FROM THE BED)

Oh, darling, you must have worked so hard. And all I do is complain and be unreasonable - sorry.

(THERE IS A RESTLESS TWITCH FROM THE SLEEPING FIGURE.

BRENDA SAYS COYLY:)

I'll stay if you like - do you want me to stay?... You do, don't you?

(SHE STARTS TO SLIP OFF HER COAT AND SHOES)

In the morning, I'll fix breakfast and then we'll do the bathroom tiles together.

(SHE SLIPS INTO THE BED. WEARING HER SLIP AND PANTYHOSE)

Don't wake up, hon. Love you...

(CUT TO RANDY'S SLEEPING FACE. HE SNORES)

DISSOLVE TO:

INT. THE SAME - DAY (Next Morning)

(BRENDA AND RANDY, BACK TO BACK ARE STILL UNAWARE OF EACH OTHER. BRENDA BEGINS TO STIR)

EXT. CAL'S HOUSE - DAY

(CAL DRIVES UP IN A PACER WITH A DENTED FRONT FENDER. HE STOPS, GETS OUT AND STARTS TO UNLOAD A BAG OF GROCERIES FROM THE CAR)

INT. CAL'S HOUSE - DAY

(BRENDA OPENS HER EYES SLEEPILY. THEN SHE TURNS AND SNUGGLES UP TO RANDY'S BACK)

BRENDA (KITTENISHLY): Darling, are you awake?

(CLOSE ON RANDY, HIS EYES OPEN, INSTANTLY AWAKE.

BRENDA BEGINS TO MOVE A HAND UP HIS SPINE)

This little piggy went to market... this little piggy stayed at home. Ca-al... Ca-al!!

(CAL ENTERS)

CAL: Yes?

(BRENDA TURNS TOWARDS HIM)

BRENDA: Cal!

CAL: What are you doing here?

BRENDA: What are you doing... *there?*

(SHE TURNS BACK TOWARDS THE FIGURE NEXT TO HER. AS RANDY TURNS TOWARDS HER)

RANDY: Hello, Brenda, what are you doing here?

(CAL STARES AT THEM BOTH IN BEWILDERMENT)

(FADE OUT:)

END OF ACT TWO

TAG

(FADE UP:)

INT. CAL'S NEW HOUSE - DAY

(CAL IS SITTING LOOKING DEFEATED. RANDY IS REASONING WITH HIM)

RANDY: You've got to listen to me. You know there's nothing between me and Brenda.

CAL: It was the nothing between you and Brenda that bothered me.

RANDY: I was so tired last night, I wouldn't have noticed if Raquel Welch had slipped in beside me.

CAL: You trying to tell me nothing happened?

RANDY: Don't be stupid. You know the way Brenda feels about me. That's why she freaked out. Not because you found her in bed with me, because *she* found her in bed with me. Go on, get after her.

CAL: No point. It's all over. Finished. Ended. She'll probably never speak to me again.

RANDY: That's the spirit, kid. Look on the bright side.

(CAL REACTS)

(FADE OUT:)

THE END